BE LEGIT

BE LEGIT

THE CRIMINAL'S PATHWAY TO SUCCESS AND LEGITIMACY

JASON GRINAGE

CONTENTS

Para Ti

FOREWORD

For decades now, many experts, specialists, doctors, psychologists, law enforcement, officers of the court, and presidents (and their administrations) have tried to pinpoint our society's peculiar proclivity for illicit drug use and the seemingly infinite ways to combat its spread. From an enforcement standpoint, we have not had much success. And interestingly, there seems to be a perpetual focus on the rehabilitation of addicts and the penalization of dealers rather than addressing the socioeconomic issues that cause individuals to use and sell drugs.

June 17th, 1971, President Richard Nixon's speech declared Public Enemy No. 1 to be illegal drugs, thus setting the stage for punitive measures for those immersed, not only in the trafficking of illicit narcotics, but in the consumption of these substances as well.

Much the same as the Volstead Act, which established the prohibition of alcohol in 1919, America's War on Drugs fueled a new era of legislation designed to simultaneously persecute the user, the manufacturers, and the distributors of illicit narcotics.

The Volstead Act cost the federal government over $11 billion dollars in lost revenue, and cost tax payers roughly

$300 million dollars to enforce. The Volstead Act lasted from 1920 to 1933.

The War on Drugs' official declaration began when Nixon made his speech in 1971, and continues to this day, over 50 years later. Imagine the costs in both revenue and expenses to enforce this protracted campaign, and how it must surely dwarf the Prohibition in cost and scope several times over.

However, it must be acknowledged that something considered taboo or prohibited by law will always have a stronger appeal to the masses than those things that are acceptable by the law's standards. This observation is only truer for capitalist societies whose entrepreneurs see the value in participating in such ventures, even if they happen to be unlawful.

And so, the formula compounds and amplifies due to its illegal nature, having the exact opposite effect on the system that intends on stymieing the refinement, distribution and consumption of these substances. Cigarettes are arguably harder to quit than heroine, and yet, Americans can drink and smoke themselves into an early grave while marijuana is still classified as a Schedule I narcotic by the Drug Enforcement Administration (DEA), meaning that it has "a high potential for abuse, no currently accepted medical use in treatment in the United States, and a lack of accepted safety for use under medical supervision."

"Primum non nocere" First, do no harm...

Physicians the nation over prescribe a steadily increasing number of Americans any and every FDA-approved medication available. We are bombarded by commercials for prescription drugs whose side effects are often worse than the affliction (if an illness even exists). But certain illicit narcotics deemed "Public Enemies" over a half century ago remain illegal. People continue to be ensnared in the endless cycle of addiction and criminality. The federal government continues to spend millions of taxpayers' dollars every year to check the pandemic which one could argue was created by the same government that classified it as unlawful.

It's puzzling to consider the number of resources that go towards funding a justice system that punishes substance abuse disorder while concurrently generating an environment of addiction and criminality; thus, fostering an incubator for illicit drug sales and abuse.

I also find it quite astonishing how literally tons of these drugs can be smuggled into the country every year, while surprisingly, our Customs agents and those assigned the task of preventing hazardous material and explosives from crossing our borders have, thus far, been successful at thwarting *any* attempts of individuals bringing biological or chemical weapons into our country.

How many lives have been lost to alcohol and tobacco? How many more lives have been decimated by drugs, their illegality, and their ever-increasing potency as a direct result of the War on Drugs? If one were to classify narcotics the way our government has, would not these substances be considered weapons of mass destruction, or forms of hazardous chemical warfare at the very least? And yet they continue to be distributed and consumed at catastrophic levels.

How is it then that these drugs manage to find their way across our borders every day using tunnels, submarines and other forms of transport yet other chemicals and explosives do not? How is it that alcohol, tobacco products and addictive prescriptions are legal while narcotics are not? Apart from regulation of some substances while others are strictly "controlled," is there any real difference between them?

Most crimes that are drug-related are due to an addict's urgent need to obtain drugs to staunch the addiction which has become such a familiar and dreadful aspect of their daily existence. These crimes are often manifested in the form of burglaries, theft, armed robbery, prostitution or any other means necessary to obtain one's drug of choice.

It is the addict's insatiable need for drugs, as well as inflated costs of the same, which then segways the drug abuser into further criminality.

The idea of writing a book aimed at helping people who sold drugs to make the transition from criminal to a productive member of society first came to me when I was still on the streets, and while I was still selling drugs. It had occurred to me that there has never been any assistance or positive forms of deterrence for drug dealers- only for the drug user. Granted, sometimes they are one and the same.

Apart from death or imprisonment, I often wondered why our options were so limited.

The United States of America has the means to subsidize farmers in every drug-producing country to grow other crops rather than coca for cocaine, or poppy to be to refined into heroine. We (The U.S.) can send millions in aid to countries such as Mexico, to combat the cartels operating along our borders and within our interior. America's Longest War in Afghanistan included resources provided to said nation to train their military personnel, as well as their civilians, in an attempt to eradicate the heroin epidemic happening there, yet it seems the only way we are able to assist our own citizens is by placing them in prison for outrageous amounts of time, for exercising, in some cases, a freedom of choice that is not their own.

Upon my arrival to prison, I realized that there were a great many people who employed a vast number of illegal activities to support themselves, as well as their families. To that end, it occurred to me that it might benefit a much larger group of people to create a process that would help criminals in general make a positive change in their lives rather than those involved solely in the drug trade. To relegate this project between drug users and dealers would be counterintuitive to my intentions. The more lives we can help redirect in a positive direction, the greater the benefits for them and for society.

Nevertheless, I will always be of the firm belief that narcotics play an integral role in our nation's future (or demise), and I could not have completed this project had I not acknowledged that fact, as well as other fundamental truths about who we are as a society. And I feel I need to stress that although I will at times be focusing on narcotics throughout my writing, this work is intended for one purpose only: the conversion of as many people as possible from lives of illegitimacy to ones of purpose, conscience, and principle.

In all my life, on the streets and in prison, I have never once come across a criminal who actually enjoyed the life he or she was living. Granted, the money is enticing, and while some may feel a sense of power or accomplishment after a successful bank robbery or drug deal, in the end, our secret hearts betray our true thoughts. I know this, as I've heard those same braggarts who were so ostentatious in the company of their peers, crying in the cell next to mine, begging God to help them escape the dismal road that they had found themselves upon.

Many of us find ourselves praying to God, asking Him to set us free under the condition that we will turn our lives around. But as soon as we are free, God is forgotten, and we revert to the criminality that we are so accustomed to. This is a hypocrisy that I no longer wish to indulge in, and I hope those who study this condition are of the same mind.

If chance should have it that you don't hold to the same religious beliefs as I, or that you lean more towards an agnostic approach, this work is also intended for you. It is my hope that you gain from this that which is most important; freedom from looking over your shoulder. Freedom from wondering when the police will raid your home. Freedom from wondering when you will finally be released from prison (or when you will be going back). Essentially, freedom from a life that was never meant for us. But circumstances being as they are, we may have found ourselves in a situation, and we don't know what steps to take to reverse its course.

Also, for those individuals who have had the prudence and fortune of avoiding the criminal lifestyle, it is my hope that those of you who read this may also gain some knowledge and insight relevant to combatting a disease that has thoroughly afflicted so many of us, *Crime and Drugs, Drugs and Crime.* They most assuredly go hand-in-hand, and they are not prejudiced or biased. They are not marginalized by boundaries of race, religion, or creed. They are completely indifferent to how they affect us and the number of lives that are affected by them; both directly and indirectly.

I often perceive these issues as things that have a consciousness and momentum of their own, rather than choosing to view them as just another form of social sickness exhibited by human beings. But in truth, to look at this problem in any other way would be folly on all our parts. We must show this in the harshest and most pragmatic of lights; thus, seeing it for what it truly is.

While I don't claim to have the cure-all for this problem, I do have the determination to do all in my power to help people overcome the belief that there is no hope for a life beyond the one in which they are currently immersed. Many criminals, myself included, have such a large and unnecessary fear of the legitimate world, due in part because we are more familiar with the processes that accompany our preferred criminal endeavors.

The prospect of looking stupid or being turned down for a job that earns far less than what we make practicing crime is daunting enough for many of us to simply reject the idea of legitimate work altogether. Why face ridicule by someone who makes less money than you? Why even make the attempt to build skillsets and obtain degrees for employment that may not even see you through to next month's rent?

One of the key problems we face as criminals is that most of us are undereducated; hence, when making an attempt at legitimacy, we usually go for the entry-level job that is completely unsatisfying in every aspect. By doing so, we set ourselves up for failure before we even begin down the path to legitimacy.

Usually after the first paycheck, or even the first day of work, we find ourselves drawing conclusions; ones that acknowledge crime posing serious risks, but the benefits far outweighing a life of lawful stagnation with no forward progress in sight.

This study will outline in detail how-to set-in motion the inexorable process of:

1. Preparing you mentally and emotionally to make the transition from criminal to civilian.
2. Give you the knowledge, confidence, and know-how to find the right job and/or career pathway that will best fit your personality and make the most out of your strengths.
3. How to remain free from legal troubles and avoid unnecessary provocation and interference from law enforcement during your transitional phase.
4. Provide comprehensive guidelines to help keep you on the "straight and narrow," as well as community and government services that are available to support you (emotionally and financially) during those uncertain times that we must inevitably face.
5. And lastly, how best to approach and assist those who may also need a helping hand in making a change in their lives once you are at a vantage point to do so.

Despite the fact that I was making a good living for myself, I was in a constant state of fear and apprehension that what I was doing would eventually lead to my incarceration or death, not to mention the burden of guilt I carried as a result of witnessing first-hand what my occupation did to those who overindulged in the substance I sold.

I can recall sitting down in front of a computer (traded to me for drugs) and trying to convey my thoughts onto a screen that remained blank for what seemed like hours at a time. Eventually my phone would ring, an order was placed, and my attention would divert from trying to figure a way out of the mess I had found myself in, to doing the very thing I was desperately trying to avoid.

As fate would have it, I now have an overabundance of time to create a template that others may follow that will hopefully lead us/them to a better life.

I can't be certain what sort of affect my work will have on those of you who read this. I hope in the end that it will be, at the very least, an eye opener. But if it can change the life of just one of us, then the effort put into it will have been worthwhile.

There has never been, to my knowledge, the creation of a detailed map to help lead us back onto the road of legitimacy. There has never been any preventative nor reentry program designed to effectively rehabilitate criminals other than imprisonment. And once you've been to prison, it only becomes more difficult to find your way back into the fold of society. I hope that this will be the beginning of the end of your life of crime.

I can't stress enough that, no matter how much the crimes we commit affect others, no matter how much hurt we inflict on society, or our families and loved ones; the ones who suffer the most and who must ultimately live with these decisions are ourselves.

Someone once told me that the "ends justify the means." In all candor, the ends are usually bullshit. And the means are what you live with for the rest of your life.

NOTE: It is now October of 2023. I've pulled this manuscript out of my closet and decided to edit it, and shell out some cash to get it self-published. Why I've waited this long, I have no idea. But the more fact checking I perform the more I'm convinced an amount of time was needed to demonstrate the effectiveness of the processes and procedures I've outlined herein. As such, I've added "**NOTE**" sections that are usually a current reflection on the past narrative, or an explanation as to the effectiveness of what was once conjecture when written (in prison), but has since proved true via its practice upon my release.

Some additional edits were made since technology and the way we job search, report to probation, etc., have advanced since I've been home for the past 9 years. Technology, resources available to us... a lot has changed. When I fell in 2008, most people were still using burner cell phones or Blackberries.

1

IN TRANSIT

"Everything comes to an end... everything."

— D.G.

WHETHER READING this on the Inside or out there in the world, know that today is as good as any to begin contemplating your future from a realistic and practical approach. As I sit here, scratching this out on a yellow legal pad with a Bic pen from my prison cell, I can't help but think that when I get out, I will have no money, no prospects, and nowhere to live. And to have the temptation of what put me here in the first place to be one of my only options that may just improve my chances of survival.

I keep telling myself, "Next time, I won't fail. Next time, I won't get caught. Next time, I'll be more careful." I keep telling myself whatever lies I have to, to hide from the reality of my situation; that I am a destitute, uneducated convicted felon whose chances of recidivism and a life behind bars is far more likely than being able to carve out a normal existence for myself.

I rarely consider my current and future states from such a pragmatic point of view. My prospects for the future seem so much brighter than they did prior to coming to this place. Until now, I didn't believe there was any hope for a life beyond the one I was living. I find it truly ironic that prison, of all places, is where I learned that hope does exist, and that a better life is attainable for us all.

Granted, one can also study how to be a better criminal, and I've taken it upon myself to learn those practices as they apply to that concept as well. But just know that that sort of knowledge, in the long-term, will always be counterintuitive to that conscientious and contented life that seems just beyond the criminal's reach. Being a better criminal simply means that your fall will be that much harder when it occurs.

Every one of us *criminals* give consideration to our futures and what end our roads will come to. We may even perform these whimsical what-if scenarios more than the average person. I think this is because our profession doesn't exactly have a retirement plan. And with the United States having the highest recidivism rates in the world, the options of either prison or death don't feel very palatable to most.

In fact, stop reading for a few moments and ask yourself just what your retirement plan is. How old are you as you consider your retirement plan or lack thereof? Have you stolen enough and sold enough drugs to live off the interest from the pile of money you've squirreled away (interest only accrues if your money is legitimately invested). How much money is enough? I hate to coin the old cliché, but crime just doesn't pay. At least, not the types of crime most of us are involved in.

I could rant and rave with the best of them, describing in detail all the stuff I had and all things I did while I was on the very top of my game; cars, homes, endless vacations, bundles of cash stashed everywhere, caches of arms in different stash houses around the areas I operated, and on it goes.

But note the use of the past-tense, *had.* The material items law enforcement doesn't seize you end up selling off at insane discounts to pay for the lawyers or simply to keep the lights on... back to square one.

There are lots of guys and gals in prisons all over the country with a serious illness known as the "I Hads." "I had the cars, the mansions, the women... I had it all!" Well, where is everything now? The fast buck goes just as quick, if not quicker, than it came. For those of you yet to go to prison, or who haven't lost everything you own, I hope this particularly sad and embarrassing fate does not become your own. I pray that prison is never in the cards for you.

Perhaps you're saying to yourself that you know people, as I do, who have the ability to run their criminal enterprises from the Inside. Are you that person? Do you have the means to dictate what takes place on the outside while you're locked away for God only knows how long? If not, then why make comparisons?

When thinking in terms of how to get out of the situation that we've found ourselves in, it's best if we don't make ourselves up to be something and someone we are most definitely not. Are you a professional bank robber, or are you merely robbing banks to support your drug habit? Do you see yourself as a successful purveyor of illicit narcotics, or are you selling drugs so as not pay for the ones you inevitably consume?

Coming to terms with where we are on the criminal hierarchy is one of the first steps to transitioning our existence. If you've practiced criminality for some time but you're barely scraping by, what's the reason behind this? A great number of us usually have some sort of idiosyncrasy of character which offsets all that money made through illicit means; e.g., gambling, addiction to narcotics, living beyond our means or, as stated previous, ensuring that the fast buck leaves just as quickly as it came.

If you are one of these types (as I was), the likelihood that you'll be arrested before your efforts have any impact on you and yours increases a hundred-fold. And, unfortunately, this only speeds up the process of your demise. I can't stress enough that we become aware, and fast, of who we are and what our weaknesses and limitations consist of. If you suffer from some form of addiction, I urge you to seek help as soon as possible, as your career in crime, and perhaps your very life, may end much sooner than the rest of ours.

I got into the business of selling drugs because I was this close (pinches thumb and forefinger together for emphasis) to being homeless, and most illegal activities normally guarantee a faster return than, say, waiting for that first paycheck to hit.

I was fortunate to not have a substance use disorder. I didn't spend money recklessly (to a point) at least not at the outset. I kept a very low profile. But despite these efforts to stay below the radar, I was eventually arrested, and everything I worked all those years to obtain was taken away in a blink.

I cannot even begin to convey how much of a mistake it is to involve yourself in any criminal enterprise for any reason other than sheer desperation. If you are still a legitimate member of society and are still holding your head above water, I implore you to stay the course. It may not feel like it, but the stress and worries folks face when it comes to keeping the lights on or paying the rent are a far cry from the worries that accompany the Life.

Whether your methods and accomplishments resemble those of Joaquin "El Chapo" Guzman (he now resides in the Supermax penitentiary a couple hundred yards away from the prison I was housed in when I wrote this), or the lowliest petty thief out there, it's important to keep in mind the two retire-ment options for 99% of criminals: imprisonment or death. Mr. Guzman has the misfortune of receiving both these retirement packages.

At the forefront of all your considerations, remember this; everything eventually comes to an end... everything. This life, the ones we love, our children, and their children- they all come to pass. But the passing of all things come and go much quicker when you're waist deep in the Shit.

THE SWITCH

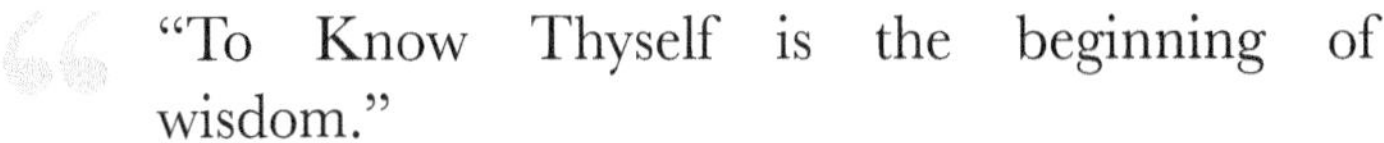

"To Know Thyself is the beginning of wisdom."

— SOCRATES

Hopefully those of you not reading this for sheer amusement (or boredom) have come to the realization that the life you're living is going to come to an end, sooner than later, and you're ready to at least entertain the idea of going legit. Trust me when I say it's easier said than done. Most of us, myself included, never think of *retiring* until we are forced to do so by way of arrest, time spent behind bars, and money lost. And for those who haven't been caught yet, I applaud you for at least considering other options apart from the one in which you are currently imbedded.

So let us assume that you've made it through the introduction; that you've stared in the mirror, considered your current state of affairs and made some self-assessments about who you are, where you are, and where you intend to go from here. Now, let's talk about making the switch.

First, it's necessary to address a few key factors in our lives that serve as reasons we started down this road in the first place. I don't know about the rest of you, but for me it was money, or lack thereof. It has and will always be about the money. And truthfully, that should be the only reason. If you're in it for the thrill, I couldn't even comprehend a criminal mind such as that reading this book or any other educational material.

If you were born into the Life via gang legacy membership, geographically repositioning yourself to another city or state might prove logistically feasible albeit difficult in other respects.

Gang members have either spread their gang's influence, or left the Life, quite successfully by joining a branch of military service. More street gangs have spread across the nation, and across the globe, due to their members joining the military and being transported to other cities, states, and countries courtesy of the federal government.

I would like to argue the point that gangbanging is dead. But to quote Ice Cube, "gangbanging will never die."

Unfortunately, it was never the catalyst for expansion by making money for its growing ranks; rather, it was created to defend and maintain small areas of real estate within the inner cities it was birthed in.

One point I will argue, until the wheels fall off, is that law enforcement loves the way rappers and so-called *studio gangsters* have stylized themselves. But more to the point, they love the way gang members have idealized these artists who imitate the Life. I tell you they love it. The reason being is because we are so much easier to identify when we are stylized as gang members in this fashion.

Criminals, at one point in time, made it their business to blend in with society, and not to stand out so as to avoid unwanted attention. Not so much nowadays. I'm not judging. I too have tattoos covering much of my body; though granted, ink is much more commonplace in the workforce, boardroom meetings, etc. I also slapped shiny wheels on my cars and installed the loudest stereo systems money could buy. Everyone, including law enforcement, could see and hear me coming from a mile away. None of these practices are good ideas if getting arrested isn't high on your list of priorities.

Making the transition may be as easy as tying your shoes for some of you, or as hard as quitting smoking for others. It all depends on the circumstances surrounding your criminal endeavors; and, in some cases, the criminal entity you've created and the obligations that accompany it.

Making drastic changes to our lifestyle, for some of us, is the most difficult of pre-steps. However, it will need to happen in order to affect change that will be correctly and permanently executed, so there's a lesser chance of backpedaling into the Shit.

NOTE: I utilize both "the Life" and "the Shit" interchangeably, as I see no difference between the meaning of each.

We can perform a number of activities (pre-steps) to prepare ourselves for the transition. I highly suggest hobbies, exercising and/or activities that hold our interest other than criminality.

Hobbies are an indirect way of channeling our thoughts and actions towards ambitions whose rewards are mostly self-gratifying. In essence, they enable us to change many aspects of daily life without consciously attempting to change the Life itself. We simply become engrossed in activities that influence and draw us away from negative practices, such as crime... without even knowing it.

Often times these activities transition into passions which other people often share. This can have a profound impact on us, and the types of human elements we surround ourselves with, or, that we find ourselves surrounded by. It helps to ensure that we're not sitting around complacently with like-minded criminals plotting, scheming, wheeling and dealing.

Virtually anything ranging from physical activity, such as exercising or gardening, to artistic practices such as drawing, music, and dance; to mental creativity that strengthen and challenge the mind, i.e., furthering one's education, a friendly game of chess, etc., are all positive activities that ensure we spend less time contemplating "doing dirt" or committing crimes, and more time redefining ourselves as human beings.

Pursuits of spiritual growth should also be considered as a

means of drastically changing our outlook and the way in which we view our criminal occupation. A simple prayer in the morning or meditation to focus your mind, body, and spirit before the day starts can be the determining factor in whether your whole day, or life, ends up productive or disastrous.

Pursuing spiritual growth in the communal sense also helps divert us from social settings where exercising criminal behavior is the status quo.

The objective here is to indulge in a positive yet sometimes constructive action, practice, or pastime. The logic being that by doing so we're already making the transition without going *cold turkey.* This helps facilitate a measured yet gradual transformation which is designed to draw us away from criminal endeavors in such a subtle fashion; that, not only are we unaware of our decline in criminality, but we welcome it- even if on a sub-conscious level.

If you have confidants, close friends, family and colleagues (FFC) who are privy to the knowledge that you are involved in criminal activity, you will find that they are a fathomless well of advice, support and ideas that may help you steer clear of trouble along the way to transitioning.

Even the family members who depended on me financially would rather have seen me go legit than see me where I am today, more so since it is those same people I now look to for support while incarcerated.

NOTE: You should be wary of those that show the slightest inclination towards disappointment in your decision to change. This isn't my favorite option to present, but if confidants are limited and you don't always trust your own advice, then consider the less-traveled road of talking to a behavioral therapist. I was court-ordered to see a therapist prior to sentencing. She helped explain to me certain triggers that caused me to feel and act in a destructive way. She was also adept at outlining routines and practices tailored to managing life's little, or in some cases, large problems. She also identified many of my behavioral quirks as verging on sociopathic, but that's neither here nor there.

But keep in mind that any ear can also serve as a crutch that many choose to lean on while continuing down the path of criminality. It can become a routine like having coffee, or cocaine in the morning to get us moving and out the door. Therapy, or any discussion, should result in subsequent action, or the appropriate inaction. Venting to anyone concerning your misgivings about life is counterintuitive to knowing thyself, much less initiating pre-steps to our transition.

STEPPING STONES

"A rainy-day fund won't protect you from the flood."

— D. PETERS

Let's discuss some steps you can take that are tangible, physical, actual adjustments in your life, your schedule, and your way of doing things. These are the first, and sometimes hardest steps that will eventually lead to a brighter future.

Prior to what I call my *final arrest,* I had begun taking half measures to avoid the criminal lifestyle. Unfortunately, it was too little too late. One of my main strategies for enduring survival in the Life was to distance myself from as many people as possible, so that when I did get caught, it would be easier to let go. My flawed logic was that there would be fewer ties to the outside world that would affect how I did my time on the inside.

Looking back, I'm sure we can all see the folly with this kind of thinking. Cut ties with everyone close to me, because I know sooner or later, I'm going to be in prison. What is that?! Instead, why not take measures to ensure that we never get caught? And while we're at it, why not take measures to ensure we'll never face the prospect of arrest because we will no longer be criminals?

As chance would have it, I did rather well, or very badly – depending on how one views progress through a moral lens – at being a criminal for over 17 years of my life. From 12 years-of-age until my 28th birthday (1992-2008) I had avoided any real serious trouble with the law, despite killings, shootings, stabbings, police raids, drive-bys, and pretty much anything else being the order of the day.

What is worth examining is that the deeper we delve into lives of crime, the further we distance ourselves from a normal existence; often times, unbeknownst to those becoming criminals.

As an adolescent I never had a steady girlfriend. I never participated in the things that might identify me as a normal teenager. I never graduated high school, and never went to prom. I wouldn't call them nightmares, but to this day I have dreams I awake from with a profound sense of loss and regret at having never graduated high school.

I never really enjoyed the activities and experiences young people are supposed to enjoy. I was too busy watching my back and avoiding detection and arrest.

If I can go into the weeds for a moment, I'd like to ask you to take measure of the things you've given up. It's such a large sacrifice for what seems like a rather small amount of financial security.

Towards the end, just prior to my fall, I met a woman who I instantly and irrevocably fell in love with.

But I still had one foot in the Shit, and with the other, I had the slightest of footholds on what felt like the beginnings of normalcy. I can't even begin to convey how much of a mistake that was. In truth, the fault was continuing with the unlawful acts I committed *after* realizing I had something worth living for beyond the world I had survived within.

Changing my cell phone number without providing the new contact info was perhaps the largest and most impactful physical act ever committed. I knew the minute I did this I would be severing contact, and a financial pipeline, that I depended heavily upon. Our mobile phone is the connection to every external contact outside of our household.

Once that number changes, you effectively disconnect yourself from any and all people with the exception of the ones who you give out the new number to. And unless your criminal counterparts know where you live, which none of mine did, the only way they can contact you is if you decide to reach out to them. If we're attempting to affect a change, and if we've made the proper preparations for that transition, there should no longer be any reason for you to contact those people.

Sure, we might encounter a customer or a meeting with one of our partners on common ground, but if that occurs, we can simply say that you're lying low for the time being. Customers will *always* find someone else to buy their products or services from, and the people we do other work with will eventually write us off as an expense rather than a contribution to their own interests.

I had a very good friend whom I had known since I was about 15 years of age who helped me get my foot in the door of the drug trade. When I was broke and living from couch-to-couch as a teenager, he took me under his wing and showed me the ins and outs of selling narcotics. Born in Mexico, he migrated to the States when he was still in single-digits. He lived in Texas until the age of 18, at which point, he moved to New Mexico. I met him in '95. In a couple years' time I surpassed him in the amount of product I was moving. As a result, he introduced me to his connection; which most dealers never do, as this cuts them out of the picture.

He kept telling me that I was heading in the wrong direction, and that selling more is not necessarily better. Selling drugs was a temporary solution (a Band-Aid if you will) to the long-term challenge of financial security. That as a result of my higher output, I had now exposed myself to more dangerous components of the Life. I didn't believe him because I could not see beyond the next dollar. I couldn't see the bigger picture he attempted to paint for me.

He eventually created a large enough cushion that he could survive, i.e., pay mortgage, bills, etc., without selling drugs for as long as needed to get his legitimate income stream flowing. He devoted every free second of spare time to pursuing a lawful career path.

To my knowledge, he was never arrested. He is now the Operations Manager for an exclusive resort in the Southwest.

This nameless friend of mine (and yes, I'll always consider him a friend) worked for one of the groups operating in one or several of the border cities of Old Mexico. (I live in New Mexico; hence we make the distinction between the nation and state using *old* and *new*).

I never saw these groups as "cartels." And I don't think those operating within these groups apply that naming convention to themselves either. They're just people- farmers, blue-collar and subsistence level laborers practicing capitalism the only way they knew how. (It's funny to me, years later, if I see someone breaking out a bag of coke to sniff at a private gathering or wherever, they always say something along the lines of, "I got this from my cartel connection.") Well, obviously if you're consuming cocaine, it made its way up the underground pipeline from South America, thence to Mexico, and finally here. Of course, throughout each stage of its transport members of some group or cartel were responsible for getting it to the noses, veins, and lungs of the good citizens of the United States.

My argument is if you can walk away from distributing for a drug cartel, you can walk away from anything. Apart from occasional phone calls and somewhat dark-humored jokes, there was never any pressure for me to continue working after I was arrested. Neither one of us was ever intimidated or threatened as a result of our voluntary or forced exit from the Life. Ultimately, as my friend introduced me, and I introduced others in their turn... we were just steppingstones for the guys beneath us to spin the proverbial Wheel of Chance when their time came.

CRIME PAYS... AND DEMANDS PAYMENT

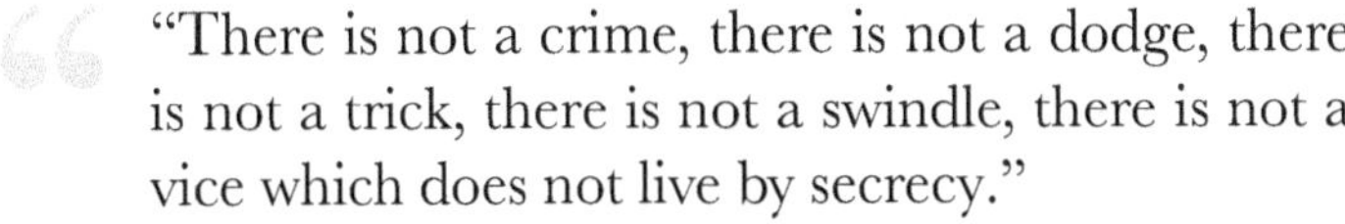

"There is not a crime, there is not a dodge, there is not a trick, there is not a swindle, there is not a vice which does not live by secrecy."

— JOSEPH PULITZER

"When a man is denied the right to live the life he believes in, he has no choice but to become an outlaw."

— NELSON MANDELA

Downsizing, downscaling, and cutbacks: these are terms and methods that corporations use when their spending and cost of operations have begun to encroach upon their profit margin. For the sake of this discussion, our corporation or company is our criminal enterprise. Our profit margin is not so much our financial gains as it is our freedom. In order to maintain a high profit margin, we must scale back on criminal practices, while simultaneously creating alternative revenue streams that will not pose risks during our transitional phase.

When performing cutbacks, we have to first make the distinction between necessity and luxury. Every penny saved is a penny earned, and the more items and services deemed as luxuries or things we can do without, the bigger and faster our financial cushion will grow.

Many of us who enter into the Life do so because we are suffering from some form of financial strain. But when the easy money rolls in we find ourselves spending frivolously on things that we were never able to afford when we were broke. These careless spending habits spiral so much out of control that we begin to lose focus on why we're committing crimes in the first place. When you continue committing crime for the purpose of supporting your high-class lifestyle, rather than doing it simply to help make ends meet, you're in trouble.

When we downsize, we're essentially minimizing our cost of living into one that is more realistic and affordable. In plain terms, this means that we have to commit fewer crimes (less risk) for longer sustainability (financial security). This doesn't necessarily mean that we have to do without certain amenities, but it does imply that we can reduce costs, and risk, by say, choosing more cost-effective phone plans, insurance bundles, etc. Everything from smart energy saving practices to grocery shopping rather than eating out can save us small but comparatively large amounts of money when we take all of our efforts at downsizing as one collective push in the intended direction.

Your financial cushion is your nest egg, your treasure trove, or your heavily wrapped and sealed packets of money that you have hidden all over the place. It's the amount of money and capital that normal folks devote their whole lives to increasing so that when they're ready to retire, they may do so without relying solely on social security checks and non-passive income.

When we cease to earn money from crime, this cushion is what we're going to depend on until we obtain employment that not only makes ends meet, but that will also produce secondary capital that should be invested in savings, retirement, and sound/safe business ventures. Remember- the less money spent on inconsequential goods and services, the more money we're putting in our pockets; thus, the faster our nest egg will grow.

Perhaps one of the most difficult commitments we can perform is humbling ourselves (once we've reached a state of criminal success), and summoning up enough courage to work a regular job during the transition. I promise it will make our conversion so much easier to fathom and ease into.

NOTE: This job doesn't have to be the career that you end up in for the rest of your life. It should just get you used to the idea of what the majority of the world does to earn their bread and butter. The realization that the masses humble themselves *everyday* in this same fashion places us in some rather familiar company.

The monetary reward for working that first 8-to-5 will be far less than what we made doing dirt- to the extent where it may appear nonexistent. But given time, the intrinsic reward or self-satisfaction will begin to take root. For some of us, it will give us that first sense of legitimacy. Once we begin going through the motions of working on a daily basis, (sometimes on a schedule other than our own), we'll begin seeing the benefits of an occupation whose drawbacks do not include taking up residence in prison or the county morgue.

So, cutbacks; how do you identify what stays, what goes, and what can be reduced in order to put a little more cream in your bank account and less in the pockets of retailers and service providers? It's about defining necessity versus luxury.

I spent thousands of dollars on clothes, jewelry, sunglasses and bullshit, that, sometimes I never even wore. I'm feeling no small amount of anger and regret when I write this.

To this day, I can't put my finger on what made me buy all of those useless rags. Watches and jewelry also took their toll (I still love watches). Cars! From the latest models to classic muscle, lowriders, you name it. They all put heavy dents in the profits I made. Strippers! God bless 'em. Hopefully some of those gals used that money to pay for an education or other investment rather than simply recycling it back into the retail and service industries, as I did.

I promise you this several paragraph's worth of ranting has its purpose. Bear with me...

I can recall waking up around noon right when my favorite sushi spot opened, and I would spend a good 70 bucks or so on breakfast alone. Breakfast was followed by another meal usually around 4p.m. (after I worked out at this over-priced gym/spa). And then a late dinner that usually cost a couple hundred bucks or more if a friend or companion joined me. Well over $1000 a week. I could've spent that money on groceries to last a good month or more.

For those of us that are not addicted to narcotics, gambling or other vices, the chances are high that we'll be addicted to *something* that will keep you dependent on profits earned from crime.

This is yet another cyclic event that occurs when easy money does not accrue through working smart and working honestly.

Something given always has less value than something earned. It means nothing to us, as we put forth very little effort to acquire it. Selling dope is by no means a walk in the park. But it was in many cases comparable to a stranger handing me something that had less value to me as compared to an acquisition I worked for and earned as a result.

Make a list of the material items and services you're sure you can live without. Sell them, trade them, or give them away to friends and family; hell, complete strangers. The first things to go for me were the extra cars I had no garages or spaces for which to park them. Some I owned outright, but in many cases the newer ones I was making payments on. We may lose cash on the trade-in to the dealership, but just think of how much cash we've already lost on purchasing items that lose a quarter of their value as soon as they're driven off the lot?

NOTE: Unless they're collector's items, (think Chevelles, Canadian Chevelles, A.K.A. Pontiac Beaumonts, 50's and 60s Corvettes, fast-back Mustangs "Eleanors," Impalas, etc.), cars have got to be one of the worst investments of all time. If we sell the ones we own outright, we'll see immediate and sizeable increases in our nest egg. Nice vehicles have almost no worth with the exception of the aesthetic value provided to the owner. For the car guys and gals throwing this in the trash, I have 1 new daily driver, and 2 oldies I just can't let go of.

I'm acquainted with a few very successful, legitimate people who would be considered wealthy by any standard. The realization struck me upon returning home that not one of these individuals owns a vehicle for which they use other than getting them from point A to point B. The vehicles they own may be a Prius or a high-end European model. But they all use them as forms of conveyance, nothing more. We, on the other hand, use vehicles as status symbols. This is one of the first pitfalls and milestones reached as a moderately successful criminal. Beware.

Successful legitimate people don't tend to flaunt their materialism as much as we do. I've always wondered why those of us who come from poor upbringings – who suddenly acquire a modicum of wealth – feel the need to advertise it when others do not.

We feel this irresistible urge to show others how well we're doing by means of a nice car, which, we at times paint and repaint with the most eye-catching custom colors; clothing, and other accessories that should be worn at galas, events, or in music videos and nowhere else.

I suspect it's because we want life to notice us. Unfortunately, when it does, the shiny rims, (country guys and gals tend to put more than necessary lifts on 4x4s), jewelry-adorned wrists hanging out the window, music heard from a mile away... it unfortunately denounces us as poor people imitating a lavish lifestyle obtained by ill-gotten gains.

We project an image of something that we aspire to be; and yet, this projection is distorted and looks ridiculous by normal standards of measuring success.

If you pair this distortion with poor money-managing practices most of us employ, it pretty much guarantees we will never reach our full potential; no matter how much money our criminal pursuits produce.

Next to go was the satellite and cable TV that I never watched.

I sold back – for always less than what I paid – watches and jewelry that I never wore, but it sure felt good having that stuff on display in my bedroom closet. I sold the custom red-felt Brunswick pool table that matched the red contemporary painting I bought off a friend that has since passed before both he and his work could be better acknowledged and more widely known outside the art community in New Mexico.

Rooms in my home that I had had entirely furnished, I completely cleared out. By the time I was finished with all this liquidating, my home, my garage, and my mind were a lot less cluttered.

I then compiled a written expenditure of every remaining bill or payment I had. The amount of money going out for bills and other expenses was drastically reduced; thus, the money made was of more worth and went to more worthy causes rather than just being given away. I made thousands more simply by spending *less*.

Those products and services I could not do without I limited to treating myself to on the weekends, or on a monthly, or quarterly basis, i.e., eating out, strip clubs, etc. I also discovered that I enjoyed these treats much more than when I indulged on a regular basis. I savored a nice meal, as well as the service that came with it, instead of gorging and drinking expensive swill simply for the sake of doing so.

In short, I began to enjoy life more as opposed to taking for granted things that most people not only find pleasure in doing, but that are used to balance the anxieties and tension that come with working a normal job and living a normal life.

When we overindulge, we begin to enjoy things at an overly-moderate pace. And, as a result, they begin to lose their appeal. We bombard ourselves with so much stimuli and pleasure that we become desensitized and indifferent to the things that we once found great contentment in doing. If your case of indulgence is extreme, as mine became, you'll find yourself spending money simply for the sake of doing so. No bueno...

Although some of us may be beneath the level of income it takes to downsize on the scale I'm illustrating, just know there are others that far exceed the level(s) we aspired to. No matter your situation, there are an infinite number of ways to reduce spending and maximize your profits. The most cost-effective, and the ones which produce the fastest results are liquidating, downsizing and cutbacks.

As mentioned earlier, if you're involved in criminal activity yet barely making ends meet, surely there is a reason that can be identified. Find out the reason(s) and create a solution. If there is a propensity in the works for abusing alcohol and drugs, deal with it before it deals with you.

Unfortunately, I was too dedicated to the lifestyle I aspired to have. I was too confident in my ability to earn to ever perceive that I had other vices – less noticeable but just as costly – that would take heavy tolls on my pocket, my overall health, as well as my sense of wellbeing.

Crime pays because it is intended to bring in more revenue than a normal entry-level position ever would. Its very nature and illegality are what ensures the profits, and stakes, are that much higher. What does crime profit us if not solely for financial gain? How much more of a gain is it really if the proceeds are spent in a careless and reckless fashion? And if the risks and penalties associated with said proceeds are higher than those that accompany honest wages, what we're really doing is working a more hazardous and protracted job than most people, and with far less benefits.

Take stock of your day-to-day routine and see what sort of lifestyle you're living when you're not out there on the grind. How do we spend our time off? Are we *investing* in our nest egg and attempting to further ourselves, or are we simply *spending* in an attempt to fill the empty void in our lives with as many material things as possible? Know the difference between spending fruitlessly and investing wisely.

If we have family, are we spending/investing time, money and effort for their sakes, or are we feeling bitter towards them; dwelling on how much it costs to keep them clothed, fed, healthy and happy? How much more could have gone towards the nest egg and the family unit if we hadn't splurged on a new car and/or new wheels for that new car? Last time I checked, they sold cars with factory wheels and tires...

How much investment could have gone to making the transition and securing a future for you and your loved ones had you not indulged in all the things we needlessly splurge on?

Identify what you need. Do away with the stuff you don't. Plain and simple.

CLOSING

From the day I began exercising, riding my mountain bike through and out of town, playing chess, reading; to the day I began downsizing, cutting back on crap I didn't need, and actively focusing on transitioning from the way I made a living, I noticed a very profound and dramatic change, not only in my day-to-day living, but in the manner in which I viewed my place in the world.

Prior to taking these steps, I had this feeling that started in my chest and wormed its way into most of my waking thoughts. At times its grip around my heart would cause me to hyperventilate, and my hands to cramp up in what I can only describe as a fetal position. It would keep me awake at night and keep the gears grinding in my head as opposed to putting head to pillow and falling asleep immediately.

I would see headlights reflected on the ceiling and wonder if it was law enforcement coming to my home. I would spin scenarios in my head and begin plotting on anyone who owed me money. I would identify and search for the slightest insult or disrespect that may or may not have occurred earlier that day or a year ago, and I would seek retribution the next day, or that night for the offense...

This constant feeling of apprehension was a direct mental > emotional > physical side effect of choosing a life of crime. It kept me alive. It kept me from getting too comfortable. But it made me hyperaware to the extent where I was unable to perform valid threat assessments versus imagined slights and insults to an egotistical and sociopathic mind-frame.

It was around this time that I knew I would never be at peace while practicing, and immersed in, the Life. It made me suspicious of the world and everyone in it. It kept me isolated from the rest of humanity apart from those who were also, on some level or another, in the Shit. It kept me from meeting individuals who I may have come to know and like; people who might have shared with me their joy and their struggles, and whom I may have gained knowledge, advice, and support from in the natural course of my relationship with them.

The moment I began to inch away from my occupation as a dealer, the more I felt apprehension loosen its grip. No amount of material possession, nor financial security, or splurging on good times would ever truly alleviate that sense of impending doom. But one small change of thought followed by actions measured in baby steps, and that feeling I had lived with for most of my life began to diminish.

Prior to actively focusing on this transition, I had tried a number of coping mechanisms that failed. The chemical route, where I was prescribed anxiety medications that only numbed me to the circumstances around me, and slowed me down to the point where it was no longer a concern if I made enough money to get by; or stayed on the streets, or went to prison. I simply didn't care about anything and had zero motivation while I was under the influence of these legal narcotics.

No matter how many different crutches, cures and diversions I tried, including ones I've mentioned that worked, to a degree, none of it came close to liberating me the way acknowledgment of my dead-end occupation's hazards and risks did.

I also came to realize that exercising, reading, and other productive activities, were, in essence, the precursor to the idea of searching for a more beneficial way to exist. On a subconscious level, I was seeking out other avenues to enjoy my free time apart from pleasure and vice.

I enrolled in a few courses at the community college, as well as in real estate classes. These small steps, coupled with other constructive activities, opened up pathways I wouldn't have thought possible.

Unfortunately, this would all come crashing down, as I had performed these steps ass-backwards.

I understood, on some level, that I was striving towards something more principle driven while maintaining as tight a grip as I could manage on the drug trafficking in the areas in which I operated. Maintaining my grip wasn't a hard feat to accomplish, but attempting to exist ethically in the process was proving paradoxical. It was comparable to jogging 5 miles and smoking 2 packs of cigarettes afterwards.

It is impossible to travel in two directions at once.

Without a doubt there are criminals out there who are more adept at business of any sort than I. Without conceit, I have to admit that I saw myself as a better than average criminal (and still do in retrospect). I also worked with a lot of individuals that were first rate screw ups, and others that managed their criminal endeavors far more admirably than most of us ever will. But I have never known one of us that does not feel torn between the two-life scenario: one consisting of normalcy, while the other is filled with everything that accompanies the Life.

Rather than suggest that we hope for the best and expect the worst. I would suggest that we Prepare Ourselves.

Find something to pursue that stimulates, exercises and challenges the mind > body > and soul. Delve into a pastime that keeps you occupied and diverted from that which earns daily bread in an unlawful fashion.

Perhaps in time we'll come to perfect what we pursue. When this occurs, find another challenge or hobby and immerse yourself in it, or simply continue to enjoy doing something well. In short, I suggest that we search out illumination and escape the saturating darkness and obscurity that accompanies our current trajectory.

Consult with our families, loved ones, partners in crime that are of the same mind, even one's attorney, on how best to affect the change from criminal to civilian according to their scope and profession. Obtain as much knowledge and counsel from these individuals as possible and utilize it.

Change our contact information and delete every contact in our directory and in our minds that has anything to do with the Life. Do not shit where you eat, that is to say, do not conduct business where you live. Move to a different city/state if you have to. Anything beats the punitive damages we incur as a result of our eventual downfall.

If we encounter people that we've had dealings with in the past, which we most assuredly will, inform them that you're lying low for the time being, and if they knew the level of heat that was on you, they should too.

NOTE: Beware of the drug user, informant or undercover that will always throw caution to the wind at the risk of looking out for *you* on this one last deal. And be sure to let everyone down easy without burning bridges. That person we sold drugs to may one day straighten their lives out, win the lottery, you name it. Our crime partners may also have legitimate contacts, as mine did, that can help us in our transition. Take one giant step towards legitimacy, that first straight job; be it construction, flipping burgers, flipping cars, or flipping houses. Host or manage a restaurant that was once frequented. Take one of your many vehicles and Uber people back and forth (I believe they have to be 4-door, and if it's high-end people will pay more per transport).

Work as an administrative assistant at your attorney's law firm, or any number of occupations that are an entry-level sure thing. And watch your opportunities, your hopes for the future, your self-confidence, and your nest egg expand.

Sometimes we're the ones drinking the wine, while at other times we're the ones picking the grapes. There's no shame in it. Embrace it as the gateway to a better existence if you must. There's nothing wrong with dirty hands earning clean money.

If you fall and go to prison, as I did, you are going to be picking those grapes for the first few years of your reentry, if not the rest of your life. It's best to get a head start and obtain legitimacy to avoid going to prison in the first place.

It takes a strong-willed individual to withstand and curb peer pressure, financial pressure, or pressure of any kind. Therefore, we must be strong and determined in the course we set, or the course we intend to veer away from. Know that whenever we bend or are swayed by another person's will, that our fortitude has just been compromised.

Choose the path that is best for you and not what's best for those that want something from us, or that depend on our efforts.

NOTE: My father grew up in West Baltimore, was in-and-out of what he refers to as boys' homes (juvenile hall), volunteered for the Army at 17 during the Vietnam War to escape the ghetto, and got into all kinds of shit there and when he came home in 1970. And here he is, a little old, mixed-race, unassuming guy that you wouldn't expect endured much of anything... all 5' 5" of him. He always told my brother and I that one of the things that got him into trouble the most was the phrase "Let's," and I couldn't agree more.

People who employ this phrase are usually ones who don't consider doing the things they want done alone. They need a little backup or support, usually because "Let's" entails doing dirt, and they don't want to be the only one taking the risk, as well as the fall.

These folks that start their suggestions with the word "Let's" can be one of the greatest detriments to your transition. What makes them such a liability – and such an influential force – is that they're usually the ones we've being doing dirt with for much of our criminal lives. If we can't convince them to transition with us, we have to simply let them continue on their own path without deviating us from ours.

There were guys I knew that never would've pursued criminality to the extent they did had I not been the one telling them Let's do this or Let's do that. Some of them fell, and fell hard, while others died from overdoses or were murdered.

Always weigh risk versus reward, actions and subsequent inevitable reactions. When we resolve to walk away from potentially dangerous situations, do so... and never look back.

2

FEAR ITSELF

> "He who overcomes his fear will truly be free."
>
> — ARISTOTLE

> "If you want to conquer fear, don't sit at home and think about it. Go out and get busy."
>
> — DALE CARNEGIE

> "While there are numerous programs available for the drug user, the options for the drug trafficker are as follows: Death, prison, and addiction to the very product they market."
>
> — DAN MARLOWE, CRIMINAL DEFENSE ATTORNEY

SINCE COMING HOME, I encounter quite a lot of people that knew me pre-prison. Many of them still have this perception about me that would fit the individual I once was. For instance, a guy I ran into was going down memory lane with me; reminding me about some guy whose teeth I knocked out at a local watering hole, (in self-defense) and about some other unfortunate case, (again, based on self-defense) in which an individual lost their life. My crime partner, and still one of my best friends, was eventually awarded a retrial on appeal and had this murder conviction overturned after spending several years in prison.

This guy I encountered had been shot himself at one point, and no stranger to every dynamic that accompanies the Life. He asked me how I made it through, well... everything that we were involved in, from the streets > prison > and now out the other side.

The truth is that people thought I was "crazy." Folks have a tendency to apply that description to those known for acts of violence at any opportunity. In my situation, nothing could be further from the truth. Everything I did was motivated by fear... everything.

If I saw trouble around the corner I would usually swing, stab, or shoot first for fear of being punched in the face, stabbed, or shot. If word got back that so-and-so intended me harm, I would go in search of that individual and deal with them before they dealt with me, out of fear.

I wasn't crazy. I wasn't preemptive out of intelligence or cunning. It was fear that motivated and moved me to action. Nothing more.

When searching for employment, the principal fear I faced was being perceived as underqualified.

The thought that never occurs to us is that this is *precisely* how almost all applicants feel when they're on the hunt; are being interviewed or perhaps even considered for a position. With the exception of those select few overachievers, everyone out there pounding the pavement looking for work feels that fear of ridicule or rejection by the individual or panel conducting the interview.

How many times have we caught ourselves half-stepping in the right direction? Searching the classifieds if you're old school, or surfing employment sites for a job or career? How many times have we found an interesting position, verging on the brink of passion, and then bypassed that position because we've never been more convinced of our underqualification? How many times have we succumbed to the harsh truth that entry-level positions, or jobs advertised with "no experience necessary" are the only ones we're suited to?

The dilemma that most of us face is that – insofar as legitimate employment goes – we *are* underqualified and inexperienced; hence, we will *always* consider the job that is going to prove loathsome and undesirable, as these are the easiest to obtain.

NOTE: They are also the easiest to vacate. Once hired, it doesn't take long to conclude that our criminal ventures hold much more promise – in terms of monetary gain – than working most entry-level, legitimate occupations.

The financial gain from criminal activity will always, initially, far outweigh the piddling amount of income scraped and squeezed out of that first laborious and completely unsatisfying piece of work. What's more is that both entry-level positions, (crime and regular work) never require qualifications of any kind from the applicant. This comparison only makes the entrapment and allure of criminality that much more appealing.

What most criminals never tell you is that the very nature of crime caps your income. Its illegality makes it harder to save and invest than legitimate revenue streams. Hence, ill-gotten currency has far less value than money earned from an honest living. To compound our problems, that time spent chasing the illicit dollar is time that could have gone towards raising our estimations in the eyes of potential employers.

I imagine your rehearsed response when an interviewer asks what you've been doing to earn a living for most of your adult life resembles my own... a complete lie.

It finally dawned on me that selling cocaine was never going to prove a solution for long-term sustainability.

I began contemplating the idea of seeking some form of gainful employment. But I faced a few hurdles. For one, I had zero work history to speak of. Apart from my GED and a couple college credits with no plan for a degree in mind, I possessed little education or trade skills. I was essentially worthless. That is, I possessed no worth that an employer would identify as valuable.

The only fix I could think of that would improve my chances of gainful employment was to create a resume, and a work history, that would prove credible should anyone decide to verify the jobs and references contained therein.

NOTE: This is what the majority of the world does when job searching- not fabricate work history, but draft in their resume the best possible representation of oneself.

I knew enough small business owners and high-end clientele through selling coke who were willing to state that, yes, I did in-fact, work as a manager at so-and-so's restaurant for the past 4 years. And, yes, Jason did in-fact function as our office manager prior to his moving on to bigger and better things. And absolutely; he was and still is, to my knowledge, a work-orientated, multi-tasking individual who takes pride in his work, and who enjoys helping others achieve their goals as well.

The sad result, however, was that when I landed these jobs, I never stayed long. The simple truth of the matter was that I was completely disinterested in maintaining legitimate employment once obtained. No matter how decent the paychecks were or the work environment itself, I had no work ethic; nor drive, nor motivation to do anything unless it consisted of making easy money through criminal acts.

I wonder if we can use some good 'ol 20/20 hindsight at yet another juncture of this study and think back to when we were either voluntold or made the decision to work for a living. Usually this was due to probation or parole's demands, or because we suddenly felt the impulse to make an honest buck. I suspect it's a combination of forced labor and entry-level positions that make for such an unpalatable experience.

We set ourselves up for failure, and knock our ambitions down because they weren't valid aspects of our true career pathway from the outset.

How long can we actually last in jobs such as these? How long does it take before we resolve to stick to the path that pays best? Have you ever heard the saying, "the world needs ditch diggers too?" Who among us would opt to scratch out an existence digging ditches when experience, and the streets, tells us we can work smarter doing otherwise?

I often feel this is the crux of our dilemma which only further solidifies our position on the criminal pathway: that first initial spoonful of hard work without reward which directs our optimism towards crime, as opposed to exerting massive amounts of physical and mental energy, and time, simply in an effort to get by.

Another component of this paradox is that we know we possess enough intelligence and capitalistic know-how to buy something for a dollar and sell it for two. However, we lack the training to use that talent in a lawful and conscientious manner.

Speaking for myself, there's a sense of alienation to conformity that occurs; a lack of accomplishment via risk and adventure not associated with an honest living.

I've often tried to pinpoint the exact moment in time when I drifted from the herd, and resembled someone who didn't abide by social norms. I used to believe it took place when we moved from Tacoma, WA to Española, NM. We became lower class and destitute almost overnight. I felt I had no other alternative for survival than to sell drugs. I now know that assumption to be completely untrue.

THE BEGINNING

I skipped a grade in elementary school (no big feat there). I think it was the 3rd grade, and began school a year earlier than most (kindergarten at 4). I was OK at math, (still am), but excelled in English, History, Social Studies, and subjects that required interest in words rather than numbers.

I remember being selected for this curriculum designed for children that demonstrated a higher-than-average intellect in areas of grammar and language comprehension. I was supposed to attend this "gifted" class at some point post-lunch and remain there until after school let out.

I went to that class for maybe a full month before I forgot that I was supposed to be going, and they eventually stopped reminding me to attend.

The seating arrangement was in a half circle (about 13 of us, and mostly kids a couple grades higher than me). The teacher – whom we were to address on a first-name basis – sat in the middle of our half circle. I thought it strange that she was positioned among us rather than opposite our gathering. And she would have to look right or left when addressing us rather than simply eyeing her subjects from across an expanse of space as a standard classroom was formatted.

We were given the impression that she was one of *us*, rather than one of *them*.She was fairly young, mid-twenties, and rather easy on the eyes. She had dark brown hair, pale skin and eyes of the lightest shade of blue/grey- a combination I still find attractive today much as I did when I was 8 or 9.

Her mannerisms were more that of a friend than a teacher, whose affability took precedence over any teaching skills she may have possessed. I never saw her anywhere in school except for in that room, which was like an extension (a nice, large office), that was accessed from the library.

Those few times I attended I couldn't bring to mind any

instances where we did any actual school work. We sat and discussed, as adults would, politics, philosophical matters, current times and events, and any other subjects that came to mind. At times, she or another student would bring reading material or a book to discuss, i.e., the subject matter or author's intent behind writing it. But beyond that, there was never any specific assignments or homework to be performed.

My regular teacher would remind me that I needed to attend this class, if, that was what I wanted to do. I eventually just stopped going. I recall looking up and seeing some of the older kids motioning to me through the window to join. I would much rather have cut up with my friends and half-assed performed the assembly line type of schoolwork in the regular classroom as opposed to associating with the, at times, aloof and somewhat introverted overachievers.

Strangely enough, when I attempted to do the things in my regular class which were encouraged in the gifted program – such as the time I moved our desks into a semi-circle and suggested that we should discuss our school work as a collective rather than singularly – I was reprimanded for disrupting the rest of the class, that is, students that were "trying to learn something."

After that, I became disillusioned with the constant never-changing schedule and uniformity that accompanied the humdrum of elementary school. There were a few good teachers that stood out, sure. But the impact of these was minuscule compared to that of the majority, and compared to the institution of education itself.

As time went on, I realized that I became bored and jaded, rather quickly, with any curriculum, program or institution that thrived on invariability.

This was a rather unfortunate sentiment I applied, all too often, to circumstances I was a part of. Considering the similarities between public schools and the majority of employment opportunities, I essentially determined I was unfit and ill-suited for adherence to the construct of life, such as it is.

From the 5th grade until I dropped out in the 9th, I ceased to absorb anything equaling educational value. It wasn't because the teachers didn't have anything of worth to impart to me. It was the manner in which it was prescribed, day-after-day, that became unbearable.

The only reason I even made it to high school was due to attendance being 50% of the grade. You can, or could, graduate simply by showing up every day. I went from a projected graduation at 16 years-of-age to dropping out years before that. The truth was I was simply not adept at playing this particular game.

From the time I was a child in the single digits and feeling no obligation to perform those tasks expected of me – for no other reason other than I chose not to – to the moment seeds of dissention and entitlement without reason began to take root, was the period I began operating in opposition to conformity.

It was at *this* point, and not at the point where I thought it had begun, where my refusal or inability to adjust to what was expected of me was to influence my outlook and distain for conventionality, and the means by which the majority of people advance in life.

If you can, try to pinpoint the exact moment in your life when you began to go against the grain. I think that we'll come to discover it was at a much earlier age/stage than we once thought. I still smile (without mirth) when I think of how I used my family's financial difficulties to justify my decision to sell drugs. I smile because I realize now that I wasn't making a brave and intelligent decision to go against the grain. I was simply following a vast majority of people down a well-traveled road to nowhere.

I was of the mind that desperate times call for desperate measures. And pride can play a major role in the lives of those who are affected by circumstance. While I don't wish to promote crime, I do think that it's necessary to conclude that for many of us, there didn't seem to be any other option; at least, not at the time. I only berate my inability to adapt to the environment I was subject to; or, more accurately, to possess the means to move from that environment to one more favorable.

My intent, though, is to help us all raise a collective awareness of ourselves, our worth, and our current circumstances. And to help us make a transition that will hopefully come before the inevitable problems arise as a result of the way we choose to make money.

It is of the utmost importance that we look at ourselves from an objective point of view; that is, if we can step out of ourselves for a moment and recognize how we are perceived, and what we are becoming.

NOTE: I use the word *becoming* because we are in a constant state of flux, and the person you consider to be *yourself* today, may not have the same opinions now as you will tomorrow, or the next day. Now that I have some decades behind me – and perhaps an equal number ahead of me – it's almost with a sense of vertigo when I recall that the 20-year-old me doesn't think like the 30-year-old me. Nor do either of these decades draw the same conclusions as my current 44-years-young version of self. And yet, I was sure my point of view in my 20s was the correct one... Such is the mind that deals in absolutism without reflection on past decisions.

Knowing One's Self will better facilitate in charting a course for where that person is intent on going, and what adjustments are required to ensure they get there.

CHESS & CHECKERS

There are members of the work force who don't display any outward intelligence whatsoever, yet they have degrees in areas of study that might seem difficult for the majority of us to obtain.

Some of these people might do very well for themselves, and may put forth nominal or excessive amounts of effort to earn a modest living in whatever field of study and work they elected to pursue.

The distinguishing factor which separates us, and those like us, from those I refer to, is their ability to play the game and our inability to do so. Their ability to foresee that adhering to the construct they are a part of will eventually yield the reward said construct provides, and almost guarantees. That attending high school and graduating from college will likely be followed by a meaningful job or career. That being used to playing this game from childhood > adolescence > and adulthood is a summation of acts, which, when culminated, will produce an outcome that is of benefit to the person who endures these often-repetitious actions over-and-over again.

When these individuals grew older, they held to the same *modus operandi* (**MO**) which they subscribed to at their introduction to education, and thence to work. Even though one's work, at times, can be the most boring, habitual, never-ending process; that career will have taken them securely (if not successfully) through their adulthood.

By performing these acts with more proficiency year-over-year, these individuals demonstrate a greater endurance of spirit than us. They possess a greater amount of fortitude than I. A greater level of foresight and prescience to see a thing through to its end.

In this instance, employees such as these will far exceed many of us who possess the entrepreneurial spirit but who never sought the proper guidance and instruction necessary to actually utilize it. Instead, we chose to use that spirit and sense of purpose towards an end that ultimately and negatively determined our fate.

Nevertheless, many of us will excel, for a time. As we have adhered to a different kind of construct. One that will promise it breaks the bonds of poverty and inexperience. That not only ensures survival, but alludes to wealth, and a sense of power and purpose beyond anything our current situation permits... crime.

When we're ready to begin our search for jobs that will prove financially and personally gratifying, we'll have the confidence, (if not the knowledge), to pursue career pathways without facing rejection for reasons of incompetency or inexperience.

Preparation is key: preparation via knowing one's self, education, experience and being confident with the light in which we choose to be illuminated by.

Preparation through knowing our strengths and how to effectively showcase them to the job market in which we will immerse ourselves, and acknowledging our weaknesses and how best to improve upon them until, they too, become strengths.

Preparation through means of life experiences that are relevant to the job being sought after. Continuing with education through aligning training, vocational skills, service, marketing and entrepreneurial techniques with the intended career path.

These are just some examples of key components of preparation which will facilitate in ensuring a successful future through honest employment.

While it may sound like a lot to do, and while it may take up a great deal of time, just think of the amount of time lost and opportunities missed when we're serving out a lengthy prison sentence as a result of pursuing a so-called career in crime.

The knowledge, experience, and intellectual capital we gain by furthering ourselves through legitimate means can *never* be taken away from us the way our capital earned through crime can. This is the one obvious truth that makes a life of legitimacy worth so much more than a life of crime. They can never take it away from us. And in all truthfulness, what reasons would "they" have for doing so?

When you're legit, you are making a contribution to society in a number of ways, e.g., a monetary contribution via the taxes we pay and lawful consumerism. Through services rendered via employment. In some cases, we provide educational contributions via training others; thus, empowering prospective employees and bolstering the job market as a whole.

When we practice criminality, the only person who benefits is ourselves, and even that is questionable.

For the sake of this discussion, never mind the arguments as to criminal behavior being *right* or *wrong*. If I can be politically incorrect just long enough to successfully argue this rationale, I'll tell you that crime being wrong has nothing to do with me wanting to stop. If it does, it lends minimal credence in swaying me towards the right direction.

The fact that I lost my freedom, my life such as I knew it, and everything I worked to obtain (because I acquired it in an illegal fashion), *that,* my friends, is the sole reason I began thinking of other ways, legitimate ways, to make a living.

I did, and I still do feel the guilt and pain from ruining people with the poison I peddled. But I was a selfish rather than selfless being, and losing my freedom and financial gain was more the cause for change than anything else.

There's a part of me that wishes I had admitted these faults publicly and when they occurred, rather than in this manuscript, and years after they happened. In any event, I thought it prudent for my own sake to voice these sentiments (better late than never), in hopes that those who read this will question their own actions; but more importantly, the validity of the motives behind them.

What will be the determining factors in your lives when you choose to pursue a pathway that fundamentally differs from the one on which you are currently traveling? What losses will you endure before you realize the high cost of doing business in an illegal fashion? And at what point will those losses become so monumental, and so final, that what's left to your pathway will even remotely resemble an ethical and purposeful trajectory?

In almost every case it will take more time and effort – than we're accustomed to – to earn an honest buck. Just know that it can never be seized or appropriated by law enforcement the way your dirty money can. The moral aspect of these truths will play a smaller or larger role in the scheme of things depending on how you build your ethical constitution towards transitioning.

There is no action performed in this world that will not have a similar reaction in spirit and intent.

I would suggest that we begin collecting "pieces of paper" that demonstrate we can play the game. This is a process I've undertaken while serving time, as time is all I have now.

NOTE: The days of the state or federal governments paying for college degrees for inmates are over. You'll have to shell out funds from your own kick if this is a pathway you're considering pursuing. The beauty of pursuing a degree in prison is that you don't have much else to occupy your time with; hence, it's a worthy investment, more so when you consider that you now have college degrees to counterbalance criminal history and lack of work experience upon reentry.

If you're of an age where graduating from high school is still possible, please consider this step. There are guys in prison in their 50s and older who are just now obtaining their high school equivalency diplomas, and then using these *pieces of paper* to secure positions upon reentry in various areas of meaningful employment. As I said, better late than never.

Most employers rarely verify basic proofs such as these. The confidence gained knowing you earned it (and can produce it if asked) outweighs the uncertainty and awkwardness that attends the knowledge that we never bothered to try.

When one of these two is acquired, (a high school diploma or equivalency) it opens the door for further opportunities of advancement in the legitimate construct by way of being able to enroll in college or a vocational trade institution. These are often the first and last stops people make before taking the skills they've learned and applying them to a trade or other form of employment.

I cannot stress enough how important it is to take the much-traveled road of education (and volunteer work, if you have the time). Many folks – young and old – graduating from college and vocational trainings sometimes don't hit the ground running. The economy and other factors can influence the speed at which this route can prove beneficial. And with student loans and other debts mounting, it can often feel counterintuitive to the favorable picture of legitimacy I'm attempting to paint.

Students can find themselves exiting college only to realize their education in the field they sought after is now obsolete, or those jobs have moved overseas. They may find themselves moving back to the nest (if that was ever an option). At times subsistence-level occupations have to suffice until better employment becomes available.

I take my hat off to those members of society who never once consider committing crime in order to make ends meet. I find it commendable that that notion never once enters their minds. Instead, they move back home, sleep in their car, get on income support (SNAP benefits, etc.), or whatever it takes to get by until that opportunity finally breaks. And when it does, they pursue it with a passion and ravenousness that only the hungry can admire.

Below are paths other than the educational route. I've spent so much time detailing this option because this is the one most often travelled, and for which we are indoctrinated into as soon as we're old enough to attend Head Start.

It's gratifying to see just how many men and women that were convicted for trafficking controlled substance(s) become successful sales reps and services providers upon reentering society. The entrepreneurial spirit (if given time to grow and flourish) has taken many of us far beyond the legitimate pathways to success that normally begin with education.

NOTE: The pathway and transition I've described thus far is one that I followed with great success upon my own reentry. But it is slow, measured and regimented... quite similar to life on the Inside. My argument is that if you can survive prison following this same path, you can create a plan and a successful reentry using a similar format, and with plenty of time to prepare.

The inconsistency and spontaneity with which I once lived could only have been experienced and practiced by either the wealthy and decadent, or the desperate and strictly criminal. It proved very difficult for me to adapt to a schedule that school, a career pathway, and normalcy demanded of me.

Again, this is the process upon which a large percentage of the population is accustom to, and has been trained to abide by for, literally, centuries. And I feel it would be to our utmost benefit to adapt and adhere to a schedule that resembles that of the masses, as we would then be aligning ourselves to the majority.

I hope we can make these adjustments sooner rather than later, as opposed to shunning them; perhaps even growing to despise or fear them, as that sort of sentiment will only prove counterintuitive to our intentions.

My only sibling was/is one of those people who never

undertook any additional education other than graduating high school. The only approach to success he ever applied was a complete dedication to the job at hand. If it required a commercial driver's license, he would obtain it. If it required additional training, he would attend until completion. He is now a regional director for a global distribution company, thus demonstrating that education is not always the beginning of every successful career pathway.

Another acquaintance of mine began her career in banking as a front-desk teller. She, like my sibling, possessed a single-minded determination that wins out over more conventional means of advancing one's career via education. She is now approaching retirement as an investment banker and regional manager of several branches across the nation with a sizeable annual income by any standard of measure.

Both of these people, like many criminals, possess an easy charm and charisma. They also represent a small yet growing minority of employees whose skills are better demonstrated by their current ability to produce results as opposed to academic achievements outlined in their resumes.

When we're saddled with a criminal record, it may take a bit more than charisma and sheer determination to secure that first meaningful employment opportunity. As such, it can be prudent to have those pieces of paper (degrees and certificates of completion) that will counterbalance the stigma of having a criminal record.

That we've taken the time to level-up on our education will serve two purposes: 1. it will give us more curb appeal when being considered for employment, and 2. it will give potential employers less pause when weighing the pros and cons (pun intended) of hiring a convicted felon.

OPTIONS

When speaking in terms of the different types of work and workers available, there are really only a few options. Our working class includes both white and blue-collar workers, i.e., those that perform menial labor, and those that perform manual labor. This excludes individuals who earn their living(s) from business ownership and the labor of others.

It would seem that most criminals possess an uncanny combination of both, a hybrid, if you will. My own criminal pathway began with an idea, which then fit into a market by turning that idea into a service, or in this case, a product.

Others cut from our cloth are those that work for a criminal organization whose structure resembles that of a corporate entity, be it a drug ring, street gang, cartel or syndicate resembling structured and organized practices in crime. Those of us in this group essentially work for a company, and advance themselves by making their way up the corporate ladder while simultaneously serving their own ambitions and interests.

While both of these work styles have their benefits, both of them also have obvious and not-so-obvious drawbacks. I recommend performing a self-analysis to determine which of these best fits your own predispositions.

NOTE: Upon returning home, I took the government employment route, as much of New Mexico's economy is government-based, national labs, etc. It wasn't until I completed more college, terminated probation early, and had some semblance of a normal life that I began looking for a means to supplement my income via real estate. I eventually transitioned from an 8-to-5 to selling real estate exclusively.It was a bit scary at first. It almost felt like I was performing drug transactions, living from one score to another. Eventually, my nest egg grew far quicker than it did from working in state government and I was able to purchase and manage rentals from which I derived multiple sources of passive income.

NOTE: Passive income, that is, income one derives from sources without having to work for it is what defines most people as wealthy. It doesn't matter if it's a few hundred dollars a month or a few thousand a month. Money coming in that you're not digging ditches or clicking away on a computer for is the ultimate goal for each of us. Keep this in mind as we progress through this study. "Passive income defines us as rich."

Be sure to do some soul-searching before committing to one or the other. And know that we don't necessarily have to commit, indefinitely. We can flow between the two as circumstances and our progress permits.

The choice we make can greatly, or nominally, impact our nest egg, our contentment, and our levels of success in whatever pathway(s) we ultimately pursue. If you are of the mind to attempt both, this may provide a broader insight as to which template best suits your current needs.

The type of person who makes their advancements in slow, measured steps via career pathways in structured corporate settings are usually those who have a marathon runner's approach. This requires getting up every day and adhering to a regimented lifestyle in order to make those measured, yet guaranteed advancements over time. Annual leave (vacation time) accrues. Health, vision and dental insurances provide security for all kinds of eventualities. But your nest egg's growth is also slow and measured.

If you have the time, patience, and endurance for this style of progress, it often proves the model that keeps us secure, content, and legitimate throughout our lifetime. Personally, I don't think I could have worked a solid decade like this had it not been for the regimented lifestyle that prison afforded me prior to my reentry.

Comparative and psychological analysis has demonstrated

that criminals bear the most resemblance to those that earn their living through entrepreneurialism. And yet, when we obtain legitimate occupations, they almost always come in the form of working for another person or company for long hours and at an hourly wage... Something to consider as we embark on this journey.

Many entrepreneurs, like criminals, lack the skills and education necessary to succeed in a corporate structure, yet they possess the drive and enthusiasm to start a business or to effectively bring a profit-making idea to fruition. That *drive* or spirit, is the very essence of entrepreneurialism, and it is also the one defining characteristic in a person's makeup that may distinguish them as a successful entrepreneur.

While many may not have the skills and the qualifications to succeed in a corporate setting; an idea, backed by determination to turn that idea into a profitable reality can very well be the accelerant that starts them down the path of a successful and lawful business venture.

Case in point. My friend, my "homie" Charles – whom I met in a federal holding cell underneath the Albuquerque courthouse after receiving the news that I was sentenced to 78 months in a Federal Prison – is just such an entrepreneur. Charles was withdrawing from heroin, had a booming voice that accompanied a Northern New Mexican accent, and was the furthest, yet most insistent thing on my mind.

He would not stop talking and had we not all been shackled, I probably would've attempted to strangle him. After sentencing, Charles was transferred to the jail I was housed at prior to being shipped off to whatever prison I was to serve my time in. I remember entering the pod during count and people throwing their hands up in inquisitive gestures through their cell windows, asking "how much time did you get?" to which I signed in response with a *seven* and then an *eight* with my fingers (78 months in prison). I remember entering my cell and rolling a cigarette (before an inmate committed suicide by hanging and the US Marshals determined smoking was the cause and banned tobacco).

Count was concluded and the cell doors popped; thus, we all commenced with another afternoon awaiting sentencing, and awaiting shipping out after being sentenced. My celly, "Droopy," had just been shipped out to a federal prison in Texas, and I enjoyed the solitude of a single cell until new inmates arrived.

Lo and behold, Charles shadowed my doorway, and yelled at the top of his lungs, "Orale perro, we're gonna be cellies!!!" to which I responded by telling the guard accompanying him, "hell naw, put him with one of the other homies that are single-celled. I just got sentenced and need some down time."

As fate would have it, I remained at Sandoval County Detention Center for months until I was eventually flown on Con-Air from Albuquerque to the Las Vegas Strip; then, to Pueblo Colorado where we were all unloaded on about 4 buses and driven to the prison complex in Florence.

NOTE: If you get a chance, Google this shithole and you'll see that this is where America sends Her most notorious offenders, including folks from other countries, i.e., Somalian pirates, mob bosses such as my friend and mentor, Vito Rizutto, Sammy "The Bull" Gravano, and more.

Florence consists of four prisons: The ADX or Supermax, which is virtually a no-contact-with-anyone prison, where inmates often lose their mental faculties due to sensory deprivation, or as I like to put it, torture.

Joquin "El Chapo" Guzman I believe is in his eighth year at the ADX... I don't wish that on anyone. A United States Penitentiary, or (USP). A medium facility, or F.C.I., often referred to as "gladiator school" by the inmates, and a prison camp where corporate criminals; Democrats, Republicans, child molesters, informants, and others with low offender points are often housed with no fence, the ability to drive into town on trash trucks, and enjoy mobile phones, drugs, alcohol, pornography and visits to the local motel for a quicky with the wife, girlfriend, boyfriend, etc.

I was assigned to F.C.I. Florence, or gladiator school.

Not long after arriving and getting my routine down, Charles and several other inmates from New Mexico joined us and swelled our ranks. Charles was essentially with me from the day I was sentenced, my entire time at Florence > the halfway house > the same probation office > and finally full freedom over 15 years later.

During that entire time, Charles always had a hustle. He'd charge inmates postage stamps or commissary (the most common currency in prison) in exchange for his laundry hustle. He'd make book for several gambling opportunities in prison, and/or he would keep a "store" or market in his cell, i.e., he would buy commissary and sell it at a markup to those inmates who needed items on consignment prior to money being placed on their account.

In short, Charles hustled and demonstrated more of an entrepreneurial spirit than most people I've ever known. When we came home, he opened a concrete business and excelled further. The raw dirt that constituted my back yard was refinished via Charles extending the sidewalks and pouring a concrete slab – complete with designs – in my backyard.

He then started a mobile car-detailing business (and managed to thrive during COVID via sending his trucks to people's houses and having them unlock their vehicles remotely so he could detail (and disinfect) during the pandemic. Huge money maker.

He now rents his original home in Las Vegas New Mexico, and manages several other rentals he and his wife accrued since he returned home... and life is good for Charles. A man with zero education, no high school diploma, no certifiable vocational training- nothing beyond his sheer will to fuel the flames of his entrepreneurial spirit... and profit from it.

Charle's story does not indicate that those who possess a criminal record, or that those who are not highly educated, are somehow destined to scratch out a living through manual labor. Quite the contrary. His story does allude to less-conventional options that can be more appropriately matched to our personalities, and our entrepreneurial spirit.

The current workforce is demonstrating that more and more managers are women (New Mexico State Government is filled with competent, affable, and professional females who are drastically excelling in their professions). Many of these people, both male and female, also come from educational backgrounds other than those of ivy league colleges (think community college).

Data also demonstrates that employers are seeking employees, and management, who focus more on high-spiritedness and empowerment of their staff, rather than the conventional methods of establishing deadlines for goal achievement and micro-management techniques that have been popular since the dawn of the Industrial Age.

So, what does all this mean for the prospective employee or entrepreneur? For one, it means that women are reaching a point in our history where they now have more power and influence to dictate the terms of the environments in which they work. It means that if you are a woman who occupies her time by making money illegitimately, you now have a better chance at success than those who came before you.

It also means that if you possess a fervor and zeal for pursuing legitimate endeavors, that you may have a much better chance than your competition at acquiring employment in today's job market.

It's not my intent to cause trepidation or apprehension for those reading this. It's my hope that when considering these pathways, there's no undue amount of unsettlement at this juncture, nor when considering change of any kind. Unless we've never made a dollar in our lives, legally or otherwise, we *have* been entrepreneurs and we *have* been working our way up one corporate ladder or another for most of our adolescence and adulthood.

If we've ever been employed in a legitimate and taxable occupation for someone else in a capacity that did not consist of free-lancing or contracting, then we were employed at a small business, a chain, and performed a variety of normal tasks, and have experience under our belts.

If you've *ever* sold lemonade as a child, washed your neighbor's cars, mowed lawns or the like, then you have acted as entrepreneurs (at a very young age), and smart ones at that. You were killing two birds with one stone: selling a product that you probably paid nothing to acquire (lemonade), and providing a service, (washing cars).

McDonalds and Walmart are corporations. If anyone's ever worked at one of these, you were in-fact working as an employee for some of the largest corporations in the world. If you've ever worked in construction – performing manual labor or administrative work – chances are the contractor was either the sole owner/proprietor; hence, an entrepreneur, or it was a medium to large-size corporate entity.

If you ever worked a route delivering newspapers as a child, you may not have realized it at the time, but you were acting as a freelance contractor for the publisher of that paper.

If you sold or are still selling dope, as I was, you are acting as an entrepreneur. I guess in some instances this action, and all associated actions, could be performed in the capacity as an employee working for a corporation.

NOTE: Depending on the scope of our activities and those we're associated with, we could very well be prosecuted under the RICO or (Racketeering and Corrupt Organizations Act), albeit this law seems to be applied nowadays to legitimate corporate entities rather than criminal enterprise.

Selling dope, while profitable, is illegal. And it is a distortion of how ethical and lawful business is conducted.

When we rob banks, extort, strong-arm, or bilk people through identity theft or cyber-criminal acts, you are exercising your entrepreneurial spirit. This is a misrepresentation of what that spirit intends. The acts I describe, and for which many of us are well-versed in, can be very profitable ways of making money. But there is zero exchange between a service rendered and/or a product sold. Those victimized by these acts received nothing in return for your "services," which is a fundamental rule of business; hence, these too are examples of distortions of how ethical and lawful business should be conducted.

NOTE: Upon returning home in 2015, working my plan, volunteering at WINGS for Life and the Santa Fe Animal Shelter, and finally securing my first job in state government (about 2 months after leaving the halfway house), I was relieved of about $3,400 in a shipping scam. I was searching for a used car and spotted a rather nice-looking Toyota Camry that would be shipped to me upon depositing money in what I thought was a business escrow account. I should've known. But the need for a vehicle, the fact that everything was going so well blinded me to the truth that the people I was dealing with were scammers. Phones still had buttons when I went away, and criminals still relieved you of your money more-or-less face-to-face... Lesson learned.

Besides the obvious victimization of others, the illegitimacy of crime is what makes it so damaging to the criminal. It undermines and devalues our worth; our strengths are squandered. We could have contributed, amplified and been a part of successful business rather than simply taking and diminishing the trust capital normally built between two separate parties.

People exchange work, products, and services by free-mutual consent for mutual advantage. When we earn income through crime, particularly in instances of robbery or theft, that fair exchange becomes null and void. It then becomes a relationship of victim and predator.

And while some of us can do these "jobs" well, they will always be distorted manipulations of earning an honest living. Because of this, and because of the very nature of their illegality, you, your life, and everything in it will become distorted, manipulated and devalued. What remains is materialism gained or taken through unlawful means; thus, whatever value we apply to it (and to ourselves) is also diminished.

CLOSING

Alcohol, like drugs, causes so much damage to the people who abuse them, and to the people who are victimized by the people who abuse them. But unlike drugs and crime there are zero damages or lives lost, or emotional and psychological impressions burned into the minds of those who are employed by the distribution or sales of alcohol.

Only by overconsumption is it made into something harmful. The distribution and sales of alcohol does not affect or shape the lives of those who sell and distribute it the way the sales and distribution of something illegal affects, shapes, and in some cases, permanently mars the illicit dealer and those who indulge in their wares.

When was the last time any of us saw a sales rep for a beer company wallowing in depression because of the life he or she is afforded by selling booze? When was the last time you heard a sales executive for nicotine vaping products say that they had to get out of the life they were living because it was ruining too many people?

I don't imagine we'll ever hear misgivings such as these because these products are not illegal; hence, questions of morality would never arise. And sales reps in legal markets will never endure the handicaps that criminals experience when seeking lawful employment, as they are not damaging their work history and moral constitution by performing unlawful acts to earn a living.

Crime fundamentally alters the way in which we view the world, and the way in which the world views us. It is an isolating and ostracizing act that alters our self-assurance and convinces us, as more time passes, of our own ineligibility with respect to lawful endeavors.

As a result, we associate more with people that share our MO- people who have the same schedules as us, and who set terms that do not conform to conventionality. This will ultimately make attempts at transitioning all the more difficult to even consider.

I'm not sure if my own reflections are similar to those of criminals reading this. But at some point, I began to scorn the Working Class. Even if the disdain I felt was barely perceptible at times, it was there. I'd feel a sense of satisfaction and pride when I considered people's sometimes hopeless struggle to stay afloat in comparison to the money I made effortlessly through crime, and by the rules and timeframes that I dictated.

I became so filled with self-pride – and contempt for those that worked for a living – that when it came time to seek their consideration for employment, I could barely look them in the eye. I knew, too, that those I once looked upon as beneath me, (or as my customers or patrons) had suddenly become my betters. And that I would now be under the scrutiny of their purportedly inferior judgment and sensibility.

Although crime affords us opportunity to utilize our skills as entrepreneurs, administrators, capitalists, and competent employers/employees, it takes those abilities and sees to it that redeeming traits become suited to one purpose only. There inevitably comes a point where they become applicable to no other circumstance.

My case that I plead to you, the criminal, is this. If we're good at selling drugs, is there any reason why we couldn't perform well at promoting, marketing and selling any legal product or service? If we are competent administrators when managing our criminal endeavors, who's to say we couldn't do well managing our legitimate responsibilities or those of others?

If you're adept at orchestrating and executing a plan on a strict time limit, why couldn't those same abilities be applied to a legitimate job that functions with the same margins and time constraints as those demanded of you when performing criminal acts?

If you possess the talent and expertise to forge documents, to hack into computer systems, etc., why could you not use those same abilities to further yourselves as legitimate members of society?

The answer, I believe, is because the crimes we commit program us, in such a fashion, that the idea of obtaining lawful employment becomes a scary and unfathomable act of the impossible. An act that could never be accomplished by people such as ourselves, with no work history; with minimal education, and who feel derision and trepidation towards those we ultimately face when attempting to acquire lawful and meaningful employment.

It is my ambition, in this instance, that we can prove ourselves irrevocably wrong.

What keeps us from realizing our potential as citizens is ourselves; our short-sightedness, and needless fears as to how intimidating getting up in the morning and working for a living can actually be. The inherent complacency that a life of crime affords is such a silent and debilitating illness which leaves those it afflicts, in many cases, permanently marred with small hope for recovery.

It afflicts us, too, in that most employers are unwilling to hire us for fear of that affliction resurfacing and causing their business untold amounts of damage.

Background checks only affirm that we have been infected with a disease whose remission is often temporary, and whose likelihood at reemergence is as inevitable as paying taxes.

This is a condition whose cure can *only* come from within. There are absolutely zero options for success with the exception of the ones that we ourselves create. While of course there will be outside sources of support we can turn to, it will remain our choice alone to affect change.

This study, along with everyone and everything in our lives that has played a minor or major role in our decision to change has almost no influence compared to the influence we have over self when we resolve to restructure our lives in a positive and productive way.

I truly believe that most of us are not the criminals we have fashioned ourselves to be. I believe we are capitalists, and entrepreneurs who need only the gentlest of nudges in the right direction. But our actions continue to define us. And if those actions are ethically and legally erroneous, then what we are, for the time being, are criminals.

I will ask repetitiously throughout this study that we each look deep inside ourselves and see what the truth is. If we're awaking every day and giving it our all in an effort to provide for ourselves and for our families, it's safe to assume we can apply this drive towards something that will eventually provide more gain, and far more security than crime ever would.

If you are the type of person who is constantly thinking of ways to increase your profits by diversifying and seeking new revenue streams – by working smarter and harder than the next person – by seeking better and more innovative ways to market products and services, and by conducting your affairs with fairness, punctuality and reliability, (even if those affairs are illegal), then I implore you to pursue an alternate form of income that does not include the indulgence of criminality. Your talents and abilities are being horribly squandered on a profession that will *never* allow you to reach your full potential.

It is my hope that all of us will allow ourselves the opportunity to grow and to use our gifts in a manner that will guide us towards the lives we've been striving to obtain but whose reality has eluded us thus far.

It is my wish that we perceive those obstacles that delay our transition. That we bypass them, overcome them, and see how inconsequential they truly are as they become smaller and less significant in the rearview. It is my hope that we can all come to realize the things that hold us back are our own fears and misconceptions about what we actually face.

I tell you truthfully that there is nothing to fear but fear itself.

3

THE HUNT

"In this world, the world in which we presently reside, where the hunter gatherer way of life is no more, and the one who earns the most money is the leader of his tribe... In *this* world, the one who successfully hunts for and obtains the right job is the warrior who arises the victor."

— ANONYMOUS

"We're not hunter-gatherers anymore. We're all living like patients in the intensive care unit of a hospital. What keeps us alive isn't bravery, or athleticism, or any of those other skills that were valuable in a caveman society. It's our ability to master complex technological skills. It is our ability to be nerds. We need to breed nerds."

— NEAL STEPHENSON

I WANTED to avoid the structuring of this work resembling anything like a "How To" guide for writing resumes, cover letters, and the filling out of online job applications, mostly because there is already a great deal of work dedicated to these specific purposes. And I felt that one more might be an unnecessary addition to a seemingly infinite well of resources.

I do think it's important to go over some rudimentary knowledge concerning job searches, resumes, cover letters, the presentation of self, how to address criminal records and lack of work history to employers.

I would go into extensive detail on the more minute aspects of job acquisition but I think it would be presumptuous of me to lecture on a subject that I am not overly familiar with but have only gleaned facts and information from by diligently studying the work of others. I suppose that most people learn in this fashion yet it seems counterfeit of me to explain an idea, or ideas, not of my own yet delivered with my character and expression.

NOTE: I have since applied the advice and methods contained in this manuscript. Upon reentering society and executing my Plan, I have been extremely fortunate in obtaining the career pathways I set out to achieve, and have confirmed the information contained herein to be accurate in its application. I also began drafting resumes in prison for guys that were going home, created a resume and reentry training course in prison, and gave presentations during annual job fairs at FCI Florence where community members and employers would also present.

Normal citizens, at some point in their lives, have exaggerated the truth, to some extent, in order to obtain something they desire, be it a job, a grant, a loan for a new car, etc. But I think it's necessary to point out that, as criminals, we practice deception on a daily basis, and that a different approach, although more difficult, might be a better way to go; especially when we consider the subject matter at hand, as well as the significance of ethics in alignment with our principles.

The majority of us utilize certain techniques at our

disposal to appear more appealing to others. Nowhere is this better demonstrated than by job seekers during the hunt for employment. But we must concede that showing ourselves in as favorable a light as possible is a far cry from embellishing to flat out lying. And if we are not as capable as we've led others to believe, then our resumes and applications may resemble a list of untruths rather than a disclosure of skills and past accomplishments.

It won't take long for an employer to perceive our true worth or lack thereof.

If you're of the mind that this is not a subject you need to fine tune then feel free to skip this chapter. But I'd like to point out that everyone, at some period in their lives, (from top business executives > to college graduates > to criminals) can always use a quick refresher/crash course in improving their presentation; be it on paper or in-person.

It became apparent when doing my research that there is a great deal of job seekers who have some preconceived notion of themselves that is unflattering to the idea of what a good prospect for employment should consist of. Criminals, by far, are more apprehensive about their criminal records than any other aspect of their character, and with good reason.

The stigma that accompanies those who have a criminal record can be a damaging aspect to our person. But there are also other polarizing qualities non-criminals possess that are unknowingly displayed, and at the worst possible time.

Therefore, keep in mind that if you have a record, it may not be the worst part of what makes you an undesirable prospect for employment. Bad hygiene, attitude, poor speaking and presentation skills, and inherent shyness or reluctance to speak around strangers, just to name a few, are handicaps that employers spot in prospective employees as soon as an initial conversation takes place.

Although some of us may have blotches on our records, we may also possess some extremely affable qualities that employers are looking for. In this chapter we'll review how to best display these qualities. We'll also examine the following:

- Personal Presentation
- Confronting and Discussing Criminal History (If Applicable)
- Job Searches
- Creating Resumes, Cover Letters & Thank-You Notes
- Job Interviews

PROSPECT

The first step to landing that first desirable job is not performed by you, but by the employer via advertising an open position in hopes of filling it with the right employee. That employee is YOU.

Knowing who you are, knowing your likes and your dislikes, your strengths and weaknesses, your character traits and flaws, your attributes and peculiarities, and everything that defines you as a human being are the things that must be identified before you even begin to search for a job or career.

"Know Thyself." These are the words inscribed at the Oracle of Delphi in ancient Greece which became the mantra and basis for the beginning of modern-day psychology. To *know* who we are, in every sense of the word, is the answer to knowing what type of job best fits you and your personality.

More often than not we end up in dead-end jobs (not because of the job itself) but because we're simply not aware of who it is we see in the mirror every day and what circumstances best showcase that person's qualities. Because of this, it's imperative that we continuously self-analyze to determine what it is that makes you *you.* This will save time and energy when considering how many jobs you might be applying for that wouldn't serve your interests (or the employer's).

Know yourself to market yourself. Know yourself to be comfortable with the right job or career choice; and let's face it, with the right existence.

I want to reiterate the fact that many whom are trying to get a foot in the door of desirable job markets these days are just as inexperienced and anxious about the whole process as we are. Even though some of them are just finishing with college, many of them have *never* worked or even had an internship before, and (unfortunately for them, but fortunate for us) their resumes are going to look just as shallow and one-dimensional as some of ours.

This is the reason why there are literally thousands of "how to" books on resume building and job acquisition. Hardly any of them were written with the intention of being of use to convicted felons, or yet-to-be convicted felons; which would imply that law-abiding folks on the hunt can be just as untested as we are.

To truly know thyself gives us a tremendous amount of headway over those who have never performed a self-analysis, or why they do the things they do, or in what direction they intend to go. The blissfulness that often accompanies a lax consciousness is such a far cry from the insight that comes with self-awareness. No matter what direction your life takes you in (or even better), no matter the direction you attempt to steer yourself towards, it is of the utmost importance that we practice the mantra of Knowing Thyself.

PERMITAME A PRESENTAR

Allow me to introduce...

Now that we have an idea of whose reflection it is we're staring at in the mirror, let's talk about how to present that person to others in a positive and flattering light.

NOTE: No one has ever been liked by *everyone*. For as much diversity and individualism out there, there is just as much bigotry, jealousy and narrow-mindedness to counterbalance this equation. Some people, through no fault of their own, may feel polarized towards some while gravitating towards others. It's simply the way of things.

This is just one more example of sociology that becomes ever more apparent at the vantage point (or disadvantage) of observing it through the microcosm that is prison. In fact, this is one of the few benefits that being incarcerated affords us- the ability to study human behavior with as much consistency and objectiveness as the fish-tank environment the Inside provides.

In prison, the wrong decisions can cost more than popularity points or your job. When seen from this perspective, it becomes easier to understand how politeness, cordiality, respect and professionalism can help speed our advancement through life, or at least ensure that life continues.

It would be to the world's advantage if we all treated people with the same respect and consideration as we do when behind bars.

Se Japones. This is a Hispanic prison term which roughly translates to *be* or *act Japanese.* This alludes to common knowledge that the Japanese conduct most, if not all of their affairs, be they personal or professional, with an extreme amount of politeness- even when dealing with some form of opposition.

NOTE: While this next bit of advice might be excessive; until politeness, patience, and respect become second nature, I would suggest that we all comport ourselves with the formality of the Japanese. And to do so with the belief that we are in prison, and that acts of disrespect or impoliteness will be dealt with with the same finality as they are on the Inside.

This particular practice has benefitted me tremendously, and it will help us to navigate throughout life, as well as the job market more efficiently. It is just one approach among many that I'm determined to make use of until the end of my days.

Whether we're in the World or on the Inside, always remember that human beings – including ourselves – are social creatures; thus, they/we are drawn to others, and involve ourselves with others for many reasons, but with the participation in the human condition as one of them.

The advantages of knowing this and understanding how to efficiently steer our way through the many mazes of sociology is one of the key factors in how we communicate and present ourselves to the rest of the world.

While we can't guarantee that all whom we interact with will automatically gravitate towards us in a positive manner, we can guarantee that the impression we leave with each will be one that is capable, affable, and professional.

The workplace is an excellent environment to hone these characteristics. Properly managing people via the proper management of self is an art that everyone should strive to perfect.

Presentation: it commences with an amount of obligatory respect and consideration for those around us. Whether they are respectful/mindful of us in return is of no concern. And whether or not people attempt to change for the better in light of our example is also of no concern. If someone has a problem, well... it's their problem. Why make it ours? If they opt for positive change in their life then more power to them. If not, then that's just one more person whose politeness, or lack thereof will never surpass our own.

It is also safe to assume that this type of person won't pose any threat or real competition for long. No one prefers negative or miserable company unless of course they themselves are miserable. Those who possess a less-than favorable air about them often remove themselves from the equation long before we begin devising ways to remediate their presence.

NOTE: Since coming home and moving up the chain in various government employment positions, I've experienced several instances with coworkers that displayed a less-than favorable disposition. Who made it their business to involve themselves with me in a negative context to one degree or another. Coming to work every day early (or on time), leaving at the right time or even staying later, and keeping positive and a smile on my face throughout, eventually won out over their snitching, wannabe-managing, and other forms of low-level cunning. It's almost as if the volume was turned down on life upon returning home, and what others might conceive as being high-level combatants or declarations of "war" in the workplace, I saw as superfluous b.s. that *always* damages the individual practicing it as opposed to the one it's intended to harm.

It's such a waste of time and energy responding to and scheming against the schemer. And it diminishes our own value in the workplace by regressing to that level. If this occurs, folks will begin to view us as part of the problem rather than the solution.

Most employers draft a Code of Ethics that employees are expected to adhere to, yet most of us learn a set of values that parallels professional codes of ethics years prior to that first job.

Throughout the course of one's life we tend to forget the simplest lessons of civility that serve as the cornerstones of social etiquette. See to it that we don't forget our own and people will always remember us for it.

Now that we have an understanding of the root of presentation which comes from within, let's discuss outward appearances and first impressions.

Speaking only for myself, the majority of clothing I possessed probably wouldn't be the best attire to wear to a job interview, or anywhere else besides the club or street corner (think 90s baggy sportswear, or suits and sport jackets that were way too shiny for an interview).

If this sounds anything like your own wardrobe, you may

want to consider shopping for about three different sets of job interview apparel.

This isn't necessarily a difficult or costly task to accomplish if we're attempting to secure a job in the menial labor force. (break out those old kakis and work boots, and use them for what they were made for!) But if your career is in sales or of a corporate nature, you'll want to look appropriately presentable, as well as professional.

For women there are other rules that hardly anyone pays attention to, such as no open-toe shoes, skirts with hemlines above the knee, etc., etc. The main thing to bear in mind is pairing one's appearance to the job for which you are applying. And not having your appearance in discord with the environement you're working in. In other words, sensible clothing for sensible employment. I would also suggest no other type of jewelry besides a watch or wedding ring. Anything beyond those two is an unnecessary adornment.

Performing some reconnaissance and knowing the type of environment we're walking into prior to the interview is a great way to determine what to wear before you arrive. Observing those who work there walking in and out will give us a good indication as to what's considered appropriate attire.

ORTHODOX

If you're the type of criminal who resembles a biker, a gangbanger, or inner-city drug pusher, chances are you're not going to look anything like your average law-abiding citizen. Certain looks are ok if you're working an apprenticeship at a tattoo shop, cast as an extra in a movie, exotic dancer, nurse or vet technician in the new tight-fitting scrubs with ink showing (I love the new scrubs). But the more typical or conventional the job, the more we'll have to level-up our Quintessentials and conventionality.

NOTE: The film industry is taking off in New Mexico. It seems studios are being built quicker than new housing developments, and the pay is usually daily or weekly, and nothing to turn our noses up at. The strike lifted as of January of 2024, and many folks that were on strike are now back full-time, either in California, on-set elsewhere, or in New Mexico. It's relatively easy to research the film industry, the unions that protect its workers, and which side of the camera you'd like to be on.

Even normal folks can have certain eccentricities when it comes to their manner of dress or appearance, such as their hair dyed a vibrant color, piercings or what have you. But just know that although these people, like ourselves, may have skills to land a job, their employer probably values their expertise more than they care about an eccentric professional appearance.

I had friends, colleagues, acquaintances, etc., that never had the slightest inkling that I was a drug dealer or that I was involved in crime of any kind. There would be times I would encounter these people at an outdoor bar or cantina, and they just could not get over the number of tattoos I brandished in a short-sleeve shirt or "wife-beater" tank top. Sometimes they would jokingly ask if I had done a stint in prison since the last time they saw me, to which I would jokingly respond, "not yet!" It seems fate is not without a sense of irony.

<u>I don't believe my civilian counterparts ever guessed at what they thought was my normal appearance was actually my attempt at blending in with the rest of society.</u> And that this appearance was also what my criminal associates viewed as strange and abnormal, or in their own words, "way too fucking pretty/preppy." One of my aliases was "Clark," due to my black plastic-framed glasses, button-down shirts, and dress shoes... pretty sure it was a nod to Superman's alter ego, which didn't bother me in the least.

The point I'm trying to illustrate is to blend. As far as appearances go, make an effort to blend with whatever style your work environment calls for. Take it easy on the facial tattoos, even though they have become more commonplace. (There is a guy sitting across from me in the prison library as I write this that has so many tattoo-tear drops on his face, a puddle tattooed on his jaw line would not appear out of place.)

Many people live separate lives from the ones that they project at the workplace. Who's to say that we can't do the same? I'm not suggesting that we continue with our lives of crime while not at our regular jobs. But I am suggesting that a more muted presentation of self can and will prove to our benefit.

If our physical presentation conforms to a standard of normalcy (whatever that may be), then we're doing well. Sometimes normalcy can come in the form of eccentricity. One of my friend's father works at a Harley Davidson dealership, and leather jackets, tattoos, long hair – even open-carry handguns – are the norm. A girlfriend of mine strips/dances to pay for medical school. I don't have to paint a picture of the different attire she wears at work versus her medical training... It just depends on what the situation calls for.

SHELL-SHOCKED

Please understand that I don't mean to admonish anyone, only to caution and advise... and level up. Most of us are not the anti-social, malevolent beings some stereotypes make us out to be. Quite the contrary. We possess a natural talent for putting a room of people at ease.

There are some of us, however, that have only become anti-social due to a life of crime; that only further alienates and perpetuates certain character flaws. Be it shyness when it comes to speaking, or flat-out apprehension and aggression towards the unknown- strangers in particular.

Towards the end of my own criminal career, I began to

feel the contrast that distinguishes normal socialization from the abnormal. I didn't actually perceive any associated anxiety or paranoia per se, because feeling anxious and paranoid came with the job.

There were times, though, when I would question a person's motives for approaching me, and I would often begin to wonder if they were agents or simply local cops doing a bit of undercover work. If I did encounter a stranger who seemed to be more interested in talking with me than usual, I would wait until they walked away before running their license plate to determine if they were actually who they claimed to be.

More often than not, they were just regular folks showing interest, trying and succeeding, at being friendly.

If this description of my paranoia resembles anything similar to what your own reactions consist of, and, if you're a class of criminal who has experienced some shell-shock due to the Life, then we may need to revamp our social skills.

Consider practicing with those whom you are comfortable socializing with. It's really no practice at all if you're being civil and holding normal conversation. You may even consider asking them what they think of you and if there are any areas in need of improvement that could be worked on. Be ready to take it on the chin and be respectful of their criticism, more so if it's constructive and positive.

Once we're ready for the training wheels to come off, we can start approaching random strangers (under the same conditions as they approach us) and see how they react to our advances. Observe how they respond when approached. If their first impression is one of apprehension (as ours can sometimes be), it may be your physical appearance that gives them pause.

Some of them, like us, are naturally cautious of people they don't know, and with good reason. These days the wolf often appears in the guise of the Good Samaritan.

NOTE: Whenever I walk through the parking lot on my

way to shop for groceries, I almost always happen across older people, or folks that might have physical challenges. I'll stop and ask them if they need help lifting that case of water bottles, a 40-pound bag of dog food, potting soil, etc., from the bottom of their cart and into their trunk. This is a daily opportunity to help a stranger in passing. (9 times out of 10 they accept my help). I make a point of jingling my keys or holding my phone when I approach so they know I'm not homeless, or an addict looking for something in exchange for my help, like running off with a bag of groceries or a purse. If they're Spanish-speaking, ask them "necesitas ayuda con eso?" and gesture towards the heavy item in their cart. "Do you need help with that?"

I try using a bit of tact when I strike up a conversation that's relevant to a common occurrence such as the weather, politics, the price of gas, what have you. And definitely make sure it's not in a dark alley, but somewhere where a brief exchange between strangers is commonplace.

NOTE: These days when I offer to help someone, or I'm just shooting the breeze in passing, I usually leave a business card with whomever I engage with. Two birds, one stone!

I think we'll come to find that most people, us included, are social creatures, if not social butterflies. And the more we communicate with them, the more at ease we'll feel when dealing with unknowns; which, of course, is what we'll be doing on a daily basis once interviewing for a job is attempted several times over.

If we learn to amplify and subtly emanate our principles with regards to our daily interactions, this will have a lasting impression on those we encounter.

An effective and lasting presentation comes from a cool, calm, and collected inner confidence, and ripples outwards with the same energy. So long as we master both – inner confidence and external presentation - and we do so with poise and genuine affability, we will always be demonstrative of people with an eye on success and positive advancement.

Employers will recognize and value upkeep on appearances and presentation, and will be quicker to place you on the frontline over employees that are overly shy and tentative. They will also be quicker to reward your efforts at being a proactive member of the team. Employees whose familiarity amongst customers and colleagues is also an extension of the business itself... and its reputation.

THE ADDRESS

"The success of your presentation will be judged not by the knowledge you send, but by what the listener receives."

— LILLY WALTERS, KEYNOTE SPEAKER

Criminal History... Background checks... Raised eyebrows when we offer a half-assed explanation as to where and when it all went wrong. What a pain in the ass. Or, more aptly put, these are the growing pains that we must come to know and experience – and even welcome – if we are ever to move forward.

So how do we confront the Big Question? If we filled out a job application instead of providing a resume, this question is going to have to be addressed much sooner than expected. I think the generalized format reads something like, "Have you ever been convicted of a crime in the past 5 years? Misdemeanor or Felony? If you answered, Yes, please explain."

I felt nervous just writing those words! Definitely not a good situation some of us have gotten ourselves into. But one way or another, we're going to come out clean and contributing on the other side, I promise.

<u>One of the best possible ways of addressing the Question is to first bypass it through the creation of a resume.</u> And one of the chief benefits of providing a resume is that we don't have to answer this question right away. Because of this, we have a much better chance of getting our foot in the door as opposed to being dismissed outright due to our criminal history. Just know that we'll probably have to address it eventually, and we'll want to be prepared to respond to the best of our ability when the time comes.

I feel that some, but not all employers that furnish this type of job app may be quicker to void an application than they would a resume which does not offer this sort of information; but rather, it only demonstrates strengths and accomplishments in their most favorable light.

It is for this reason that I suggest we create and submit resumes (if the employer accepts them), rather than walking in, wasting time filling out a dismissive application by default, and then possibly eliminating ourselves before we even get the opportunity to successfully market who we are as employees during an interview.

When we inevitably reach the juncture of responding to the Question – either on paper or in-person – I usually answer with a simple, "Yes, but will explain during interview if eligible," or if there's room, "Yes, but many years ago, and can provide clarifying responses to further questions, hoping my candor does not exclude me from the interview process."

If we do fill out an application and answer truthfully, *and* we're asked to an interview, that's a good indication that we're not only eligible, but that this particular employer may be willing to overlook past transgressions in light of current performance and capability. This is a good sign, and we'll want to be ready to accurately respond to any questions, (including the Big Question) in a way that will quiet any fears about hiring someone such as ourselves.

Also know that the further in your past your criminal

history is the better your chances are going to look at rationalizing the existence of a criminal record. By the time I'm released from prison, the offense that put me here will have occurred over a decade ago. That's ten years in which I haven't been involved in any criminal activity whatsoever. That's huge. Granted, we all know I spent that time in prison, but so what.

The time will come when prospective employers' human resources departments will begin running background checks on me. And they'll see that my life of crime ended quite some time ago. I'll of course have to account for a rather large gap in unemployment, but my educational experience gained since incarceration will greatly counterbalance lack of employment history, as well as my criminal background (if it even surfaces in background checks).

NOTE: Since returning home, I've found there are several websites and applications created that employers use to research a prospective employee, i.e., Been Verified, social media platforms, etc. Often times a background check might consist of one person performing a rather cursory attempt at researching another person (yourself) via Facebook, entering your name in a Google search, or maybe checking the local detention center (a year back) in the city you're applying for work in. If you were locked up in state or federal prison, and for some years, simple searches are not likely to yield anything. As my crime was federally prosecuted, even though I was honest about my past, human resources staff usually informed me, after I was hired, that nothing ever surfaced concerning the convictions I was prepared to explain. Go figure.

This is why education is so important, particularly for those of us who have convictions on our record; and more so for those that have been to prison. It shows that we have been doing *something, anything,* to improve our lives rather than picking up more charges and learning how to be better (or worse) criminals while behind bars.

When I am asked about my convictions, I intend on explaining that mine were a long time ago, and that the person I once was (and his lack of principles) no longer resemble the person I am now.

"Frankly, I view that person as separate and dissimilar compared to the one I am today... a person who only exists on paper."

It was easy to disassociate myself entirely from, well... myself.

What we are doing by responding in this fashion is making a clear distinction between our old selves and new selves; both in measurements of time and ethics. We are also establishing a sense of conviction that the person(s) we are now are no longer criminal; nor a liability to the employer that hires you. But rather, an asset that can be utilized and relied upon for profit's sake and the continuity of the employer in question.

While different crimes may call for varying explanations, the root answer is the same. Be as forthcoming as possible and as convincing as possible. In the Information Age, knowledge is capital, and people are going to find out either way. As we are already privy to this knowledge/power, we have the ability to bestow it to others in the best light possible, as opposed to someone debriefing, questioning, and perhaps judging you on what you already know about yourself.

No matter how much education we acquire, or how long we've kept our noses clean, there are going to be some opportunities for employment that are not suited to our particular pathway. Handling rejection can be difficult, or as easy as letting it roll of your back like so much water in the shower. Accept that that opportunity was never meant for you in the first place; hence, it was never *your* opportunity.

If we're turned down subsequent an interview, the best reaction is to respond with thanking them for the opportunity to interview, and to keep you in mind should circumstances change. This is often best performed via a thank you letter by way of an email. (See examples at the end of the chapter).

Handling rejection of any kind, with humility and grace is a trait that anyone can come to admire, including the person rejecting you. A rejection does not necessarily mean that we weren't the right people for the job. Often times company policy dictates the decision(s) of those doing the hiring. They may have wanted to hire you, but work history, education, interview quality, or a combination of the three did not meet HR's criteria.

Turning a negative response into a positive learning experience will always benefit those whose reaction is a continuation of applying one's self to the lesson's intent.

Making a federal seizure of several hundred thousand dollars, and a 7- year prison sentence, was the government's (an employer, if you will) reaction to a substandard employee's performance (me), and what was ultimately a decision on my part to turn that rejection into a positive learning experience.

Rather than allowing multiple rejections to be the cause for losing hope, try to optimize each experience by leveling up your interview skills subsequently. Do your homework on the employer for which you're considering employment, i.e., if they hire felons, if the pay and benefits packages are even something you're willing to consider. This will save us time and energy looking for employment in areas that wouldn't even appeal to us at the outset, or, because of our criminal backgrounds.

SEARCHES

Finding out who hires and who does not hire people with criminal convictions is as easy as calling the employer in question and asking their Human Resources Department what their hiring policy consists of. Learning which employers hire felons is also as simple as performing an online search.

www.Hirenetworks.com is a website that has key re-entry and employment information for all 50 states with data ranging from which companies hire felons, to federal assistance initiatives such as the Federal Bonding Program, and tax benefits for companies that hire individuals regardless of their criminal history.

There are literally dozens, if not hundreds of websites that help people in their search for the right job and/or career pathway:

- www.monster.com
- www.directemployers.com
- www.careerbuilder.com
- www.employment911.com
- www.nationjob.com
- www.careerflex.com
- www.careerjournal.com

These sites not only provide a means of obtaining employment, they also have other features such as job search suggestions, career assessment tests, resume and interview advice, and much more.

There are also a few sites designed specifically to help those who have felony convictions find employment:

- www.indeed.com
- www.jobs.felons.com
- www.jobsforfelons.com
- www.jobs2careers.com

There are also a range of websites which provide means of testing oneself in order to determine which jobs or career pathways best fit specific character traits. One of the more widely used assessment tests is the Myers Briggs Company Personality Assessment Test at www.cpp.com

NOTE: If you're currently incarcerated and do not have internet access to websites, you can check the validity of these upon release. Truth be told, I had to update the above listings, as some of them were no longer valid.

While the internet is by far the most accessible and the most informative, there are other options that should not be overlooked, such as the classifieds, job fairs, and networking. I can recall Chris Rock doing stand-up (I think it was his Bigger and Blacker tour), where he states that "90% of the people in this room got a job because a friend recommended them!" One of the things that makes comedy so hilarious is the validity behind the humor - Mr. Rock's assessment was probably spot-on.

Networking; that is, using and expanding a group of trusted friends, family and colleagues (or crime partners) (FFC) to our benefit is one of the best possible resources at our disposal. Seeking employment is often times a matter of exposure. The more potential employers we expose ourselves to, the better. And the more people in our network aware of our search, the greater the likelihood that they will put us in touch with someone looking to hire.

Set realistic quotas as to the number of interviews and people you expose and market yourself to each week. For me, (10 resume/job application submittals a week) should yield, in time, about half that amount in interviews for following weeks. That's easily over 40 submittals in one month that should result in at least 20 interviews later that month; not to mention follow-up calls, emails, etc. That's a good deal of exposure by any standard.

In fact, the amount I've stated above might be somewhat extra if the career pathway you seek is a bit more specific; hence, limited in nature. And we don't want to be expelling energy applying for jobs in an assembly line fashion (and performing poorly in too many interviews) simply for the sake of exposure, or overexposure.

We're not targeting every place in our radius that has a Help Wanted sign in their window. You don't want employers calling for interviews and subsequent job offers that wouldn't suit you to begin with. Be precise and selective (and honest with yourself) with the types of jobs you seek. If we're saturating the job market with applications and resumes, without even thinking about who we're sending them out to, you'll spend/waste a great deal of time answering and responding to inquiries and interviews that will veer us from the path we intend on taking.

I'm not saying it will, but overexposure could cause us to miss out on an opportunity we could have landed had our mission objectives been clearly defined.

RESUMES AND COVER LETTERS

Typically, there are two types of resumes; one is the Skills Resume which outlines your skills, education, achievements and work history without listing them chronologically. The other is the Chronological Resume which is an exact timeline of your past work history, as well as other accomplishments.

The chronological resume is designed to display a person's strong work history and is intended to demonstrate a steady transition and advancement from one job to the next, with little or no gaps in between. Typically, if there's a gap in work history, you should expect to give some kind of explanation during the interview. This style of resume more-or-less, mirrors the standard job application that most employers provide.

The skills resume tends to work a little better for people who lack employment history because it showcases their skills, talents, and education in a way that does not reflect the minute amount of employment experience a person may have as a result of their criminal activity- or any other instances which may have prevented them from establishing a solid work history, such as continuing one's education or performing volunteer work.

A blending of the two different types in a hybrid can also work if you feel that that's what the situation calls for. It all depends on what you're comfortable with or what demands you feel the potential employer has in mind. The examples provided at the end of this chapter are ones that I had created for people who were preparing to reenter society, and who wrote me to tell me that the resumes I had made for them were one of the determining factors that helped them to 1. gain interviews, and 2. gain employment. While I was grateful to know that I was able to lend a hand, I also felt it was necessary to remind them, (and you), that their presentation and performance are the things that ultimately landed the job.

Most of the guys that I helped draft resumes for had almost no work history to speak of, *unless* we listed jobs they had while on the Inside. Two things that seemed to really help with their job acquisition was the amount of education they had received through courses they took while incarcerated, and volunteer work performed as soon as they hit the streets.

Some did have a bit of work history, and I was able to provide, in a few cases, both a chronological resume and skills resume; or a hybrid of the two. Both types are preceded by generalized (rather than targeted) cover letters, because they weren't sure just who it was they were going to seek employment with.

Time is of the essence when coming home from prison. We're going to have probation officers and halfway house employees breathing down our necks, pressuring, threatening and basically strong-arming us to get a job, any job, before they lose patience and violate us back to the can. It is for this reason that having a generalized resume and cover letter already written – *before* hitting the streets – is one of the best ideas conceivable... it gives you some breathing room before the "walls of freedom" begin closing in.

Many of us upon release get the first job we find just so we can breathe a little easier by relieving the suffocating feeling parole/probation places on us. But it's that first undesirable job, and every unappealing quality it possesses, that steers us back towards the easy money.

Instead of desperately rushing around from a defensive posture, submitting as many applications as possible, and settling for the first job offer that comes our way, consider how much easier it is dropping off resumes at the employers we've set our sights on? It's such a better approach than, say, hitting up every store in a strip mall and spending 20 minutes in each trying to accurately fill out a resume and remember the from *when-to-whens,* on each job you ever worked.

NOTE: Just before release, or immediately after it would be prudent to have a few custom cover letters and resumes, i.e., employer-specific addressed to those companies we really dreamed of working for.

Custom cover letters should have the name of the person for whom the resume is intended. They should be slightly more engaging and personable (yet professional) as compared to the generalized version. No "For whom this may concern." This is when our research will come into play to determine who it is that is doing the interviewing, and who it is, specifically, that we intend on working for.

In some instances that one person may actually be a few people, in which case we would send out a cover letter addressing the name of the employer followed by "Interview Panel." We want to be as personable as possible so that we can give those interviewing us the distinction and autonomy they deserve.

Once the cover letter and resume processes are complete, you'll come to see just how much easier and timely it is submitting resumes, either on paper or electronically. I think on some intrinsic level, <u>it gives us more confidence in pursuing</u>

<u>desirable positions at better companies via submitting tailored resumes.</u>

Creating our own resume is very similar to creating any artistic conception, in that the intent of the artist is to capture the eye and consideration of those viewing it. Sometimes we commission a work of art to capture the eye of one person only. Our cover letter(s) will often serve as the component of our work that stands out from countless other works of art that have attempted to do the same.

When interviewing, avoid some of the more common idiosyncrasies of character I've listed below:

1. *Gesticulation of the hands.* My mother is Hispanic and Italian. That side of the family uses their hands to talk, probably more so than their mouths. Dad is of mixed-race, primarily English/French and North African descent. Needless to say, my cousins in Baltimore are probably just as animated as those on my mother's side, albeit with different gestures. One of my Baltimore cousins claps out every word for emphasis when she's trying to drive a point home... Hilarious. Be that as it may, we have a mouth, lips, tongue, and vocal cords to annunciate the spoken word. These should be the only parts of our bodies in motion when conveying our thoughts. Take a comfortable position while seated, and place one hand over top of the other.
   - **NOTE:** I keep a notepad and a pen in my lap for two purposes: to keep my hands from doing the talking, and to write down notes if someone is providing a clarifying response to one of my questions.
2. *Fidgeting.* I suppose nail-biting and hair twirling fall under this category as well, and any other thing that constitutes a fidget. I fidget a lot so using that

notepad to write rather than fidget really helps. I also get cotton-mouth when interviewing and so I'll keep a bottled water handy to wet my whistle. An occasional re-crossing of the legs (or ankles) or reminding yourself to sit upright all help to demonstrate an animated individual without too much unnecessary movement.

3. *Repeating the question that was just posed to you.* This one nuance I find myself doing during interviews, be they in-person or online. I suppose it's ok to do it once to allow us time to calibrate a response that fits the question. In fact, it's better than asking an interviewer to repeat the question.

    ○ **NOTE:** This was a tactic I employed when being interrogated by law enforcement when I was very young, and a poor one at that. Simply refuse to speak until a lawyer is present and then your lawyer will also advise that you say nothing. A detective's job is to investigate; so, let them investigate without volunteering any information that would incriminate us. Unfortunately, this tactic won't work during an interview. Instead, try practicing with a friend so that your answers will come automatically and smoothly, without any hesitation or possible repetition of the question posed.

4. *Asking about pay and benefits.* The job posting usually provides these details, and/or they are often times discussed at the introduction or end of the interview. If this is a subject that doesn't make it into the conversation, and when the interview comes to a conclusion, it is at this point that we're usually given the opportunity to ask questions ourselves.

- ○ **NOTE:** Politely inquire as to pay; is it based on salary, hourly, commission, etc.?

5. *Keep everything out of our mouths except words of wisdom.* This too is a practice I have difficulty with.

   - ○ **NOTE:** I'll keep a small chip of a cough drop or breath mint in the side of my cheek to help cope with the dry-mouth, along with occasional sips of water. Anything other than that is extra and might be distracting.

6. *Don't let your guard down.* I have a tendency to be way too open and friendly with folks I should be exercising a bit more circumspection around. Again, if the job calls for being a greeter, host, or presenter; customer service or the like, then reigning in our sunshine probably isn't as necessary.

   - ○ **NOTE:** If your interviewer is the boisterous type who utters an occasional curse word, that's fine, but it isn't an indication that you do the same. For my last interview, my future director was this older, well-spoken black gentleman who had managed a much larger city before coming to Santa Fe and greatly improving our town's economic development department. He and his panel snuck in a couple of "bullshits" and one "fuck" before they finally asked me if I could handle an animated office whose staff often used curse words. I laughed and repeated their phrases in which they used profanity to demonstrate that I was no stranger to it, but not to the extent where I exceeded their own usage. They got the gist of what I was implying... I also got the job.

7. *Checking the time.* I don't think there's any action more damaging to our chances of having a good interview than looking at the time on your watch or phone, or the clock on the wall when someone is speaking to you. Doing this during the interview lets the interviewer/interview panel know that you're not taking this opportunity seriously, and they'll write you off as someone who won't take working there seriously either.

We can, and should, always work with FFC to see if there is anything they notice about our oral and physical presentation that could possibly use some improvement. Practice might not always make perfect but it will definitely bring you a little closer to perfection.

If you do receive a call for an interview, it's imperative that we only answer when there are no distractions that might hinder our performance such as background noise, loud music, screaming children, etc. If there's a number on your phone you don't recognize – chances are you've been leaving your contact info on applications and resumes – it could very well be someone calling you back to make an appointment for an interview.

If *now* is not a good time to answer the phone then don't answer it. Check your voicemail so you can respond to any missed calls at a time when there are no distractions that might affect the conversation.

NOTE: If you have voicemail (VM) set up on your phone, make sure it's a professional greeting rather than an automated response. Also make certain that your inbox isn't full, and that you can actually receive VMs.

This will also give you time to put your proverbial game face on instead of being caught off guard and stumbling when we should be dancing. Whether it's over the phone or in-person, be on even terms with the interviewers. Employers seeking good employees favor bold, inquisitive and well-spoken interviewees. As long as these qualities don't supersede our professional presentation as opposed to augmenting it, there's nothing to worry about.

One of the most common and unfortunate occurrences during an interview is allowing the interviewer to take the lead during the *entire* course of the proceeding. Granted, most interviews are of the Q&A variety, and they most often commence with the interviewer giving us the broad strokes as to the job responsibilities themselves. But it also behooves us to be active listeners; to know when to engage, to provide intelligent responses, and to include clarifying questions in our responses when appropriate.

Interviews should *never* be a monologue where one party talks and the other simply nods and listens. No bueno. There must be a dialogue between two parties where we, at certain junctures, are given the opportunity to convey our worth as potential assets to the employer.

Have you ever tried to have a conversation with a person who, frankly, isn't very good at reading the ebb and flow between each party? And did you find yourself becoming slightly irritated at their inability to exercise one of the easiest forms of social interaction? The same rule applies to job interviews.

Granted, an interview isn't exactly your normal form of chit chat with someone we already know. Rather, it consists of similar elements of a conversation with someone we're meeting for the purpose of determining how compatible we'll be, if our mannerisms and sociability are up to par. And most importantly, if we're able to demonstrate that our efforts are productive with favorable results.

In essence, our interview is the conversation that convinces our target audience that we are the best person for the job. The proper responses from the interviewee combined with a good presentation are the key factors that usually determine whether or not they'll get the job. The facts about yourself that are listed on paper should only be a back-up component, or affirmation of who we are as a whole. Never let our resumes do all of the talking when we ourselves are able to do so in-person.

Remember also that, for the interviewer, conducting interviews may not be an ideal job responsibility either. And that people who are engaging and responsive will *always* be easier to interview as opposed to those that need coaxing and steering in the right direction. When it comes time for us to ask our own questions, we'll want to be prepared to use this opportunity to demonstrate further interest in the job and the people interviewing us, in an effort to appear that much more appealing in comparison to those whom will interview before and after us.

The questions I've included below have worked wonders when I've interviewed for positions/promotions in the state and local government job sectors. In fact, I've also drafted several of the questionnaires since working a regular 8-to-5; thus, I have been on both the giving and receiving ends of several interview panels:

1. *What is the most challenging aspect(s) of the position for which I'm being interviewed?* This is a question that shows your interest in working for this employer hasn't diminished since the interview began, and that you're still enthusiastic and up for the challenge.
   a. *What are the most rewarding aspects of this position?* This is the follow-up question to the first and shows that not only are we up to the challenge, but we're mindful of the rewards as well; be they monetary, intrinsic, or otherwise.
2. *What would you consider to be the greatest contribution(s) I could make in the position for which I'm applying?* If

everything hasn't already been explained in detail, this is a great way to squeeze a bit more truth out of your interviewers. Usually, at this point, our questions are off the record, and it gives the interviewers a chance to drop some of their formality and exercise a bit more ease in their approach.

3. *Where do you see this company, office, bureau, firm store, shop, etc., in 5 years? Do you see the position I'm applying for taking on any new roles/new responsibilities?* These questions are in direct response to the question often posed to interviewees, "Where do you see yourself in 5 years?" It's meant to glean an understanding of your intended advancement, either in life, working for the employer you're interviewing with, or both. Your response to this question is important. But asking something similar is indicative of your own estimations of them as an employer; and as such, may be the more important of the two inquiries. It shows that not only are you interested in your own personal outcomes but in the outcomes of the entity with which you'll earn a living.

4. *If considered for employment, when is the soonest I could start? And will I have a chance to provide ample notice to my current employer?* This is a great way to demonstrate that 1. you'd like to start as soon as possible, and 2. You're already employed; hence, another company (possibly even their competition), is losing a valuable asset.

5. *Are there any more questions you might have for me that would help you gain more insight as to my character, or why I'm applying for this position?* This truly gives them the chance to go off script and ask you questions they were unable to ask due to policy, adhering to HR-

approved interview questions, etc. It's also a double-edged sword, and they may ask you about your criminal past or any number of things, so just be prepared. You'll rarely experience interviewers pass up the chance to see a bit more of your daily humanity, and they will remember you for it.

Once they thank you for your time, stand up, shake hands, tell them you look forward to hearing from them, and step out of the hotseat. We did it!

CLOSING

Presentation, Preparation, Self-Confidence, and the best possible responses followed by tailored questions are your strong suits during the interview process. Combined, and when used correctly, they are the very qualities that will guarantee job acquisition.

Perceptiveness and understanding the ebb and flow of the interview is essential in knowing which direction it's going to go before it even gets there. Take the reigns when appropriate to let those who are interviewing you know that not only can you listen and follow instructions, but when necessary, you can also direct, lead, and mitigate circumstances in a way that demonstrates your abilities both in social and occupational settings.

Address your criminal past with the utmost level of honesty. But be sure to impress upon everyone – that includes you – that it is definitely in the past. Convince others, and convince yourself, that that part of you no longer exists, and it will be so. Confront and discuss your past mistakes as an unfortunate act, or series of acts, in bad judgment that all people consider at one point or another in their lives. The people you're sharing with will be sure to relate, even if that relation only occurs in their minds.

Be conscious of your ability to practice beginner's psychology, as we have been doing roughly since the age of three. Know who our audience is within the first moments of meeting them to appeal to their personalities and curtail any behavior on our part that might appear objectionable to their sensibilities.

Know thyself. Know every aspect of your makeup and be conscious of both your inward and outward appearance to ensure that you are exceptional by any standard of presentation.

Be Japanese! Obviously, this isn't to say that those of us who come from other backgrounds are not mindful or respectful of others. It's simply an indication that most of us are aware that that particular culture, and people, are renowned for their ability to be respectful and polite, even in the face of adversity. And it would benefit us if we could keep this in mind when managing our own lives, as well as the people that exist in them, no matter how long or short their involvement with us.

Being Japanese just means that we treat *all* people, be they your parents, siblings, friends, interviewers, coworkers, adversaries, or complete strangers with an equal amount of politeness. Being familiar with people shouldn't cause us to take certain liberties with them simply because we're on friendly terms. Rather, that shared familiarity should be valued and appreciated as opposed to taken for granted.

Use the right handshake with the right hand, literally. Even lefties know that everyone shakes with the right. We're not the president so no grasping the hand that we're shaking with our free hand in an attempt to convey a closeness that doesn't exist. We're not courtiers from centuries past so no kissing the hand of those conducting the interview. Give a firm yet relaxed handshake that's not too loose and not bone-breaking either. Think of firmness and dependability without nervous strength or flimsiness.

NOTE: There was this old Vietnam Vet/biker I knew that had a Traumatic Brain Injury, or TBI, named Jerry. Jerry was a sweetheart of a guy and super friendly with everyone he encountered. He never had a tattoo in his life, but left a shop of mine covered from the very top of his head to the tips of his toes in tattoos. In any event, Jerry had a bone-crushing handshake that he would then hold you in while staring into your soul with his glittery blue eyes. It was unnerving to say the least. And it took me awhile to get used to his style of greeting. He wasn't trying to be intimidating or overbearing. It was just the way he greeted people. I realized this after watching him shake several people's hands other than my own, and often seeing people, both male and female, slightly wince from his handshake. But it's the perfect example of how *not* to shake hands during an interview. Another example of what not to do would be the very opposite of how Jerry greeted people, i.e., a loose handshake with zero eye contact. Another acquaintance, Barry, has the oddest handshake I've ever tried to manage, and I finally gave up on trying to shake this dude's hand. I now settle for the dap with Barry, and even that he struggles with by either punching too hard or missing the mark every-single-time. Jerry and Barry... go figure.

Eye contact is also key. But it's not a stare-into-their-soul kind of thing that Jerry would do. The eye contact should be just as brief and held for the same time as the handshake. I'm a bit cockeyed with my stare so I'll usually clasp hands, smile enough to show some crow's feet, and transition my eye contact from one eye to the other before releasing my hand and searching for my seat. The entire process takes about two seconds.

I often have this sense that the formality that accompanies a job interview is most often the thing that can make it a nerve-racking occasion, more so than the reality that our very survival may depend on landing this particular job.

We tend to forget that the ones conducting the interview

are just as human, and prone to worry and anxiety as the rest of us. We also tend to overlook the fact that they also had to endure this very same process in order to be in the position they're currently in.

The fact that our lives and our very standard of living can be affected, enhanced, and temporarily or permanently altered from gaining employment are the reasons that should make an interview an important occasion; *not* the prospect of being interviewed or interrogated by strangers. But rather than be nervous, make an attempt at transforming that anxiety into eagerness at a brighter future.

Let the enthusiasm for advancement in life show in every action (verbal and physical) that we perform. View the person conducting the interview as one of the means to obtaining that future, and not as someone who is casting judgment upon you.

Applying this outlook when being interviewed should help alleviate most of the fears and anxieties that one faces during this process.

Be presentable and be prepared to perform at your highest level on the day of your interview. If you get passed over for the job you're applying for, think about what might have occurred that affected this outcome and make the necessary adjustments. Also know that being passed over may have been a result of another interviewee being more qualified than us. Be positive in the face of defeat in order to learn, adapt, and to turn those defeats into future victories.

Above all, we must remember that we may be turned down for employment by our own doing, by employer policy, or by fate. But this by no means suggests that we weren't qualified. It simply means that that particular job was never an option in the first place. Even getting turned down or passed over should be seen as stepping stones and advancement, provided, we learn and move forward afterwards.

Always compose and send thank you letters/emails post-interview. Even though an employer may choose not to select you, they'll remember you, as well as your having gone the extra mile. And you could very well be referred by them to another company, or even another position within their own.

Take into account that it is almost always our own fears that keep us tethered to our current existence. And that it is that same apprehension and anxiety – when coupled with determination and educating one's self as to the job for which we're applying – that can often be the perfect fuel for current and future successes.

When we're sitting in our car, in the lobby, or at the bus stop, take a moment to practice some positive visualization. We've already memorized our discussion about the position, the employer, and our standardized responses and post-interview questions. Now's the time to visualize a positive, easygoing (but sometimes technical) conversation with a person whom we've never met but who we intend on engaging through intelligence, professionalism, and politeness.

Visualize yourself already working there, going through the sometimes hum-drum day-to-day routines, completing daily tasks and planning for next day's assignments. Visualize the life that obtaining this particular job will afford you, and it will be so.

COVER LETTERS

A cover letter is basically the inner-sleeve of a book cover. In essence, it should convey to the reader the contents of the book which they are about to read, which, in this case, is your resume. It should also assert your intentions and eagerness at pursuing employment with the target company, as well as express to the reader a few facts about the author (you) that are relevant to the desired position of employment. Cover letters should *always* be addressed to one particular person. It is because of this that you should do as much research as possible to find out who it is that you're going to be sending your resume to.

Only in instances of absolute uncertainty should someone submit a generalized cover letter. Or, as is the case with many of us whom are reentering society, where time is of the essence, a generalized cover letter would be better than none at all.

And if it's a simple job rather than an attempt at a career pathway, a generalized cover letter will not, by any means, be viewed as impersonal or inconsiderate, more so when we consider that for a standard run-of-the-mill gig, most people automatically ask for an application to fill out as opposed to submitting a resume, much less a cover letter to boot.

Finding out the name of the individual who will review your resume and perhaps even interview you can be a fairly simple task. Place a call to the employer and ask for the name of the person(s) conducting the interview for that particular job posting.

Again, this is yet one more part of your story, or manuscript if you will, that when added to the whole, should make a nice and informative read. The construction of cover letters, resumes, and thank-you notes should never be a stressful task to undertake. And yet, I have seen many people struggle with creating these. Granted, there are challenges, but they are challenges that should exercise and strengthen your ingenuity and creativeness, rather than frustrate and test our patience.

NOTE: Drafting resumes and cover letters for guys before they left prison eventually became the manner in which I earned a little extra for commissary and other necessities. My function as an unofficial jail-house attorney eventually took a back seat to fine-tuning documents for guys that were intent on making a successful reentry. I envision e-publishing this work for the purpose of those needing resumes and other associated documentation. Simply copy/paste the applicable examples and then replace and plug in your own information.

Have fun and gain some insight as to the kind of person you are, and the sort of employee you want to present yourself as on paper. If you're not the "fun" type, then get serious. And in our seriousness, create something that conveys intent while capturing the interest of the reader. And remember that works of art, no matter how appealing they may appear to some, may seem rather uninteresting and bland to others. The more you know about the person(s) you're submitting your cover letter to, the better an idea you'll have as to capturing their attention through the written word.

Cover Letter (Specific)

Dear Mr. Brown,

Please see my attached resume and references. I submitted my application via the City's online platform, but thought it a good idea to provide you with a resume as well.

I have been employed in State government for over ten years with a background in contract management, Medicaid MCO oversight, legal research and writing, and of late an emphasis on bureau-specific presentations to the Governor's Office during legislative session.

I also spearheaded the State's efforts at streamlining processes and procedures via working with an external review team to outline previous workflow charts, and then create new ones with the technology and support available to us. This effort drastically reduced the steps necessary when performing functions using antiquated methods.

I recently received notice from a friend and colleague, Lucinda Garcia, who informed me that the City's Economic Development Department was looking for new ED Specialists. If a job entails helping people, I'm all for it, and would love to see what the City's Economic Development Department has in store for the people of our small, yet growing municipality.

Thank you for your time and consideration. I look forward to hearing from you and your team.

> In Candor,
> Jason Grinage, Contract Manager
> New Mexico Dept. Of Health
> Epidemiology Bureau

Cover Letter (Specific/Cont.)

Jason Grinage

123 Calle Sin Nombre • Santa Fe, NM 87500 • (505)-456-7890 • Jason.Grinage@gmail.com

---

March 25, 2024

Carl Katz

Kentish Inc.

123 Siler Rd.

Santa Fe, NM 87501

Dear Mr. Katz,

A rewarding and successful work (or educational) experience motivates me to bring my commitment to Kentish Incorporated. I offer four years of experience, dedication, and productivity in shipping and receiving, sales, and customer service.

I have recently left my position as head shipping and receiving clerk at TMCI in Albuquerque, and it was by the suggestion of Mr. Ken Martin, my supervisor, that I submit my resume to you.

As head shipping and receiving clerk, I developed new initiatives which were successfully implemented into our daily distribution plan that enhanced our monthly output by 15%, without negatively impacting customer service. I also helped to create our "Source to Customer" plan which enabled clients to communicate directly with our warehouse staff via telephone/text/email in order to provide real-time updates as to customer orders, readiness and delivery.

My experiences at TMCI have also permitted me to do the following:

• Work in a team-orientated environment where multi-tasking and meeting deadlines were the standard for day-to-day operations.

• Communicate with customers and warehouse staff to convey successes, pain points, and challenges to management to ensure that everything from purchase orders to deliveries were carried out as efficiently as possible.

• Empower team members by providing them with the tools, training, and skills relevant to accomplishing duties without the need for micromanagement on my part or on behalf of upper management.

I have enclosed my resume for your review. If you have any questions or require further information, you may call/email me with the number and address provided. I thank you for your consideration in this matter.

Respectfully,
Jason Grinage

NOTE: The only difference between these two cover letters is that I asked Mr. Brown in the first sentence to review my resume and references while informing Mr. Katz of the same at the end of the second cover letter. Albeit names of the target audiences, companies, etc., were changed, these were actual cover letters created by me and submitted for positions I sought after subsequent my return home. They were also positions I acquired, and worked, until I was promoted or resigned to pursue a different pathway.

RESUMES

The examples provided are ones that were constructed for guys who were getting ready to reenter society. For reasons of privacy,I've given my name for each. Some of the educational experiences listed were pursued by me or other inmates on the outside, or were classes that were taken through correspondence courses and/or programs available in the federal prison system.

In some instances, guys had been incarcerated for quite some time, and a **skills resume** displayed their proficiencies in a manner that would not cause doubt or speculation due to a lack of work history.

In other instances, I had constructed resumes for people who weren't even in prison for longer than a year or a few months' time, because of a probation violation, or the like, and their work histories were more compatible with a **chronological resume**.

Others were more challenging to customize as their work histories and skills were good, but they were also coupled with poor educational backgrounds, so a hybrid of the two proved the better option.

Remember that in cases of long to moderate duration of imprisonment, the skills resume may prove a bit easier to construct, albeit a chronological resume can also apply. (much of this depends on how you spend your time in prison, working jobs, taking classes, or playing cards and politicking). If your jail time is minimal and you've had some steady employment to camouflage your criminal endeavors- No. 1, you're already several steps ahead of the majority of us. And No. 2, a chronological resume is going to better showcase your work history timeline.

No matter what a person's work history, or lack thereof, bear in mind that resumes are designed for the sole purpose of making yourself appealing to the job for which you're applying; because of this, you're going to need to customize resumes that better reflect a person whose talents and capabilities parallel the requirements of the position you want to obtain.

Think about how many jobs are out there and the range of diversity that separates one from another. If you have only one resume, designed for compatibility with only one area of work, there's a high probability that that resume may not be as well-matched to other fields of employment. Always be prepared to make adjustments, have multiple resumes labeled for specific job opportunities, as well as a generalized resume so that your exposure, and the presentation and reception of that exposure, will always be in our favor.

There were instances where I had to add, "References will be furnished upon request," or "Please call for references," within the resume. Not only is this an acceptable statement for people who don't wish to have their references bombarded by an overly high-level of phone calls, but if you don't have any people to return home to, or if you have been imprisoned for so long that you don't have any references, then this will give you time to create a network of people that you can rely on for references and recommendations, when the time comes.

I would use caution when entering too many "graphics" into your resume to the point where the reader becomes dizzy. I used an old clunker of a desktop computer in the can, and had to get permission from the library guard to print them out; hence, some of the options for bulleting work history and other details were a little limited, thus, superfluously used. I've seen plenty of resumes with a page border (which is fine) and more than three font types, which proved unnecessary. We don't really need to put a signature at the bottom of the resume if our name is already included at the top, i.e.,

Jason Grinage.

Jason Grinage (chronological resume)

123 Calle Sin Nombre • Santa Fe, NM 87500 • (505)-456-7890 • Jason.Grinage@gmail.com

Experience:

2022-2024, JMB Builders, Longmont, CO
Contractor(General and Foundation Applications)

- Form setting
- Foundation layout
- Finishing

2020-2022 Amber Homes Denver, CO
Superintendent

- Front-end Superintendent
- General construction oversight
- Final walkthrough and build inspection

2017-2022 Snappy ADP, Grand Junction, CO
Regional Sales Rep

- Executed regional company sales in Southwestern U.S.
- Product Development Consultant
- Customer service

2015-2017 CB Commerical Property Main., Thornton, CO
Properties Mgr.

- Grounds Keeper
- Safety and quality control
- Assessments for primary systems, i.e., boilers, HVAC, plumbing, etc.

Computer Skills:

- Microsoft Office, PowerPoint, Excel, Word
- Apple (Mac OS)

Certifications:

- HVAC, Plumbing, Journeyman
- EPA Certified for HAZMAT Class I and II
- Business Administration Certification

Education Volunteer Work:

- Vocational training, Building Trades, Pueblo Community College (PCC)
- Vocational training, Green Energy Applications, PCC
- Business Administration Certificate, PCC

Jason Grinage (skills resume)

123 Calle Sin Nombre • Santa Fe, NM 87500 • (505)-456-7890 • Jason.Grinage@gmail.com

Skills

Construction

- I have worked in most all fields of construction ranging from commercial/residential foundation builds to finished applications, i.e., paint, plumbing and electrical/lighting.

Building Trades

- I have recently completed a training program via Century College for both Building Trades and Industrial Housekeeping with the expectation that the knowledge gained from these programs would be relevant to employment in a construction-related field. My expectation is that, by familiarizing myself with specific aspects of the construction industry, my education will help counterbalance deficient work history.

Driving Record

- Please see attached driving record for review. I also have a valid commercial driver's license (CDL) that has benefited past employers who also depend on transportation services.

Education and Training

- Building Trades, Century College
- Industrial Housekeeping, Century College
- Electrical Wiring Certification, Pueblo Community College (PCC)
- Vocational Training, Custodial Services, PCC

(Note how my educational experience while incarcerated drastically improves my appearance on paper by counterbalancing my lack of work history. Granted, it's not much, but this is how many skills resumes are drafted by high school students and others with no work history or internships to show. Even though my skills resume does not detail **one-single-job**, my skills and time spent in training are demonstrative of one who has been preparing himself for the workforce via education.)

Jason Grinage (hybrid resume)

123 Calle Sin Nombre • Santa Fe, NM 87500 • (505)-456-7890 • Jason.Grinage@gmail.com

Skills & Certifications

- Associates, Business Administration, Pueblo Community College (PCC)
- Green Energy Applications Certification, PCC
- Microsoft Office Certification
- Apple (Mac OS)
- Bilingual (English/Spanish)

Experience

F.C.I. Florence • Instructor/Law Clerk • 2010-2015

- Created course curriculums and tutored students on subjects ranging from criminal justice, high school equivalency diploma preparation, legal research and writing, and resume building.

Dawn-Smith's • Asst. Mgr. • 2009-2006

- Managed and trained a team of 8 sales and customer service reps
- Created bi-weekly work schedules for sales team
- Inventory Mgr.

Santa Fe Paint & Body • Paint Technician • 2006-2004

- Customer Service
- Body prep work
- Finishing

Education and Training

- Basic and Higher Education Instructor • F.C.I. Florence • 2010-2015
- Business Administration • Associates • PCC • 2011
- Electrical Wiring Certification, Pueblo Community College (PCC)
- Vocational Training • Painting/Spraying • Dept. Of Labor • Florence, CO 2010
- Management and Training Program • John-Edwards • Los Angeles, CA • 2007

(This is almost identical to the hybrid resume I used upon my release from federal prison. Simply copy/paste, and replace the company names I used with your own, and you have some of my work history prior to incarceration, as well as my job duties while incarcerated. Submitting this resume resulted in callbacks for interviews and job offers, but I opted for public service upon my release rather than sales or labor).

THANK YOU NOTE

A Thank-You Note is not only professional, but a welcome form of notifying your interviewer(s) that you valued the interest they showed in you, as well as the time they spent out of their day conducting interviews. More importantly, it demonstrates continued interest – even after being interviewed – to pursue employment with their company.

While emailing a thank-you note is more common these days, know that it's also ok to drop off a hand-written or printed note. You may have a contact within HR that you could email the thank-you note to, and/or address it to the "Interview Panel." If the interview was conducted by one person, then a typed or hand-written note may be just the thing to deliver. Use your discretion and instinct to determine which is best.

A Thank-you Note should be up-beat, professional, and to the point. All of our Q&A sessions should have been worked out during the interview. So rather than posing more of them in your note, use it as a means of showing continued interest, intent, and gratitude for the opportunity, nothing more.

Dear John Smith,

I want to thank you and your staff for taking the time to see me. The interview was extremely informative and only further instilled my beliefs that working for your company would be a positive and productive opportunity for all parties concerned. Your thorough explanation of the position I applied for indicates that this would be a chance for me to not only demonstrate my skillsets, but an opening where I might also prove a productive member of your team. Again, many thanks for your consideration. I look forward to hearing from you soon.

In Candor,

Jason Grinage.

(A short thank-you email can influence the decision to hire you. 31% of qualified applicants do not send a short thank-you note after every interview and 7% of applicants never send thank you notes at all. A survey by CareerBuilder determined only 57% of applicants send thank you notes after an interview.)

ENTREPRENEURISM V. CORPORATE ADVANCEMENT

Generally speaking, there are two types of breadwinners in the workplace. One is the entrepreneur, and the other is the person who makes advancements through working their way up the corporate ladder (public or private sector). An entrepreneur is essentially a risk taker. This is the type of person, who, through an idea, finds a way to create transaction by turning that idea into a marketable product or service.

Both approaches have pros and cons. Speaking for myself, obtaining employment in the public sector (government) provided a regimented lifestyle that probably facilitated terminating my probation early. It kept me on a normal schedule, helped to build my credit (slowly but steadily), provided a great benefits package (full health, vision, and dental coverage), but never increased my nest egg and savings at an acceptable pace. These of course are the "velvet handcuffs," which is to say, any arrangement designed to provide favorable benefits so as to discourage a person from choosing to leave that arrangement.

Sure, it's great if you're entering government employment in your late teens or fresh out of college, and you have 20, 25, or 30 years to devote to 8-to-5 drudgery in order to reach retirement. Otherwise, you're working the majority of your life away.

THE ENTREPRENEUR

The benefits and drawbacks of entrepreneurism are as follows:

- *Opportunity.* The opportunity to share, and have a part of, the true American Dream (not some watered-down version of it) is a tremendous allure. Many people may not have the skills, or education to work, successfully, in today's complex corporate structures, but they do have the initiative and drive to create something; market that something, and earn a nice profit. Being an entrepreneur offers more opportunities for advancement than working for others.
- *Profit.* Profit is another important reason to become an entrepreneur. WIlliam Henry Gates III, or Bill Gates, the Co-Founder of Microsoft, is one of the most successful entrepreneurs in the world.
- *Independence.* Many of us simply do not enjoy working for others. But we can take something that motivates and inspires us (such as writing this manuscript), and act on it without having to seek permission from an employer; or, having to do so on someone else's schedule.
- *Challenge.* Some folks are under the impression that entrepreneurs are people that thrive on high-risk ventures. But many of them take moderate, calculated risks that are more likely to yield modest levels of income as opposed to recklessly gambling one's holdings away. Entrepreneurs normally welcome a challenge. More importantly, they create the challenge and outline the parameters in which such challenges can be defined, overcome, and profited from.

Drawbacks include:

- *Long hours.* Being an entrepreneur is often comprised of long hours of hard work. Granted, it may not seem like work to the one willing to see their dream become manifest.
- *Monetary risks.* An entrepreneur can risk everything for success. They can also lose everything. Be sure to have a realistic business plan in place before investing large amounts of time, sweat equity, and money into something that may or may not produce a profit.
- *Large start-up costs.* Some people find that although they have an idea, product, or service that they are willing to bring to market, they don't have the necessary funds to put their plans into effect, and getting a loan or finding investors who can be sold on your idea is often times easier said than done.

THE EMPLOYEE

Being an employee who works their way up the corporate structure can prove extremely challenging yet beneficial. Much of the benefits depend on how much of ourselves we're willing to invest in the employer we work for. Working for a company has many upsides and can provide much more security than entrepreneurship, but this too comes with drawbacks.

The benefits and drawbacks of working for others are as follows:

- *Security.* Working for a company normally comes with much more security than working for yourself. When we work for an established corporate or private entity, we are pretty much guaranteed a paycheck. When we work for ourselves, there are times when you're not paying yourself anything in order to continue supporting the business.

- *Benefits.* Most employers offer a wide range of benefits including health insurance, paid vacation days, sick leave, pensions, 401k and deferred compensation plans.
- *Advancements.* When we work smart, hard, and consistently for an employer, our achievements are usually recognized and rewarded by way of a pay raise and a higher position within the company.

Drawbacks include:

- *Scheduling.* Working for someone else also means working on their terms and their timetable. Showing up to work late, being sick too often, etc., will normally bring about some form of reprimand. Deadlines that are expected to be met will often take precedence over our personal lives.
- *Slow pace of advancement.* Some employers are so large in scope and size that it takes a lot of hard work and initiative to be recognized as a valuable asset. While we may have secure positions of employment, our pay raises and forward advancement may come rather slow.
- *Micro-management.* When working for a company, we may run into the type of manager who is always looking over your shoulder or issuing directives and then immediately checking on us to make sure those directives are being met. This is perhaps the largest drawback of working in a corporate structure. It is also perhaps the most negative aspect of corporate employment that makes entrepreneurism so enticing to many people.

So how do we decide which route is best to take? It all begins with us, and what form of work we're most comfortable with. The qualities it takes to become an entrepreneur may not be the ones that are needed in order to succeed when working for others. We may have managerial and leadership skills needed to run a team. However, we may not have the characteristics required of us to assume all the risks, and rally others to follow our dream. Such traits can be harder to learn than academic skills are.

Generally, people who have the entrepreneurial spirit have a few tell-tale signs. They are as follows:

- *Self-directed.* You should be self-disciplined and comfortable being thoroughly immersed in processes of your own creation. You alone will be responsible for your own successes and failures.
- *Self-nurturing.* You must believe in your idea when no one else does, and be able to replenish your enthusiasm and conviction. When Walt Disney endeavored to create a full-length animated feature, "Snow White," the cartoon industry balked and criticized. His personal commitment and enthusiasm caused Bank of America to finance his venture. The rest is history.
- *Action-Orientated.* Great business ideas are not enough. Almost as important – if not, more so – than the idea is the burning desire to realize, actualize, and build your dream into reality.
- *Tolerance for uncertainty.* Successful entrepreneurs take only calculated risks. Still, they must at several stages be willing to take *some* risks. Many entrepreneurs fail several times over before they become known for that first success. The late great Vince Lombardi – whether knowingly or not – summarized the entrepreneurial spirit when he

said, "We didn't lose any games this season, we just ran out of time twice." New entrepreneurs must be prepared to run out of time, and other resources, a few times before they succeed.

Different characteristics apply to those individuals who are more suited to working for a company in a corporate setting. While entrepreneurs may have the "spirit" and drive to come up with an idea and turn that idea into a profit, it does not necessarily mean that they possess steadfastness, patience, endurance, and strength of an individual who can start at an entry-level position, and slowly work their way up the chain of command until they are one day at the top.

Generally, there are a few attributes in people who possess the skills that it takes to make it in today's competitive corporate world. They are as follows:

- *Foresightedness.* The ability to see an employer's Big Picture is key to working our way up the ranks. Taking into account the skills we've applied and perfected as ones that will yield results as we advance our career pathways working for others.
- *Multitasking.* Employees who can perform a variety of tasks at once without getting sidetracked or allowing themselves to simply shutdown are traits highly sought after by employers. They help assure that we can complete our work, as well as help others within the company achieve their goals. Employers see staff with traits such as these as possible management material.
- *Team-orientated.* Working for others means just that. It usually consists of working with a great many people. Whether they are directly involved, are comprised of support staff, or even people we never see yet communicate with constantly via

phone or email. Possessing the ability to work synergistically should come naturally to all corporate employees.

ENTREPRENEUR READINESS QUESTIONNAIRE

Each of the following items describes something that you may or may not feel represents your personality or other characeristics. Read each statement and then add the response 1-5 that most nearly reflects the extent to which you agree or disagree that the statement seems to fit you. 1=agree completely 2=mostly agree 3=partially agree 4=mostly disagree 5=disagree completely

Looking at my overall philosophy of life and typical behavior, I would say that...

1. I am generally optimistic. _
2. I enjoy completing and doing things better than someone else. _
3. When solving a problem, I try to arrive at the best solution first without worrying about other possibilities. _
4. I enjoy associating with coworkers after business hours. _
5. If betting on a horse race I would prefer to take a chance on a high-payoff "long shot." _
6. I like setting my own goals and working hard to achieve them. _
7. I am generally casual and easy-going with others. _
8. I like to know what is going on and take action to find out. _
9. I work best when someone else is guiding me along the way. _
10. When I am right, I can convince others. _

11. I find that other people frequently waste my valuable time. _

12. I enjoy watching football, baseball, MMA, and similar sports events. _

13. I tend to communicate about myself very openly with other people. _

14. I don't mind following orders from superiors who have legitimate authority. _

15. I enjoy planning things more than actually carrying out plans. _

16. I don't think it's much fun to bet on a "sure thing." _

17. If faced with failure, I would shift quickly to something else rather than sticking to my guns. _

18. Part of being successful in business is reserving adequate time for family. _

19. Once I have earned something, I feel that keeping it secure is important. _

20. Making a lot of money is largely a matter of getting the right breaks. _

21. Problem solving is usually more effective when a number of alternatives is considered. _

22. I enjoy impressing others with the things I can do. _

23. I enjoy playing games like tennis and handball with someone who is slightly better than I am. _

24. Sometimes moral ethics must be bent a little in business dealings. _

25. I think that good friends would make the best subordinates in an organization. _

Scoring: Give yourself one point for each 1 or 2 responses for questions 1, 2, 6, 8, 11, 16, 17, 21, 22, 23

Give yourself one point for each 4 or 5 responses that you

circled for questions 3, 4, 5, 7, 9, 12, 13, 14, 15, 18, 19, 20, 24, 25.

Add your points and see how you rate in the following categories:

21-25 Your entrepreneurial potential looks great if you have suitable opportunity to use it. What are you waiting for?

16-20 This is close to the high entrepreneurial range. You could be quite successful if your other talents and resources are right.

11-5 Your score is in the transitional range. With some serious work, you can probably develop the outlook you need for running your own business.

6-10 Things look pretty doubtful for you as an entrepreneur. It would take considerable rearranging of your life philosophy to become one.

0-5 Let's face it, you may not have what it takes to become an entrepreneur. Still, learning what it's about won't hurt.[*]

---

[*] Source: Kenner R. Van Voorhis, *Entrepreneurship and Small Business Management*(New York: Allyn and Bacon).

4

INCOGNITO

 "Mediocrity is the best camouflage known to man."

— BRYCE COURTENAY, THE POWER OF ONE.

THROUGHOUT THE FIRST few chapters I have been stressing the ability to blend, to conform, and to adapt, to ensure that we ourselves are in some measure of harmony with our surroundings, and the manner in which the public in general interacts with one another, and with us.

As people - and probably more so as Americans – we've been using our style as a form of expression since before we were a nation. Granted, if the same person was using the same fabrics to make the same clothing for the same group, the style is going to be in accordance with the seamstress's or tailor's available resources. Many of us wore what was available, or what was "handed-down" as a result of older siblings outgrowing what clothing options were available.

Before the Industrial Revolution occurred – and with it, mass production of cloth and textiles – there was the Frontier. There were European settlers. There were Indigenous Nations of people populating virtually every region in the North

American Continent, each with their own style of dress and adornment. There were Chinese immigrants who came to and helped connect the East Coast to the frontier of North America while escaping the economic chaos that was occurring in China during that period. There was slavery, and with it, the peoples that were brought here in bondage from the regions of West Central Africa in modern day Angola, Congo, and the Democratic Republic of Congo. And with this forced exodus came perhaps one of the most predominant cultural expressions whose effects continue to ripple outward from North America into the rest of the world.

There have been successive waves of immigrants coming to America ever since. Each bringing with them and contributing to the collective melting pot of style, dress, mannerisms, cuisine, architecture, culture, and other ingredients that make up our nation as it is today.

As a collective, we have a tendency to overly promote our outward expression in an effort to display what I can only think to call our "united individuality." A form of expression that has manifested itself time and again, and in so many different ways, it really is quite amazing to behold- like an inconsistent species of flower that blooms each time into a different shape, size, and color. A flower whose impulsive inconsistency would lead one to believe that it could not possibly be the same plant that bloomed the day before, and yet it is.

The way we dress is what makes us unique, or in some cases similar. It is often one of the first things others notice about us. It helps those whose outward expressions of their inner selves find common ground with others before conversation ever takes place. Often times people either gravitate towards, or are polarized by someone because of the manner in which they dress. (think sporting events, team memorabilia, the film The Warriors, salsa dancers, mechanics, butchers, painters, business men and women, you name it.)

But a strange thing has happened, a thing that I find to be crucial to the demise of criminals- how they are identified by non-criminals, and how their individuality has become an iconic gesture of such normality that anyone can spot us out of any crowd or social construct... The unique and outlandish has become mainstream.

Certain telltale signs that were once only distinguishable by other criminals have now become typical to the extent that anyone can spot a crook. This has its advantages as well as its drawbacks. It allows us to blend into society with ease because more people are dressing, acting, and posing as criminals.

Simultaneously, this makes for identifying an unsavory character (or one who wishes to be perceived as unsavory) a much easier task to accomplish.

While it's amusing to me that certain people would want to idolize and emulate someone who makes his or her money by breaking the law, it's also a bit saddening to see that this trend has been gaining traction amongst our youth for quite some time.

It's also a sure sign of the deterioration of morals and ethics that accompany the present. Through sheer suggestion, propaganda, and the power of marketing, the ability to have others believe that the Life is a glorious existence; and an intentional pursuit by those immersed in a desirable lifestyle.

Some of the most prolific examples of this glorification of criminality are perpetrated by movies, TV shows, and certain elements of the music industry. While I love gangster rap more than any other genre of hip hop, the one thing I abso-lutely abhor is a studio gangster or "wannabe" who projects an image of successful criminality in order to market music to people whose susceptibility to such tactics is almost assured.

And while I love a good gangster movie (who doesn't?) I think it's important to point out that actors have been portraying other people, some real and some fictional, for their entire careers. The very idea of killing another human being, robbing, or making drug deals to earn money is unthinkable. More so I imagine, after they've performed research on the criminal characters they portray, observing and becoming immersed in sociopathy in its purest forms.

We all possess the ability to choose and differentiate from that which is fiction versus the things that define our reality. But I do think it's necessary to single out and isolate the current glorification of crime, more so for those of us who have yet to grasp the enormity that accompanies this lifestyle.

NOTE: One of the more disconcerting occurrences I've witnessed is reality imitating art, i.e., criminals practicing self-deception, and emulating the fictional characters that movies and music portray which were initially created to imitate the criminals themselves. What happened there?!

An associate of mine whom I'm currently serving time with just cannot get enough of the "Novelas" or Mexican television series that, in some cases, glorify the Life as it is portrayed in Old Mexico. He's serving a life sentence for, allegedly, trafficking large amounts of narcotics from Mexico to the United States. And although he is one of the people that these shows emulate, they never cease to amaze and entertain him with their open veneration of what he describes as a "very ugly business."

And what's more, to my associate's incredulity, the younger generation of Mexicans who are entering the federal prison system actually believe that this fantasy lifestyle portrayed by the Novelas is, in fact, the reality that is attainable for any up-and-coming drug trafficker.

Very few of these young men, myself included, ever reach the level of success depicted on television. But I imagine that to an eager and impressionable mind, these lifestyles look a hell of a lot more obtainable than, say, a good-paying non-laborious job in Mexico, or as an illegal immigrant seeking employment in the United States.

The sad state of affairs though, is that most people are

right in assuming it's an easier route to instant financial relief. It's not only easily-influenced youths resolving to pursue unlawful acts in order to capitalize off of crime's high profit margins.

We hear about people every day, well into adulthood, being arrested for crimes that are quite obviously illegal, e.g., Ponzi schemes in which thousands of people are bilked out of their life savings. Insider trading, insurance fraud, bribery, online scams, just to name a few, are some of the most common criminals acts committed by those we would consider to be normal upstanding citizens.

The difference between these perpetrators and your average criminal/gangster is that these people will *never* conduct themselves with the stereo-typical outward attitude that is expected of the modern criminal. They will never act, dress, or speak like criminals, even after their stint in a minimum-security prison camp.

In their minds there can be no comparison between themselves and your average thug – or someone whose criminal acts are more obvious – rather than the grey area in which these white-collar villains operate.

There are many reasons for this internal and outward denial of criminality. For one, conducting unlawful acts under the guise of legal business proceedings tends to give a person a kind of buffer zone between their conscience and the victims of their actions. It is also easier to justify white-collar crime, because, as is often the case, many people make bad investments and it's convenient to use this as a defense when in fact, the victims are being deliberately misled and defrauded. And in some cases, white collar crimes do not necessarily impact individual people, but rather, companies and corporations which can sustain heavy damage and still rebound subsequently.

NOTE: August 1, 2019 – A 50-year-old man from Lithuania, Evaldas Rimasauskas, pled guilty to a phishing scam that fooled tech giants Google and Facebook into giving him over $100 million in the course of two years. Essentially, what Mr. Rimasauskas did was create an account with the same name of a tech support company already contracted with his targeted victim. He then sent Facebook (Meta) invoices for "services rendered" which Meta then paid to Mr. Rimasauskas' account. I have to admit, there's a part of me that feels no small amount of jealously and admiration for someone who could think of a scheme as simple as that, and then make that kind of money simply by sending an emailed invoice.

Some of these white-collar criminals were raised and educated in environments that fostered a sense of self-entitlement where it was, in fact, a privilege for others to invest and do business with them. They were convinced, or they convinced themselves rather, that others were there to provide them with capital, and whether their "investors" saw any return was inconsequential to their own pursuits of success.

I'm sure practicing narcissism to such an extent would cause us to reason, even when spending years behind bars, that we've done nothing wrong, and to classify us as criminals would be an unfair act of persecution towards an otherwise law-abiding citizen.

Such a state of affairs is somewhat comparable to ours in that some of us choose to believe that because we were born underprivileged that that apparent lack of opportunity gives us the right to justify our criminal actions as a means of survival. When viewed from that perspective it becomes a bit more difficult for me to cast judgment on others simply because they were at a financial advantage over my own circumstances.

And who knows, perhaps Mr. Rimasauskas was no more entitled than the rest of us. He simply developed a scheme that was more profitable, and far less risky than the template we've followed.

But when you go from middle-class to lower, or if you were brought up destitute, chances are the types of criminal elements that surround you are ones that tend to advertise their gains in a way that alludes not only to success, but successful criminals. Most often times the underprivileged do not hide their unlawful acts under a pretext of legitimate business; at least, not initially we don't. Instead, we choose to flaunt our accomplishments in a way which suggests achievement through criminal enterprise.

This often occurs because of the factors of social elevation that are so enticing to the lower classes. These are similar to the dynamics of lawlessness that encourage us to dress flashy, drive flashy forms of conveyance, and to look equally flashy when they're pushing our heads down while being stuffed into the back of a police unit.

Know that we will *never* be convicted of running a Ponzi scheme, or of taking hundreds of thousands of dollars in bribe money for our political campaign, or for insider trading in which we made millions. The reason for this is because – as a product of our base-criminality – and the manner in which we advertised our resulting success, we will never reach high levels of legitimacy which would then provide opportunities for high level white-collar crimes. The majority of us will remain on the same consistent plane in which we began.

NOTE: I would also like to believe that those of us who are able to elevate ourselves to such an extent – where our legitimate occupations fall into that of the more prestigious categories of earned income – would be smarter than to squander those opportunities pursuing illicit gains.

As long as we give the impression of someone who came from the gutter, and who exhibits behavior of a street criminal, we will unwittingly remain in the lower levels of the Life. As such, circumstances and opportunities will never permit us to achieve an amount of privilege enjoyed by those who acquired it through education and honest work.

Shedding our outward display of criminality is like a snake shedding its skin. And like a snake, we'll find ourselves having to shed that external appearance over-and-over again if we're not careful.

IMAGERY

"If outside validation is your only source of nourishment, you will hunger for the rest of your life."

— UNKNOWN

Question: What images come to mind when you think of a criminal? Or even better, what images come to mind when you think of a street-level drug dealer, gangbanger, outlaw biker, pimp, etc.? The stereotypes that accompany these images are so well entrenched in the minds of the average citizen that it becomes difficult to be a criminal of this sort without, on some level, displaying a quality in your outward appearance that would be recognizable to anyone.

Mirror exercise No. 2: No matter where you're reading this, be it in prison or at your home, disregard the surroundings that you're in, find a mirror, and take a look at the reflection staring back at you. What does he or she resemble; a normal citizen or something else? Are there *any* telltale-signs whatsoever that would lead you to believe that the person staring back at you is involved in criminal activity? If not, then you're already taking steps in the right direction, even if those steps are taken for the sole purpose of appearing to be normal and avoiding detection... you're definitely taking steps.

I look at myself in the mirror and I can spot a few indicators. For one, my forearms are covered in tattoos (this can be fixed with long sleeve shirts). Granted, tattoos are much more commonplace these days, so there's that.

Besides ink, facial tattoos, etc., all other indicators are

usually nothing more than mannerisms, style of dress, speech patterns, or criminal "swagger," often exemplified by a bit too much emphasis on expression in some way shape or form.

A lot of us don't realize that as a result of doing dirt for so long we've garnered some bad qualities. Perhaps the most obvious to others, albeit not so obvious to us, are the idiosyncrasies of character exhibited as a direct consequence of being hyper-aware. We tend to take up defensive postures in social settings that others might perceive as "flanking" or gaining a tactical advantage, when in fact, we're just being aware of our environs, as well as those circulating near or around us.

Do you ever find yourself at a club with your back to the wall, scrutinizing everyone in the vicinity? When you walk into a restaurant do you insist on taking the chair whose back faces a wall and which gives you a vantage point to observe the entire dining room, as well as the entries and exits? This behavior is called Threat Analysis or SWOT Analysis which is short for Strengths, Weaknesses, Opportunities and Threats. More often than not, we're not even aware we're doing it, but the people who observe you, be they law enforcement, fellow diners, some old war veteran, waitstaff, etc., are on some level, semi-conscious of the fact that our level of awareness is higher than those around us.

NOTE: I was at the gym the other day doing bicep curls and staring into the mirror at my reflection, not unlike any gym douchebag, when I noticed another guy, (Black dude) uphill-walking on a treadmill, facing another mirror on the opposite side of the gym, and staring at everyone behind him. We must've locked eyes a few times before I realized we were both performing our respective SWOT Analysis. At some point we ended up in closer proximity to each other and I asked him if he ever served in the military, to which he laughed and stated that he was one of the last troops to make it home from Afghanistan. He immediately asked me if I was in the military and I told him that I had did a stint in prison. I told him that I observed his hyperawareness to which he responded that he also observed mine. We both drew parallels between our two recent lifestyles that required a heightened sense of awareness in order to survive the experience...

First-rate criminals, cops and folks that have been in combat situations are able to perform SWOT Analysis without others even perceiving their attentiveness. The majority of criminals have a tendency to advertise their criminality; hence, their alertness becomes yet another "tell" of their character, their occupation, or worse, what they're about to do.

I can picture some of you reading this with a knowing smile on your face, because this fits your character to the "T." If this does sound like you, make a conscious effort to loosen up a bit, at least externally. Turn that deadpan, thousand-yard stare into an easy smile. If there's a chip on your shoulder, remove it, for to draw attention to ourselves by putting our vigilance on display is counterintuitive to the art of conformity.

Always keep in mind that the intent here, for us, is to conform and not appear unique, but ordinary. *Never* forget this. Although you may view yourself as singular; although mom or grandma confided that you were special and unique (she told all the grandkids this), it's necessary to present an image of normality. And if you have the urge, like many of us, to stand out, remember that your idea of individuality is probably being emulated by thousands, if not millions of people just like you. And what we're doing is anything but extraordinary.

Once we've performed a self-analysis on our external appearance and behavior, apply the same analysis to other external aspects of our life, i.e., the vehicles we drive, the volume at which we play our music, (announcing our arrival into whichever neighborhood we're entering), and make the proper adjustments.

REFINEMENT

 "Let 'em see you shine!"

— LUCIOUS PETTWAY

 "Five thousand on the paint just so life will see you."

— WILLIAM LEANARD ROBERTS II (I WON'T
CALL THIS ARTIST IMITATING THE LIFE BY
HIS STAGE NAME BELONGING TO ANOTHER).

 "You can't polish a turd, but you can roll it in glitter"

— UNKNOWN

"Notice me! "See me shine!" "We didn't have a pot to piss in or a window to throw it out of, but look at us now!" "Kiss my rich ass!" While these statements may seem amusing, they are also what many of us are saying in our minds when we demonstrate an outward facade of keeping up with the Joneses. They also perpetuate a way of thinking that often leads to forms of expression that are sure-fire ways to get noticed.

This is why so many of us become engrossed and obsessed with immersion in the material world. We've been assured that only through material possessions can we convey a sense of success, not only to others but to ourselves as well. Imagine this paradox if you will- the need to convince one's self of success via convincing others that we are successful...

The problem with this is that law enforcement, the opposition, and everyone else will also get the message we're intent on broadcasting. Did we not think that along with the rest of the world, law enforcement wouldn't receive our All-Points Bulletin?

Was it not our intent to announce victory over poverty? Was it not our intent to display our trophies of war, earned by each battle, each successful transaction? If not, then why were we doing it? Why is it so difficult to see, in the moment, that it is our declaration of success which takes those successes from us through the blatant announcement that we are criminals?

I cannot think of a more efficient means to end a life of crime than by advertising it to the world before it even has a chance to be of true benefit to us.

Most of us never perceive that our speedily attained affluence is a cyclic event that forever keeps us in a holding pattern at its most infantile stage. Prior to my imprisonment, I often reflected upon what I thought was my rise to the top. I know now that that climb was a descent, and my estimations of the top was yet another illusion designed by an ego that led me to believe I was advancing rather than regressing.

I was never climbing the proverbial ladder of success. I was scratching and digging my way into the deepest of pits.

There are no stages of early growth in the dope game, or any game in the Life, followed by expansion, growing pains and an even arc of consistency and achievement, concluded by a maturity of enterprise that is sound and strong in its old age.

If at any time we can be arrested, if at any juncture in life the materialism we gained can be taken away; and if the fall that awaits you towards the maturity stage of your pathway is just as severe, if not more so as the consequences at the outset, how could we possibly perceive the Life as being associated with any sort of advancement?

I stress conformity so much in this chapter, and indeed, in life, because to stand out as a criminal is to end your career as one. I've seen cops break their necks watching someone on full display driving in a vehicle and with a disposition betraying them as anything but a law-abiding citizen. I've seen that aforementioned neck-breaking followed by a traffic stop and an excuse to search that almost always concludes with an arrest.

There were times I found myself driving down a street (often coming from or going to a deal) in one of my nondescript vehicles, with a baby seat in the back, a college sticker on the rear windshield, and no tint to speak of. At times the local gangsters would pull up in the lane next to me. Their urgent need for acknowledgment was evident in what they drove, how they stared at me (needing me to stare back), and the music they blasted through every open window, the recording artist proclaiming "set trippin" a virtue, and death to "n!ggaz from the other side."

They *wanted* to be noticed. They *needed* to be noticed. They'd cause an incident simply to get noticed. The reason being is because these types of criminals have no worth with the exception of the value society bestows upon them via acknowledging their existence as criminals.

I often wondered during these encounters what they would think if they knew the unassuming guy driving the jalopy next to them was the chief contributing factor to their status as drug dealing gangsters.

I urge those still in the Life not be *that* sort of criminal. I assure you their fall comes just as fast, or faster, than their ascension. I say this being currently imprisoned with thousands of them.

THE USUAL TYPICAL STANDARD OF COMMON ORDINARY MEDIOCRITY

> "Make money, act broke.
> Be humble, say less."

> — BOB MARLEY

Is it necessary for me to give a kind of tutorial which instructs people how to dress, what sort of vehicles to drive or how to conduct themselves in public? By no means. The necessity comes from identifying threats, internal and external, before danger becomes palpable. The necessity comes in the form of detailing my own mistakes and thought processes so that you can head trouble off down the road.

While there's no denying that the biggest danger is the pursuit and engagement of criminal activity, there are also associated dangers that amplify the consequences and hasten the pace of getting caught. The false reality that success can only come from acknowledgment and demonstrations of that success is, in my opinion, one of the most damaging concepts I have ever come to identify.

Our success comes in the form of effectively putting an end to the Shit before it puts an end to us. Our very survival is dependent upon conformity and our ability to blend in order to minimize our exposure to danger. Our triumph over poverty and the criminal mindset begins with making the transition – from criminal to civilian – and becomes manifest in our eventual and legitimate accomplishments.

If we choose to display our newly-acquired prosperity, as I did, in a manner that draws attention rather than promoting anonymity, we then set the stage for the curtain drawing much sooner than we initially anticipated. If your idea of success is presenting an *image* of the same, you're in trouble.

Strip away the illusions of grandeur that accompany the

poor man or woman's idea of success. In fact, disregard society's ideas of what it means to be successful; for to be successful in this age requires acknowledgement of others that we have indeed "made it." This simply isn't true and is a sure fast-track to ruin.

Understand the difference between art imitating the Life and vice versa. Know that certain actors and recording artists are just that; people who make millions emulating and glorifying the abhorred shit that sometimes accompanies the precarious lives we live. If it were that lucrative, we would not be out there hustling, robbing and scheming every second of every day.

Any person who proclaims the message of success through criminality – while actually obtaining their success through legitimate means – is probably the business model you should be following. They are highly intelligent people who have created an image; packaged it, and successfully marketed it to the masses, and have made millions of dollars as a result... *not* from doing dirt.

NOTE: Doing dirt = dirt wages. Marketing ideas to the entire world in the form of a service, product, movie, song or other forms of expression = millions $$$.

Know that it's OK to be ordinary. Or even better, to *appear* ordinary. Know that if you are extraordinary yet you can blend with the herd, it will prove more difficult to single you out.

In nature, we see that predators – both strong and weak – prey upon *only* the weak, the sick, the dying, the old, and the very young. It takes so much more energy to prey upon the strong and is counterintuitive to serving their purpose as predators if they are not thinning the herd and keeping it comprised of strong healthy, reproductive-aged adults.

When we're in the Life, no matter our level on the food chain, there are predators looking to devour us. There is *always* a bigger fish. There is always a bigger and badder criminal. The better we camouflage ourselves, our activities, and our earnings, the less of a chance predators will have of distinguishing us as prey.

Showcasing our accomplishments via displays of extravagance that far outshine the environment in which we live and operate is akin to letting every predator within proximity know that we are vulnerable; that we are sick, old, young, and feeble. And our enemies, along with our troubles, will multiply.

It is the weak among us who feel the need to be recognized. It is the weak and naive who believe acknowledgments must accompany achievement in order for those achievements to have real meaning.

In the words of Malcom X, "We've been tricked. We've been had." We've been led into thinking that identifying ourselves and our accomplishments are requisites to proclaiming individuality and success.

These acts, regrettably, reveal who we really are and what we have in the way of assets. It also ensures law enforcement, and other predatorial components in opposition to us, will have a clearer picture of the trophies they'll relieve us of once we're taken down.

And so, I continue to advise us to seek individuality through individual thought. Pursue singularity while practicing external conformity.

Many people today see themselves as a rebellious minority going against the grain. If the majority are thinking this way, are they really moving in a different direction, or are they traveling the same path as those with the same ideas? So too does this apply to us.

At the time I began selling drugs, I somehow got it into my head that what I was doing was not only profitable, but that it was somehow unique and that it displayed a sort of defiance against the conventional methods of surviving in this world, which also made it *special*.

I thought the manner in which I dressed was different, and in some way, special. I thought that the tattoos I had begun adorning my body with at the age of 13 made me different and extraordinary compared to other 13-year-olds. My face reddens with embarrassment when I realize I am a 44-year-old male with a "thug life" tattoo on my rear-right shoulder blade, the lettering materializing as smoke issuing from a pistol barrel.

I reasoned that by committing acts of violence and using them to settle disputes, that my methods were different, special, and in some way unique in comparison to other ways of obtaining concession... and my enemies multiplied.

What I didn't realize at the time, was that I was restructuring myself in such a way that, yes, I was no longer ordinary in the usual sense. But what I became was nothing more than an ordinary run-of-the-mill criminal.

Not only did I devolve into a state of criminal normalcy, but I became so commonplace, and so regular, that I lost many of my attributes that people recognized as the things that made me unique.

My individuality was smothered in my attempts to go against the grain, and I became completely ordinary.

The proof in this perception is the number I wear on my chest as a means of distinguishing me from the thousands of others who wear the same uniform as me. Who live in cells that are exact replicas of the cell I live in. Who dressed as I dressed on the streets. Who have similar tattoos as mine. Who possessed the same ideas of individuality as me. And who are now living by the same ordinary and preordained schedule as mine until the end of our respective sentences.

Upon reentry to society, I can hopefully make the right decision, to choose a path that is truly unique, even if it parallels what others are doing. Or I can continue down the well-trodden path of criminality; a path I might add, that will classify me as just one more part of a failed whole.

The more I consider the methods people utilize in an attempt to be different, the more I'm convinced we've been acting exactly the same.

COWBOYITIS

 "Oh, I should've been a Cowboy."

— TOBY KEITH

 "People do that shit they want to be caught! It's called cowboyitis!"

— TONY SOPRANO

"Cowboyitis..." much more dangerous to the criminal, and humankind, than, say, laryngitis, meningitis, hepatitis, or any other kind of "itis" that afflicts us.

Cowboyitis occurs when we become so enamored with our own image that we forget, as criminals, we're not supposed to have an image. Least of all one that singles us out from the masses.

Cowboyitis is the culmination of decades of movies and pop-culture influence, status symbolism, misplaced ideology of what it means to be "somebody," and the need for recognition of an existence that supersedes the one we currently occupy.

The initial symptoms of this disease are, at first, subtle, and they bear a strong resemblance to accomplishments and victories rather than ailments. Symptoms first manifest as precursors to bills and other expenses being paid well in advance rather than allowing them to fall into delinquency. Bills and debt that were once nightmarish skyscrapers of paper on your coffee table or inbox, that seemed not only to take up residence in your home, but in your mind as well.

These precursors soon manifest in material acquisitions that heretofore, were unattainable luxuries, difficult, if not impossible to obtain by people such as us. They then encourage confidence in that the acts we're committing are indeed profitable. They instill conviction in our decisions, now no longer based on fear and apprehension as they once were. Instead, a bold certainty and sense of absolutism tells us that whatever choice we make will be the right one, and with the right outcome.

Our lives seem better because of this disease. They *are* better. Our standard of living far exceeds the one that we were in only months ago. We are now in the position to provide, not only for ourselves, but for those we care for. Hell, there's even money to spare, to burn if the illness strikes with sudden impulsiveness.

And because of this overabundance of cash on-hand, we indulge. We indulge in things that we really don't need, but our convictions sway us into believing that there's really no harm in treating ourselves. For if you don't treat yourself, who's going to??

It wouldn't be such a bad thing if that self-recompense wasn't expressed with such gaudy eccentricity. But damn it, we want and need to express our individualism now that we can afford to do so.

This malady ultimately creates a distorted image of one's self. An image that would have been created a long time ago had we only the means to construct it. An image that defines us, that *is* us, that lives through us- that is the very essence and material reflection of our spiritual self.

This image is unique and powerful. It conveys wealth and prosperity. It is the personification of a successful human being; one who doesn't take any shit, who's popular yet feared, has sex appeal, and can demonstrate these qualities through being charismatic, generous, and extravagant.

In almost every single case, this illness/image not only

expresses individualism, but does so with either a subtle, or not-so-subtle undercurrent of criminality. For what good is a proclamation of success if you can't publicize to the world the MO that made you successful? The cowboy/cowgirl living inside you needs to have their time in the limelight, and what better way to achieve this than by the introduction of that entity via their fame, fortune, and success?

The people we once were did not receive an introduction in this fashion. The people we used to be evolved since their birth, and as a result of their upbringing and immediate environment. We were never presented with the ceremony, bells and whistles that announced the arrival of our alter ego. Nor did we receive the same warm reception that almost always accompanies that of the thriving criminal we became.

The old versions of Us had to work ceaselessly to convince others that we were of any worth, as opposed to having those same people readily acknowledge our significance simply by looking at us.

If this depiction resembles anything similar to your own advancement (or digression, depending on points-of-view), there's a strong chance you developed a case of cowboyitis.

The cure? There are only two treatments, and one is much more difficult to endure than the other. The difficult treatment comes by way of prison, property loss or seizure, and of spiritual, mental and physical anguish. Even after enduring all these, there is no guarantee that a stint in prison will have alleviated the illness itself.

The other procedure is a simple injection of reality, of modesty... a slice of humble pie, if you will.

Humbling ourselves in order to strive for the things we want – without the pretentious ideals of status and public recognition clouding our judgment – is a sure means of inoculation from this disease.

It's so much more arduous to achieve success and individual thought with the accompanying burden of cowboyitis clouding our judgment. This sickness makes the pursuit of success, and happiness, so much harder to attain, because it adds an unnecessary component to an already complex equation. Not only are we striving to make it, but we are now doing so with an illness that requires of us an additional and unnecessary level of extravagance.

LAST CALL FOR BOARDING THE INDEPENDENCE

I cannot counsel any of you on what measures to take that will ensure a pursuit of success that is unlike any other ever attempted. If I did that, then the ideas I've presented will not be your own. Consequently, they will not be unique either.

But more to the point, who am I? Who is anyone to proclaim your pathway as either singular or commonplace? Some of the best and most profitable ideas ever conceived were done so by people that simply improved upon an invention already created by another person. And if you're following a path that another has already walked, who's to say that that pathway is not new to you; hence, so too will be the outcome?

Camouflage yourselves with an outward facade of insignificance so that your creative spirit will require of itself alternative methods for conveying the unique and extraordinary within you. During your transition, conceal your criminality to the extent that you eventually smother it entirely. And the reemergence of the person you once were – accompanied by some new features and upgrades – will be comparable to the rebirth of the finest version of Self.

Disregard the acknowledgment of others and pursue the acknowledgment and understanding of self. Forget for a moment what it means to have the recognition, praise, and envy of your peers and gauge your victories by the positive or negative outcomes they provide.

Realize once and for all that to seek the recognition and

acknowledgment of others is to seek the ruin and assassination of self. Strive to become an inscrutable nobody whose unremarkable appearance is contrasted only by the effectiveness of your internal creativity.

When we seek to be *somebody*, we marginalize ourselves. Because other people have to acknowledge that we are a businessman/woman, an accountant, a drug trafficker... that we are *somebody*.

If you insist on recognition, see to it that it is acquired only through positive action, productivity and a code of ethics that is applied to everyone, including yourself. Be known and be celebrated for adherence to your principles, rather than by an image that metastasized into a parasite that seeks fame and acknowledgment no matter the cost to the host.

To pursue criminality and to be somebody while doing it is, in truth, to be completely ordinary. To practice success under the guise of ambiguity is to assure unrivaled fulfillment in a way that will not cost us our freedom and independence. But will only promote and venerate the intrinsic individuality we were born with.

Whether you need recognition of your accomplishments is ultimately up to you.

5

OUT OF THE
FRYING PAN

WHEN WE EXIT the Life due to imprisonment, we are either still fully-immersed or put on a shelf; depending on choices, the prison's current political environment, and our propensity for being "criminally activated."

Upon our discharge and reentry into society, there is rarely any time for a gradual transition. This can be a frightening prospect for some of us. So much so, that many would rather abandon the regulations that Probation and Parole (P&P) prescribe for us, return to the Life, and face the consequences down the road.

I'd be lying if I said I wasn't nervous myself. I can recall talking to my older sibling, and feeling other people out for entry-level positions that would placate my probation officer and provide a bit more room to breathe upon returning home. But truth be told, and with the exception of our own resolve, help from any quarter is going to pale in comparison to our own decision to hit the ground running.

The associates I had on the streets seemed to have better offers for me than the ones presented by my non-criminal contacts. But to accept those offers is to concede defeat before even attempting to exist legitimately.

I experience no small amount of anxiety thinking about some of the limitations I heaped upon myself as a result of my delinquent work-history, my criminal record, and the pressures that accompany being on federal probation for 4 years.

I tell myself, "There's no way in hell I'm going to flip burgers or bust my ass for minimum wage on some construction site just to appease the powers that be." But the powers that be are the ones that will be controlling major aspects of my existence for the first four years of freedom once I leave the frying pan of prison, and enter the fire of probation.

From what repeat offenders tell me, there is nothing more alluring than that first taste of liberty after years of imprisonment. It is perhaps the main expectation on every convict's mind... Freedom. But when I exchange bars and razor wire for the prison that P&P provide, I know that what I'm experiencing is the illusion of freedom, a mere whiff of possibilities yet to be realized.

Probation and Parole are simply another form of managing a prison populace that isn't quite ready to be recycled and fed back through the prison industrial complex. Rest assured that if we're on P&P, we are most assuredly still a part of that population.

To yearn for; or worse, to indulge in freedoms that society enjoys is to simply feed oneself back into the prison system a bit earlier than intended. For to indulge in the full spectrum of freedoms that others are allowed is, in most cases, a violation of some rule or regulation that P&P insists upon.

NOTE: Now that I've been home for about a decade, I can honestly advise others not to be misled by the illusion of freedom that you can feel all around you upon reentry. Just because we can feel it, it does not make it ours. We cannot allow our senses to give us the false impression that we are free. We are anything but...

LONG LEASH + SMALL YARD = TOO MUCH ROPE

"I am my own worst enemy. This, more than any other trait, proves my fundamental humanity."

— DEAN KOONTZ

The concept of P&P is to ensure that those convicted of crimes – after having served their debt to society – are no longer a threat to the community in which they're returning to. As such, it keeps us on a pretty tight leash. It also provides just enough length on our tether to jump the fence and strangle ourselves.

Any notions of gradual reintegration by the proper "guidance and instruction" is a misrepresentation of the facts. While P&P may sound like a good idea in theory, the practice itself is a bit harder to define as functional.

The very concept of probation alludes to supported and supervised reintegration; yet, its reactive nature to violations keeps the prison industrial complex alive and thriving. P&P officers' jobs are not to support, nor to help the returning citizen. Rather, they are the administrative gatekeepers that help ensure one more business in America remains functioning with balance and consistency.

If Probation Officers (PO)s were there to provide guidance and instruction, I imagine the rate of recidivism would be far less than it is today. Administrators that guide, support, assist, and instruct should not block avenues of opportunity for their "clients" through limiting freedoms and job opportunities (think of employment in a sales position at a liquor distributor or marijuana dispensary, or as a server of alcohol at a bar or restaurant).

NOTE: I have to say that my PO, Jeff Martinez-Spelech, was the exception to the stereotypical PO. I was blessed to have him. He was very supportive of my reentry plan, and congratulated me from my first government job, to buying my house, and receiving promotions while I was under his supervision.

I was also transferred to the chief PO, Domenico, who was definitely more your typical PO. He was gruff, to the point, and no nonsense. But to his credit, he was fair. I believe much of a PO's outward demeanor is a direct result of their being overwhelmed with heavy caseloads, administrative burdens, etc.

The institution of probation itself is where the difficulty lies. The halfway house staff made it strenuous at times for me to hold down my first government job by calling me to make sure I was there (even though my ankle bracelet confirmed my whereabouts). If they called my "color" I would have to drive to Albuquerque after work and provide a UA, then drive back to Santa Fe and resume my preparations for the next morning's drudgery.

Some of us were required to attend AA, NA, or other counseling where appointments were only available during work hours; hence, you had to choose between possibly being terminated from jobs you were required to work, or being in violation of probation and sent back to prison for failing to attend prescribed meetings. That's a bit of a paradox, and a difficult one at that.

If you pair some of these unrealistic requirements with a less-than accommodating PO, you've got problems.

This is the combination that steers many towards self-medication, lawlessness, and of course, what-we-know-best.

When P&P insists on adherence to policies that may result in termination of your employment, which in turn is also a violation of P&P, which segways into whether they're going to revoke you and send you back to prison... It's at this point where our fight or flight response begs the question, "What the hell is really going on here?"

I imagine the same rule that applies to cops, judges, law enforcement, and criminals can also be applied to POs. They're not all bad. The key to successfully completing P&P – or possibly even early termination – is to understand their function. Probation officers are there to protect the interests of the public via supervising and monitoring the actions of the returning citizen... You.

They accomplish this task by submitting case work on their rather heavy caseload of offenders returning home.

NOTE: The less of an administrative burden you pose to your PO, the less work they have to do; thus, <u>the amount of supervision and time focused on you will lessen.</u>

I outline P&P in the manner that makes sense to me. To view them any other way is going to leave us feeling unjustly victimized by public servants and by a system that we are at the tail end of concluding our affairs with.

P&P is not structured around you, or me, or us. It is structured around the welfare of those who pay taxes in hopes that their investment will protect them from people, and actions, such as the ones we practiced.

My intent is to raise your awareness and to help, guide, support, and instruct you the way your probation or parole officer should, but cannot. My goal is to also see us break the habitual cycle of going against the grain, which in turn, only buttresses the thriving prison industry, and assures the job security of your friendly probation or parole officer.

The goal is to use any and every opportunity available to us that our circumstances provide, rather than identifying, loathing, and *resisting* every negative aspect that the institution of P&P forces upon its recipients.

Keep in mind that to oppose something while still subject to its authority is counterintuitive to freeing ourselves from its control. More so when we're opposing something as strict and as unyielding as P&P.

Only after you are no longer subject to an institution can you afford to make attempts to change its policies. But more often than not, we tend to forget the hell we were in once we're no longer in it, and the people who are still burning are of no concern.

OUTLINE

I have not researched how states implement their reentry policies. Concerning the feds, you almost never leave prison and head straight to the streets. They place you in a halfway house which is intended to help you get back on your feet before full-immersion into society. Once you've completed 6 months at the halfway house, you are then placed on federal probation for however many years until completion.

NOTE: I enrolled in correspondence courses through the International College of Bible Theology (ICBT) while imprisoned. Because of this, I was not required to seek a job while at the halfway house. They simply set an outdate for me of March 30th, 2015. I left prison February 9[th]2015... I spent less than a month out of the 6 months I was supposed to reside there.

PRO TIP: If you enroll in school, you can leave the halfway house without doing the full 6 months, and without paying 25% kickup from working.

The concept of the halfway house is such that it is supposed to allow for time to look for a job, and time to save up enough money to move out on our own once we have the means to do so. But here's the catch: every federally approved halfway house takes 25% of our earnings to pay for "room and board" and other expenses. Even if you have plenty of money and don't need the services the halfway house provides, you must still serve your time there. You'll see why in a minute...

If we accrue enough funds before the six-month period, we can leave the halfway house and remain on house arrest (ankle monitor) until the remaining time left over from the 6 months has ended. But you *still* have to give the halfway house 25% of your income for the bed that you're no longer sleeping in until the end of the 6th month period.

Because of the profits generated from this policy, federal halfway houses strive to receive as many intakes – followed by discharges – as possible. This ensures that countless numbers of people are giving that same halfway house 25% of their income to pay rent on the same bed that many individuals are paying for at the *same* time.

In essence, you have fifty beds with fifty people actually occupying each bed. But we then have to take into account an additional 200 or more people paying 25% of their income for each one of those fifty beds they have already vacated while living elsewhere on house arrest... and we're the ones who are breaking the law?

Be that as it may, we are at the mercy of policies such as these, and by the people who remain employed by enforcing them. Because of this, it is of the utmost importance that we explore every option available to us, and that we also create alternatives that ensure our reintegration is a successful one, rather than a failed attempt through our own capitulation, or by the hands of those vested in the prison industrial complex.

NOTE: One of the best ways to beat the halfway house trap... deny your 6 months early release and see to it that "they" don't get a penny more than what they've already taken. Veterans of the federal prison system will always advise novices not to take the early release to the halfway house. I hope I've explained adequately why serving your full sentence (by a few additional months) may prove more beneficial to some of us.

This method ensures that we head straight home (wherever that is), and report directly to probation, negating the 25% kickup of your paycheck to the feds, daily piss tests, and house arrest if discharged prior to the 6-month requirement.

SEA LEGS

"To live is to suffer, to survive is to find some meaning in the suffering. "

— FRIEDRICH NIETZSCHE

So our sentence is up. We've served our time, paid our debt to society, and we're ready to move on. But before we do, understand that our sentence is by no means completed. You paid your debt to society, but society wants more. Society still owns a big chunk of our collective asses, and we won't be moving on with anything until we successfully complete P&P.

I once heard that "To live is to suffer." Well, to make it through the streets, prison, and finally to P&P, is to die, be resuscitated, and to suffer some more. Surviving this particularly painful method of scourging requires familiarization of oneself with it. And to be well-prepared for your continued suffering at the time it's being administered.

I urge us to view our time with P&P with as much detachment and indifference as humanly possible. To take our plights personally would be giving too much credit to the working class responsible for continuing our regimented lifestyle.

It would also imply that we are unique, and that the circumstances surrounding our torments are in some way unique. To the contrary. The maltreatment you may receive through P&P has been administered to millions of Americans in the exact same way, and with the same amount of objectivity.

Growing accustomed to circumstances is comparable to

being on land for the majority of your life, and suddenly being cast into the role of a sailor, forever out to sea. Perhaps an even better euphemism would be living free for the majority of one's existence and suddenly being placed in bondage. It's all a matter of how quickly we can adapt... how long it takes for us to "grow" our sea legs.

If we are entering P&P subsequent imprisonment, then we already have an idea as to going about adapting, living, and indeed, thriving in the environment that P&P will afford us.

To thrive in captivity is to adapt to a way of life that human beings were not made to exist within. This is why imprisonment is applied to those who break the law. It is a punishment which effectively removes the offender from the environment in which the offense was committed; thus, protecting those *offended* by the offender.

To be released from prison and placed back into society, under the supervision of probation and parole, is a difficult challenge, more so for those who have no intention of reverting back to the Life. One of the causes for this difficulty is due to the strict limitations imposed through P&P that do not necessarily promote behavior nor provide an environment that encourages its clients to thrive in a way that is both productive and lawful.

It limits us, rather, to pursue bottom-of-the-barrel jobs which will provide bottom-of-the-barrel existences; even less-than once 25% has been deducted for room and board at the halfway house that we may or may not be living in. It doesn't take long for the average offender to realize that the pursuit of crime will at least allow for a better existence until we're once again arrested and sent to prison.

"Throw it to Crazy"

Surviving prison is in itself an accomplishment. If you

have come out the other end, I salute and commend you for your efforts.

To survive prison without adopting certain character flaws that will only make it more difficult to reenter society is a feat achieved by only a marginal portion of returning citizens. The majority of us leave with a Prisoner's Mindset.

The prisoner's mindset is one that was established for the need to survive in the environment of prison. This mindset is a specialized and altered version of the one which most people utilize in normal social settings. The need to defend oneself, and to more closely analyze the things people do and say is much more prevalent with the prisoner's mindset. And as such, we're more attuned to identify intended slights and insults that, in prison, need to be addressed and dealt with instantly, and with more finality than in the world.

Turning off the prisoner's mindset and not taking ourselves – and each perceived threat or insult – so seriously, is the key to surviving the rigors of P&P. For to confront, head-on, every difficult person, problem, or dilemma, rather than circumventing these issues, is to fail in our attempts at adapting to probation, parole, and life in general.

"Throw it to crazy," is a term and approach to life that people use in prison when confronted with a problem that might not be worth the trouble of addressing. This is the one scapegoat that inmates use if they feel that solving the problem would, in effect, bring upon them more problems as opposed to simply letting the matter rest.

Throwing something to crazy is comparable to shrugging your shoulders and saying "screw it," or refusing to lend credence to a person or thing that does not merit your full attention.

Things only affect us if we allow them to. It is only through our negative reaction to external stimuli that causes it to be a negative occurrence. It can be onerous to view someone giving us a tough time as inconsequential, more so when we consider what it took to get to this point of our reentry after five, ten, twenty, or thirty years behind bars. But their attitude and treatment of you is only negative if you acknowledge it as such.

To refuse to acknowledge maltreatment for a few more years from people whose authority we are subject to is to drastically undermine the influence and negative impact they can have on our person. And to view these individuals objectively; as one more bump in the road designed to slow our roll just a bit, is a far superior approach than to feel threatened by them or their actions.

Seeing this institution or people working within it as a threat only makes our predicament seem much more intimidating and hopeless than it actually is. Once we're out from under the thumb of P&P would it be prudent to file complaints, change the system, or make certain individual's lives as complicated and as difficult as they tried to make some of ours. But leaving this chapter of your life in the rearview is perhaps the best course of action moving forward.

It's important to note that, in most cases, it was our decisions and the resulting misfortune of those decisions which placed us under the authority of these people in the first place. As such, my approach to circumventing the recurrence of such a deplorable experience is to take steps to ensure that it does not happen again, rather than fighting it every time I subject myself to this cyclic event.

Pro Tip: The best revenge is a good life...

I would also hope that once we're free from these policies that we would aspire to be on a level of financial and personal prosperity that would far exceed the ones our criminal pasts afforded, and which placed us at the subjugation of people who misuse the authority provided them rather than administering to their clients in a fair and equitable manner.

Is it not also presumable that these people will only be a hindrance so long as we are operating at a level on par with their own? Or that we will only be subject to repression so long as we continue to demonstrate a need to be repressed?

It is my fervent hope that each of us subjected to P&P will view it as nothing more than a minor bump in a long road home. Take whatever they give us, roll it up into a ball... and throw it to crazy.

... and Into the Fire

When freedom can be taken away for something as trivial as missing an appointment, getting a speeding ticket, or simply because it pleases someone to do so; know that we are by no means free.

Power of any measure can be displayed in insignificant actions, and power can also be wielded on much grander scales. Perhaps the most demonstrable power is people's understanding that others have it, sometimes in vast amounts, and yet, they choose not to abuse it while others can't help but to do so.

Power mongers come in varieties. Sometimes they are motorists driving aggressively or using their position in traffic to hinder another's advancement; thus, they exercise what they consider to be positional leverage over a stranger.

Or they come in the guise of public servants, such as those we've all had to endure at the MVD, or some other office whose function requires its employees to interact with the public and provide services rather than hindrances.

This low-level exercise of power often accompanies those who realize their occupations are necessary ones, when the arrangement their job provides is such that it offers a means to fulfill a lawful obligation vital for the public to accomplish.

When this understanding crystallizes in an employee's mind, it becomes the realization of power. And when that power is wielded by a self-serving individual of low cunning, it can make the rest of our lives difficult.

Where these people come from, or how they came to be the way they are is of no importance to us. How we effectively deal with them, and how we ensure that we do not become jaded and similar to them is what's imperative to our welfare and peace of mind.

When dealing with a difficult probation or parole officer, it's first necessary to determine what it is about *you* that gives them such a bad disposition. If it's something we're doing, then we need to identify and resolve. If the problem goes away because of adjustments we made, then all the better.

If problems don't lessen, but increase, then we have a challenge ahead of us. Not a challenge that we should let hinder our progress or destroy our lives, not after how far we've come. And not something that we should evade or confront with an aggressive defense or offense. But simply a challenge, or a means to make ourselves stronger and improve our methods of survival and interaction with our fellow human beings.

POs can sometimes have a bad disposition that's meant to convey a no-nonsense style of communication. This could also be an indication that they're not going to be the ones who continue to enable us to screw up our lives.

I would argue that the majority of them are good people. If they're being somewhat obstinate, it may stem from the knowledge that if they're not tough, many of their clients will backslide into the Shit.

It's up to us to decide if they are, in fact, being tough for the sake of our salvation, or if they are merely being difficult in hopes that they will share in and be the mechanism of our failure.

Our own personalities or appearances notwithstanding, there isn't much you can do that would cause your PO to have an aversion towards you, at least, not from a professional standpoint. However, your conviction may be another issue. We'll never know if our POs have a loved one who is suffering from some form of substance abuse disorder. And if you were convicted of trafficking, as I was, they probably won't be cutting you much slack. They may have a wife or other relative that was subject to a bank robbery while working as a teller, and if you've been convicted of armed robbery... need I say more?

The goal at this juncture of our journey is not to make a demonstration of our willingness to change but to show that we already *have* changed. That the Life is in our rearview, and that our PO need not waste additional time, energy, and resources on the likes of us.

I won't go into another lecture on conformity, but I'm sure it's becoming apparent just how much it's going to be of benefit in every setting we find ourselves in. The advantages of being a mediocre and hassle-free client will always outweigh the perception of a problematic, disadvantaged ex-con that will need a bit more control and supervision as they make their way back to the streets.

SOME OF THE BEST ADVICE I EVER HEARD

At my sentencing I was informed by my judge of a few things. I was told that I was now "committed" to serve 78 months (six and a half years) at a federal prison. I was told that I would not be able to possess firearms for the rest of my life, and that I would be placed on probation for a term of four years.

I explained to my judge – much to the dismay of my attorney – that I disagreed with the concept of probation. That – if I had already served out my sentence – how is it legally plausible that I would then have to serve another sentence (of possibly four years) if I violated the imposed probationary period?

Would this not constitute a ten-and-a-half-year sentence rather than the six- and one-half years I'm already "committed" to? And if so, why could he not just sentence me to a full ten years without any probation subsequently?

While my last question posed may seem a bit imprudent, I assure you it makes sense. And those of you who have already been to prison will know why. Because a great majority of us never successfully complete probation and parole before being sent back to prison. Either because we were accused of violating the terms of P&P, or we picked up new charges, which only strengthens the severity of our next "commitment" since we were on P&P at the time of our latest offense.

My judge knowingly smiled after I made this argument because he also knew why I would prefer more time in prison as opposed to dealing with probation. And I would rather have gotten ten-straight years behind bars, than to be released, only to have to go in and out of prison – either as a result of my own actions – or because my PO has a strong influence in swaying which direction my life will go.

Many convicts choose not to be released early on parole because it only provides a false impression of autonomy, which can be quickly stripped away. That freedom of choice, though, is fast becoming a fantasy, as it is pretty much policy that we continue our extended sentences via probation and parole.

Imagine for a second, if you will, returning home, being reunited with family and friends you haven't seen in years; getting a job, buying a new car, a new home, and earning a new existence. And then having your PO wake up on the wrong side of the bed and violate you back to prison for some slight, real or imagined.

Many who recidivate also find themselves wondering why they even strived for early release in the first place. Would it not be better to serve one solid sentence and then worry about rebuilding once we're finally, permanently, and irrevocably free from getting fucked over-and-over by the long dick of the prison industrial complex?

My sentencing judge explained to me that I seemed a decent enough person, one who hopefully wouldn't be subject to the cycle of going in-and-out of prison numerous times throughout my life, despite the system's structure of making this the most likely of occurrences.

I remember him peering down at me and asking if I was listening, because he was going to give me some of the best advice I ever heard.

He told me when I exit prison and the halfway house, and when I'm finally on the last stretch of my sentence – four years of probation – to purchase a pen and a notebook.

He told me to log every visit with probation, i.e., what was discussed, what advancements I had made since the last visit, such as building credit, earning promotions, going to church, exercising, etc. He advised that I should politely inform my PO what I was doing (documenting my probation experience) and who it was that made the suggestion to do it (the judge who sentenced me). And politely ask him to sign. If not, I would sign it in his/her stead, documenting my POs decision to either sign or not.

Anytime I gave a urine analysis I was to record the date, time, and outcome. There should only be negative UAs. My judge further explained that after a month had gone by, I should enter a brief synopsis of what I did that month; and the following month, and so forth until a genuine logbook began to take shape.

He explained that whether my PO liked me or not, or whether he disapproved of the crimes for which I was convicted was of no consequence. The logbook would be a testimony of the life I've chosen to live moving forward. He stated that when I was halfway through with probation (2 years), I should contact my attorney (or any attorney) and request a hearing for early termination. And that at that hearing, I would present to the court my logbook demonstrating two years of clear conduct and legitimate advancement.

NOTE: Please see the attached Early Termination document at the end of this chapter. As it happens, I did not need to request a hearing; rather, federal probation had a huge caseload at the time I reached my halfway point. And seeing how my first two years were of clear conduct, it was determined that I be released early. I'm not sure if my request, my clear conduct, a combination of both, or their caseload initiated the decision to cut me loose. I assume the administratively burdensome lift of so many offenders coming home – and the majority of them reoffending – was probably the greater determining factor than any good behavior on my part... I may never know.

Nonetheless, this statement was an act of unfathomable charity, for it is a rare occurrence when someone will give you inside information pertinent to combating the system that they themselves are a part of. Normally, judges tend to lace their sentencings with admonishments and reprimands, not so much for the sake of those being sentenced, but for the audience present and the concept of justice the office of the court is tasked with upholding.

This advice is perhaps the best defense against P&P, as well as being a surefire way of escaping a controlled and limited existence before our predetermined date. With that logbook, we possess the proof – endorsed by our PO in some cases – of our compliance, signed by the very person who may one day accuse you of performing otherwise.

PROBATION AND PAROLE DO'S AND DONT'S

While there are a few things that we can do to make ourselves a favorite target of our probation or parole officer, know that there are just as many things we can do – to not only avoid unwarranted attention – but also, to make ourselves appear as miniscule as possible in the eyes of P&P. The intent isn't so much to project an image of an ordinary, non-threatening minor concern compared to others that are also a part of our PO's caseload. <u>But not to project any image whatsoever.</u> This is to ensure that we are the last thing that comes to mind when our PO is asked to submit their monthly report as to which clients are concerns versus those that are adhering to policy and procedure.

Probation and Parole officers need success stories in order to advance their own interests. Why not make our success story a small part of theirs?

The list of do's and don't are as follows:

1. *Presenting an attitude of nonchalance, or, "I don't give a fuck."* This particular disposition may have been the thing that's helped us cope with many a bad situation in life, but it will only make our PO more dedicated to ensuring that we start giving a fuck by placing us in every type of program and therapy session in their arsenal. This is in hopes of breaking our belief system that to not give a fuck is to not acknowledge the situations we've placed ourselves in time and again. It will also give POs the impression that we don't take P&P seriously, and because of this, they will not consider the options to give you more freedom and leeway seriously as a consequence.

2. *Missing appointments of any kind.* Failing to keep appointments with POs is often times perceived as

a strict violation of policy or even absconding from justice. My opinion is that when we miss appointments, we are messing with our POs schedule, which is probably just as tight and difficult to adjust as any prearranged timetable. As a result of such strict enforcement of policies and procedure, we can be charged with escape and receive more prison time if we fail to make our appointments, or any other arrangements they may have "voluntold" us for, such as community service or therapy sessions.

Look at it this way- we really don't have a life or any other obligations that supersede those imposed by P&P. Paying the rent, buying groceries, and holding down a job are inconsequential if they interfere with reporting to P&P. If we fail to report, and they violate us back to prison, then we've failed in holding up to those obligations anyway. And now they mean absolutely nothing, as matters of importance in the free world are once again no longer our concern.

I know this may be a hard reality to manage, but it is of the utmost importance that we inform everyone, employers included, that P&P comes first. We absolutely cannot create a schedule for ourselves that would infringe upon our dedication to P&P. You *might* be able to pick up the kids from school. You *might* be able to take the car to get maintenance. You *might* be able to make it to the family reunion. But nothing and no one can take precedence over our commitment to P&P.

The sooner we convince ourselves and those around us that they cannot rely on us for much of anything – until we've finished with P&P – the better off our relationships with them, and with P&P will be. To wholly commit ourselves to something else while we're determined to successfully complete probation and parole is to commit ourselves back to prison, plain and simple.

3. *Argue, debate, or resist – more than once – a decision your PO has made that runs contrary to your work schedule and/or free time.* Let's assume that we've been informed we are now committed to attending a drug prevention class once a week. Not only does this obligation fall on the same day you stay late at work to complete mid-week work deadlines, but it's also the night your significant other has off, and for which the two of you go out to dinner.

We need to politely rationalize with our PO that – while we thank them for being concerned with our overall rehabilitation – our job is one of the main reasons we are still on the straight and narrow. And if that job is compromised for attending a superfluous treatment program that you've gotten along just fine without, that that would seem counterintuitive to your rehabilitation. Suggest that they give us more UAs that only take 5 minutes to perform at various windows throughout the day that would not impinge upon our employment.

NOTE: Often times POs aren't even aware of which client has been convicted of what crimes because their case-loads are so heavy. Are you the addict that robbed banks to support your habit before getting caught, or are you the trafficker that sold drugs, stayed sober, and made a successful living as a result of both? It might be a relief if we actively facilitate in guiding our own reentry.

However, if no amount of logical discussion will sway them from their decision, we've simply got to throw it to crazy and be as positive as we can concerning our participation. This will serve two purposes: it will make what we're doing less difficult if we're thinking positive about the benefits, rather than fighting it. And it may also cause our PO to desist from assigning us more of these programs if they deem it a waste of our respective time.

4. *Succumbing to peer pressure.* Prison, the halfway house, and life in general will always come with various forms of pressure from our families, friends, crime partners, and the like. It's vital to understand that while we are on P&P, we are not as free as the average citizen. As such, we are also not subject to the same laws as they are.

The average Joe/Joney can smoke a little pot after work, or have a few drinks with their co-workers without losing their freedom over it. They might even get into a scuffle at a bar or club with no more of a consequence than being eighty-sixed that night... not so much with us.

If we're seen at a place that serves alcohol – even if we're not drinking – we can be thrown back into the clink. To do any drugs not prescribed is often followed by a violation right back to federal or county holding until a judge decides how much of our remaining probation will be served in prison.

To fight on P&P is to pick up felony assault charges, whereas most people would simply get slapped with battery or drunk and disorderly, if they receive any punishment at all.

To succumb to peer pressure of any sort is to succumb to other influences that are going to get us into trouble. This is not to mention a direct reflection on our constitution and how difficult or easy it is for us to waiver from our principles.

NOTE: I mentioned in Chapter 1 that anytime we bend to another person's influence, our fortitude and integrity are weakened as a result of our acquiescence. And that if we let someone do this once, it will only be easier for them, or another, to do it again. We may get away once or twice with taking a hit of some bud or a welcome home shot of liquor, but what once started as an occasional indulgence will catch up to us.

Pro Tip: Don't let something as trivial as the whims of other people take away your freedom.

There's not that many Don'ts besides the obvious ones mentioned. Don't break the law. Don't miss your appointments. Don't place anyone or anything above your personal obligations to secure your freedom. Don't *not* give a fuck, and don't succumb to peer pressure.

Although it does happen on occasion that we'll fall under the authority of a particularly dedicated PO, know that most of them are just people trying to get by in the world, and the less work-related stresses they have to deal with, the better.

The less you make your PO work, and the less of a concern you are, the more you are going to reside in their peripheral thought as opposed to the forefront of their concerns; hence, the more freedom and leeway they'll provide. Demonstrating not just the facade of legitimacy, but the conviction that exudes from within and is reflected in our speech, our mannerisms and our progress, is key to successfully and serenely surviving the rigors of probation and parole.

The things we can do that will help guarantee an easy introduction (and completion) to this final stage of the prison industrial complex are virtually infinite. What's more, is that most of these practices are nothing more than acts of common courtesy, though some require a bit more finesse than others. They are as follows:

1. *Make use of a logbook.* Some of the best advice I ever heard is only good advice if it's actually being used. I spoke with a friend of mine a few days ago – whose release was some years behind my own – and who confided in me that his PO likes this concept, and was even thinking about providing a notebook for all of his clients so they might take a more hands-on approach at participating in and being the authors of, so to speak, their P&P journey.

NOTE: Associating or even speaking with another felon while on P&P is a violation, but he and I weren't conspiring to commit further crimes; we were simply discussing tactics and strategies for a successful reentry. I can't stress how important it is to keep a record of your visits with your PO should you ever need to show proof of where you were and what you were doing; more so if a crime was committed and fingers are pointing in your direction.

I can give several instances where returning citizens were violated back to prison because their PO was on vacation and *verbally* advised them it wasn't necessary to report. When those same clients were noted for not reporting that month, it was deemed a violation; hence, they were ordered to turn themselves in and face a sentencing review. If instructions were only verbally given, there is no proof to substantiate why you didn't report.

Perhaps the earliest retelling of this constructive form of revocation was by my father. He was revoked back to custody as a pre-teenager to the Baltimore Training School for Boys.

Pro Tip: Always request hard copies of any instructions from your PO that deviate from your normal routine.

2. *Communicate.* The strength of all relationships (personal and professional) is based on proper communication and trust capital. Only through healthy, honest interaction with others can we hope to have any sort of productive communication with those in our sphere of influence; or those whose influence we are subject to.

Learning how to effectively communicate with your PO provides much more than just a healthy relationship between two people. It can very well be the thing that guarantees your freedom and peace of mind for the remainder of your time with P&P.

Granted, many POs don't necessarily view their relationship with their clients as a two-way street, but rather, a supervisor/subordinate association. Nonetheless, successfully forming this relationship is good practice for the workforce we're about to enter, as well as the relationships we'll form with those that employ us.

If we perform as a self-motivated employee, our POs will recognize this and devote more of their attention and supervision to those "clients" that could use more performance improvement projects (PIPs). By performing well, we are in effect, *communicating* to our supervisors that they need not direct us with the level of management others may require. In time, we'll begin to see the benefits that our competence and efficiency will produce.

Be it a personal or professional relationship, obligatory deference needs to be extended in order for that same deference to be received. While your PO might not give you the immediate respect you give them, by remaining steadfast in your professionalism, and in your commitment to stay out of trouble, you'll begin to receive consideration in the form of leeway and trust capital. That trust will be evident in them loosening the reigns and restrictions during those first few months of P&P. Thus, you will have earned their respect.

Communicate with your PO. Do not come off as someone with a chip on their shoulder, or worse, as someone who is complaining or groveling. This will only make your position as a subordinate, and a weak one in need of supervision, more prevalent. Convey *only* needs that are necessary for your PO to consider; necessities that your PO can help you obtain and for which you'll be a more productive client, one who does not create more administrative lifts for your supervisor. You may very well find your requests being granted due to the professionalism you've demonstrated, as well as the way in which you've communicated your needs.

3. *Be punctual.* Have you ever had a girlfriend/boyfriend, husband/wife, friend or business partner constantly arrive late to a meeting, lunch, date, or travel departure? How did that constant disregard for your consideration and time make you feel? This is the same sentiment your PO will begin to experience every time you are late.

NOTE: My Black cousins in Baltimore jokingly refer to people showing up late as being on "Black People's time." And while this assignation may apply to those who are constantly late (rather than them being Black), it should never apply to those of us that are on probation.

It might be safe to assume that if you miss a meeting with your PO, or show up late, that it's going to make them suspicious of you and your ability to properly conduct business.

Pro Tip: Being punctual *is* being professional.

The steps we can take that will improve our experience or make it easier for us to interact with our PO are the same ones that we've applied in every social setting we've ever found ourselves in. When someone holds the power of freedom over you, this should only further instill the determination to win that individual over, or, at the very least, prove ourselves to be committed to whatever it is they expect from us.

Probation and Parole are battles that can be won through accepting that your antagonist is stronger than you, for the time being. And with that acceptance comes the realization that riding the current will win far more concessions than swimming against the tide.

Some cases, however, are going to prove difficult, no matter how well you interact with others. While I don't have any illusions of finishing my own probation without a couple of snags, I do feel confident that the knowledge I've gained from past experience – as well as facts learned from others – will empower me to perform to the best of my ability.

ONCE BITTEN TWICE SHY

When I was a child my parents had this beautiful cast iron wood-burning stove in the living room that they used to help heat the house in the winter time. It had a row of four little windows along the broad side that faced the living room. I remember being completely captivated by the way the fire rolled inside those windows, almost as if it was made of liquid. I would stare through the glass until my face became so hot that I had to back away lest it burned me. I became so entranced by the appearance of that fire that I actually looked forward to those days and nights when using the stove became necessary.

There came a time, not long after my 5th birthday, when I could've cared less if we ever used that stove again. I would rather have froze to death than to have seen that liquid fire doing its dance and slow roll within the depths of those windows. I can't remember if my brother ran past me, or playfully pushed me, or if I tripped, or what. But I ended up placing my hands on the surface of that stove to avoid burning my face when I somehow lost my balance.

My father had to forcefully pull my hands off as they became stuck to the surface. It was a solid two months or more before my skin started to heal. I learned the old proverb many people apply to those things harmful to them... "If you play with fire, you're gonna get burned."

It's amazing to me that to this day I'm wary of fires, even if only on the most subconscious of levels. I love sitting in front of them and allowing the heat to comfort me, or send me into a lazy haze of thought. But they never lull me into a sense of complacency. If anything, they sharpen my senses, and cause me to think about the day that same life-sustaining heat caused the most severe pain I've ever experienced, and death for others less fortunate.

What's even more amazing to me is that the burn and suffering we endure from the result of our criminal lifestyles never seems to sear our bodies and souls bad enough for us to consider stopping. We often pursue these acts over-and-over, only to be further burned and marred by the consequences. I believe this is because – much like fire – these acts provide a sense of security to those who practice them.

They afford a level of comfort more so than any other method we've practiced. And we bask in the warmth and protection that crime surrounds us in. But this too, lulls us into a sense of complacency, and when we fall asleep at the wheel it burns us; scars, and in some cases, kills us.

It also assures that we will forever be subject to lives that are directed, supervised, and lived under the control of institutions such as the prison industrial complex. And as such, we will be subject to those who work in these fields, as well as their proclivities, flaws, and mercy, or lack thereof.

It's important to understand that we as criminals created these fields of employment. Our actions are also what created such unfavorable existences as the prison industrial complex provides. Without us these career options would not exist, at least not at the level they currently operate.

We are what makes them relevant. We are what defines their profession, and the responses they provide when others ask what they do for a living.

If we've become the type of people who allow our criminality and time in prison to become the common denominator that defines us, then we are lost. All we've become is a means of job security for someone else. For it is that direction and control of our own lives that provides security, meaning, and relevance for theirs.

It is necessary for us to believe that we are in one category, one margin of existence, that must be controlled and property managed in order for their own survival to be assured; and nothing serves this purpose more effectively than a lifetime of supervision under the prison industrial complex.

I have come to realize many things about myself that, heretofore, I would never have known had I not experienced imprisonment first-hand. Perhaps one of the most shocking was the level of compassion I have for the people I thought I disdained the most.

There's a part of me that feels empathy for the ones that arrested me, that judged me, that guard me and sometimes go out of their way to make my stay in prison that much harder. And I feel grateful for what I view at times as misguided efforts. Because they're only making me a better person, which, in some cases, I'm sure is not their intent.

The agents, cops, snitches, guards, and probation and parole officers; they'll never escape this life. It will forever define much of their existence. It's what makes them a necessary unit of measure in the present scheme of things. And because of that I feel no small amount of melancholy for their chosen pathway. As well as for anyone that earns their living from crime, and those a part of the system which attempts to control it, which they most assuredly will never do.

My time in prison and my life as a criminal will never define me. It was just a job, a means to an end, and I believe I would have come to a much worse end had this particular chapter of my life not come to such an effective closing. All those that contributed to putting me here, and keeping me here... they are still in the thick of it. This is their daily life until they reach that twenty-five, now thirty-year pension.

As I write this, I guess you could say I'm still in the thick of it, but it doesn't feel that way. And if you're in prison reading this – with a release date at the end of the tunnel – you shouldn't feel as if you're in the thick of it either. On the contrary. We're on the home stretch.

PEACE TREATIES

I'll continue to emphasize the importance of identifying our own character flaws and making the proper adjustments before we identify the flaws of others, and subsequently condemn or judge them for their shortcomings.

It's so easy to pin a label on someone and then use that label to provide us a synopsis of everything we'll ever need to know about that person. It can be a simpler route to categorize someone as either a likable person whom we gravitate towards, or a useless and exasperating person who isn't worth our efforts.

I suspect this is the one disruption to the line of communication between a probation or parole officer and their clients that is the foremost deterrent to a successful relationship between the two: our automatic classification of them as a hindrance to our freedom, and their habitual classification of us as convicts in need of supervision, both of whom are not often given the benefit of the doubt.

A rigid form of classification of one's character is used by people when we come across an individual whose personality is abrasive to that of our own, or when we encounter someone whom we've already reached a conclusion about based on previous knowledge, e.g., their criminal record, or their employment with the prison industrial complex.

Often times we categorize people under two designations-those we like, and those we dislike. This is usually based off first impressions, not realizing our own ability to be dexterous and flexible when dealing with different personalities is what's needed in order to – not only effectively communicate our needs to others – but fully understand what they're attempting to convey to us as well.

More often than not, people define themselves (and others) based upon what their occupation is, or on the title that comes with that occupation. This is part of the principle that many Americans (and people throughout the world) use to measure their worth; that is, their status and the amount of success they've achieved based upon the revenue and standard of living such statuses provide.

As criminals, our material wealth can only parallel the amount of money we make. Through this system of social elevation, our only other means of obtaining a higher status comes from the titles we possess in whatever fields of occupation we find ourselves in.

Some place a high level of status on occupations that measure a person's worth based on what they contribute to the rest of society, and not so much the amount of revenue their position generates (think law enforcement).

In some instances, people measure status by the amount of obligatory respect and/or influence a particular job title is associated with, i.e., criminals, law enforcement, and individuals employed with the prison industrial complex.

For example, I sold drugs. To most, that makes me a drug dealer. That's it. That's my title. That's who I am. That leaves no room for any other description other than someone who sells drugs. The characteristics that most people apply to drug dealers are not very positive ones, nor are they multi-dimensional. All that's left for a stranger to distinguish me by is my profession and the amount of influence it wields.

The title of Drug Dealer also provides that instant respect and influence to those that know who and what you are. It provides perks and opportunities that would never have come my way had I not earned and maintained that particular assignation.

I'm convinced this same formula applies to legitimate jobs with titles and responsibilities that command a certain amount of respect and influence, such as law enforcement, where the status level can be high, yet the income is not.

So too is the level of negativity and stereotyping that accompanies law enforcement as it parallels that of the criminal.

I've encountered some pretty wretched members of law enforcement in my time. The two narcotics officers in Santa Fe that operated at the same time I sold drugs were arrested by the FBI for robbing drug dealers and using the proceeds to improve their own standard of living.

The lasting impression these two detectives had upon me was that *everyone* who makes a living in law enforcement are terribly corrupt, power hungry, and committing crimes under the Color of Law.

But I've also come to know some who were in fact, genuinely good people; and held themselves to a higher standard – both personally and professionally – than I ever held myself to at that moment in time.

I know many today, men and women I grew up with that pursued careers in law enforcement and later in politics, public service, etc. They are a far cry from the stereotyped, standardized version of police I painted in my mind's eye.

Prior to going to prison, I viewed good police officers and agents as the exception to the rule, and a small exception at that. Since coming home my perception has reversed, as has theirs.

I've been pulled over a couple times for speeding when merging from an on-ramp onto a highway. One state trooper (real buff guy that barely fit into his uniform) asked me to step out of my vehicle. He told me I wasn't in any trouble and didn't have any warrants, but wanted to show me his laptop in his unit to make sure the profile he ran was actually mine.

He could not believe the rap sheet that his search

produced belonged to the Hyundai-driving, lanyard-badge wearing, nerdy-dressed, glasses-sporting guy he pulled over. We shot the breeze for a good 15 minutes outside our cars. We both bitched about working in state government, the velvet handcuffs it provides, and where we saw ourselves in the future (I don't think I had obtained my associate broker's license yet).

We exchanged business cards and I haven't seen him patrolling that part of the highway since.

I've met law enforcement and probation officers either through work or just happenstance, and when we finally share one another's pasts, it's interesting to see how many parallels we drew; how rooted they are in the lower-middle class, and all that comes with it.

It occurred to people on both sides of these discussions that the exception to the rule is in fact the majority, and that our relative occupations, and the stereo typical negativity that accompanies them are, more often than not, the elements that cause prejudgment of one another.

In time, and through fostering these relationships, we came to understand that the bonds that formed between us were founded because we're all just ordinary people; not supercops or mega criminals. For the time we spent together, we were on neutral ground, and both parties became freed from the judgments and persecutions that we assigned to the other... and that normal citizens assigned to both sides.

The more I considered these discussions – usually on the side of the road or at a restaurant after work – the more I came to realize that perhaps it's time as a society to measure people's worth as people, and not by what they do to earn their bread and butter. And that the old system that implies status or commands respect through job titles might be due for an overhaul.

We all come into this world by the same means, and we will all leave it by varying degrees of the same conclusion. To make distinctions between yourself and another is to further alienate ourselves from our fellow man/woman. And it will only serve to make our commitment to P&P and other constructs that much harder to endure.

Possessing the ability to adapt to various personalities we encounter, without prejudgment, will make probation and parole that much easier. Perfecting this ability when interacting with your PO will bring your term to a positive conclusion, rather than a negative and continuous loop of frustration.

To express your sentiment of transition to your PO through intelligent thought, action and accurate communication is to convey our intent at being a positive element of their profession, a success story that they too might share with their colleagues and supervisors.

We might not receive praise or gain a new friend by these efforts, but by making their workday easier to tolerate, we could very well gain a colleague, or an advocate who might facilitate in gaining our freedom that much quicker.

I would wish good luck to all of you in your struggles with P&P, but that would base each individual outcome on something that has little to do with the control we possess to maneuver our lives forward in the intended direction. That would imply that our fates would be dictated by people and elements other than ourselves.

Instead, I would simply ask that you plan for your release to the halfway house, and probation and parole similar to the plan I've outlined in this chapter; one that is specifically tailored, not to the person you are, but to the one you aspire to be.

Keep P&P and the rest of the prison industrial complex, not only in the rearview, but within the margins and boundaries they were designed for. And our own lives will eventually possess minimal barriers of their own.

A CITIZEN OF THE REPUBLIC

Possessing Roman citizenship was one of the highest standards of status and protection any normal person could hope for in that age. It would guarantee safe passage in any Roman territory or province, and it could protect such a citizen from unlawful persecution at the hands of non-Roman peoples, groups, or governments.

But that coveted citizenship could also be stripped away if they were found guilty of committing certain crimes. The convicted could spend the rest of their lives as slaves to pay off debtors, or dying violently as gladiators to appease the masses.

In the Republic of the United States of America, in which we are subjects, and indeed citizens, the protections and punishments are still there – structured under a democracy quite similar to that of Rome before it became an empire – yet both protections and punishments are more subtle. And their effects can be more difficult to perceive by those being protected... or punished.

Rest assured that the enslavement and loss of citizenship we're prescribed as convicted felons are just as commonplace, and just as lethal as the punishments that a citizen of Rome endured in antiquity.

When another citizen, or group of citizens, can strip you of your rights and freedoms, you have essentially lost the protections as a full-fledged citizen of your country. When you are discriminated against because of a past conviction, know that your safe harbor under federal and state laws has been forfeit.

When another citizen can point a finger at you, or pick up a phone and call the police, and have you placed under arrest, the citizenship you hold is substandard compared to that of the person who accuses you. And when we find ourselves going in-and-out of prison time and again, know that we are not considered by anyone to be lawful citizens of this country.

What we have become are valuable units of measure; or slaves, to the prison industrial complex. We have become assets, stock, and monetary units that are traded, bought, sold, and moved around from one location to another in order to keep the full-fledged citizens working, secure, and conciliated.

When our level of citizenry has been reduced to the point where our sole purpose is to fulfill the needs of others, without receiving any recompense, we've proven ourselves to be essentially worthless from an economic and sociological point of view. More to the point, we have become economic burdens as the crimes we commit and taxes we don't pay are satisfied at the expense of contributing members of society. Their obligation and subsequent freedoms are greater due to ours being nonexistent.

The solution is to transition us from worthless to valuable while protecting society from our negative effects. This occurs by converting criminals into assets that will provide others with job security while isolating us from those whose contribution to the whole are assured by their lawful acts of paying taxes and obeying the laws in place.

I understand that many of the things that happen to us as a result of the lives we were born into (or chose) are unjust, and are by no means dictated by any laws. But to view these occurrences for what they truly are – as simply a formula to solve economic and sociological problems – is to take away the abuse heaped upon us as personal, and to see our criminal pathway with a more clinical mindset; one that informs us that our treatment results from actions that negatively impact the collective.

The criminal pathway, and no other, is what has unwittingly enslaved us and marginalized our lives under a strict form of control, while we believed the opposite- that we had liberated ourselves from the bonds of poverty we were subjected to prior to our lives of crime.

This is the *why* behind why we were stripped of our citizenship. This is why we have received the assignation of substandard; thus, receiving substandard treatment from those who possess a higher level of citizenship than our own.

I think another significant parallel worth pointing out is just how many of us have suffered and died within modern day coliseums that make up this nation's jails and penitentiaries. Those of us that are released also have scars to bear, some apparent, and others more subtle.

Identifying the wounds the prison industrial complex has left upon some, if not most of its gladiators is trivial compared to the awareness that we must use these lessons, and our survival skills, to reacquire our full citizenship.

Using these experiences in furtherance of strengthening our resolve is key to reacquiring full citizenship after criminal convictions. Being aware, also, that we must make selfless contributions upon returning home to receive recompense is also compulsory.

Do not come to loathe every negative aspect of existence and control that has been assigned to us through the prison industrial complex, and by our own choices. Instead, view the scourging you've endured as a form of training that will only better prepare you for any and all unforeseen events that will surely come our way.

Our pathway is not by any means unique. And it is becoming a path that more and more citizens are traveling. But it can be a higher path, trodden by those fortunate enough to have lived a more thoroughly experienced existence.

We can choose to be so much more than subjects of the prison industrial complex. We can choose to be the rightful citizens of this country. We can choose to live lives that contain more meaning and more fulfillment than those we've found ourselves living. We most assuredly can do better than this.

UNITED STATES PROBATION OFFICE
DISTRICT OF NEW MEXICO

Margaret Vigil, Chief   *Ron J. Travers, Deputy*

333 LOMAS BLVD. NW, STE 170
ALBUQUERQUE, NM 87102-9844
(505) 348-2600

800 EAST 30TH STREET
BUILDING 5, SUITE A
FARMINGTON, NM 87401
(505) 325-7507

909 METRO AVENUE
GALLUP, NM 87301-5384
(505) 726-1660

Richard Bohlken, Assistant Deputy
Chris Hill, Assistant Deputy

100 NORTH CHURCH STREET
LAS CRUCES, NM 88001
(575) 528-1900

500 NORTH RICHARDSON
ROOM 309
ROSWELL, NM 88201
(575) 637-7929

120 SOUTH FEDERAL PLACE
ROOM 304
SANTA FE, NM 87501
(505) 992-3872

March 7, 2019

Reply to: Santa Fe

Jason Grinage
6384 Jaguar Drive
Santa Fe, NM 87507

RE: Termination of supervised release
        1084 1:08CR02126-001

Dear Jason Grinage:

This letter is to inform you that you received an early termination of supervised release on March 6, 2019. You satisfactorily completed all conditions of supervision, and have no further obligation to the U.S. Probation and Pretrial Services Office. Enclosed, you will find information concerning your loss of rights as a convicted felon, including firearms restrictions, and how to apply for a Presidential Pardon. As you have satisfied all conditions of supervision, under New Mexico Code, Section 31-13-1, you now have the right to vote. Should you desire to vote, please present this letter to the County Clerk's Office in your county of residence.

Should you have any questions, please contact me at 505-980-0935.

Sincerely,

Dominico Encinias
USPO

Felony Resriction Form
Enclosure

UNITED STATES PROBATION OFFICE
DISTRICT OF NEW MEXICO

Margaret Vigil, Chief   *Ron J. Travers, Deputy*

333 LOMAS BLVD. NW, STE 170
ALBUQUERQUE, NM 87102-9844
(505) 348-2600

800 EAST 30TH STREET
BUILDING 5, SUITE A
FARMINGTON, NM 87401
(505) 325-7367

909 METRO AVENUE
GALLUP, NM 87301-5384
(505) 726-1660

Richard Bohlken, Assistant Deputy
Chris Hill, Assistant Deputy

100 NORTH CHURCH STREET
LAS CRUCES, NM 88001
(575) 528-1800

800 NORTH RICHARDSON
ROOM 309
ROSWELL, NM 88201
(575) 637-7020

120 SOUTH FEDERAL PLACE
ROOM 304
SANTA FE, NM 87501
(505) 992-3872

FELONY RESTRICTION INFORMATION

ATTACHED TO TERMINATION LETTER OF   March 7, 2019

Jason Grinage
6384 Jaguar Drive
Santa Fe, NM 87507

The following information is important to you in order to avoid any future difficulties with law enforcement agencies:

Even though you are no longer under supervision, your felony conviction remains unchanged. This means your rights to hold public office HAS NOT been restored. As for firearms possession, the Gun Control Act of 1968, pursuant to Chapter 44 of United States Code Title 18, makes it clear that any person convicted of any offense punishable by imprisonment for a term exceeding one year MAY NOT receive, possess, or transport any firearm, including handguns, rifles, shotguns, or ammunition. To do so could result in a new felony conviction punishable by a fine or imprisonment, or both. Should you be granted a Presidential Pardon, all rights would be restored to you, including the right to use a firearm. You are now eligible to serve on jury duty pursuant to NMSA 38-5-1. There are no expenses involved in obtaining and completing an application and the services of an attorney are not needed.

If you are interested in applying for a Presidential Pardon, please read the following instructions:

> To determine if you are eligible to apply for a Presidential Pardon, contact the Pardon Attorney, U.S. Department of Justice, Washington, D.C., 20530. This information can also be found at www.usdoj.gov pardon. Include in your letter the date and place of conviction, nature of offense, sentence received, when released from prison (if sentenced to confinement), and when released from Probation or Supervised Release. If you are eligible, the Pardon Attorney will send you forms to be completed and returned. The United States Probation and Pretrial Services Office can assist you in completing the forms, if necessary. You will not be eligible to apply for a pardon until at least five (5) years from the date of your conviction or from the date you were released from confinement, whichever comes later. In some cases, such as those involving violation of narcotic laws, violent crimes, gun control laws, income tax laws, perjury, violation of public trust involving personal dishonesty, fraud involving substantial sums of money, violations involving organized crime [and] other crimes of a serious nature, a waiting period of seven (7) years is usually required. The length of the waiting period is determined by the Department of Justice.
>
> Should you need additional assistance or clarification, please contact the United States Probation and Pretrial Services at (505) 348-2600, and request to speak to Dominico Encinias.

6
FOOTING

"If you want to succeed in the world you must make your own opportunities as you go on. The man who waits for some seventh wave to toss him on dry land will find that the seventh wave is a long time a coming. You can commit no greater folly than to sit by the wayside until someone comes along and invites you to ride with him to wealth or influence."

— JOHN B. GOUGH

"America is the land of the second chance- and when the gates of prison open, the path should lead to a better life."

— GEORGE W. BUSH

I'VE ALWAYS THOUGHT of myself as bi or tri-partisan, belonging to no political party yet favoring those ideas coming from each side of the isle that seem to ring true, and be of most benefit to those for which each proposed bill was created.

I was taught at a very young age – when voting or considering one politician over another – to always choose the lesser of two evils – but to not vote defensively, if performing the two simultaneously is even possible.

While my family has always been staunch blue-collar Democrats, they seem to be voting more towards the other side since my incarceration. Or to be fair, we seem to be the new middle, separated from the far extremes as both sides slid to their respective ends of the spectrum.

I loved Obama, and I loved how he always seemed to handle interviews with a certain grace and poise. I remember the guys banging on their cell doors when the election results came in late that night (for Obama's 2nd term) as we were all listening to the polls on our AM radios.

Obama reduced the "Crack Law," and guards would come into the law library or the yard and yell out an inmate's name to pack up and go home due to sentence reductions.

I feel one of the primary flaws in both Obama administrations was their foreign policy. I can recall when the Arab Spring occurred, and all these countries had this "awakening" as to the strict control their governments exercised over their citizens... and the Obama Administration(s) pretty much did nothing with the exception of oppose our favorite puppet leaders in some nations after they were exposed for crime or corruption (think Egypt and Syria).

I've always found it perplexing, if not entertaining in a jaded fashion, the way most Americans favor and then seek to elect those who will be dictating the many aspects of existence. Not only do we vote from a defensive posture, but we vote for the politician that we "like" the most, i.e., whose public relations campaign best appeals and parallels our way of thinking.

A certain amount of shine and affability, accompanied by a winning smile and campaign slogans seems to be the prerequisites for gaining our collective trust and confidence.

At the time I write this, I've lived through six different

administrations (1980 through 2013). Carter and Reagan I barely remember (with the exception of Nancy Reagan's "Just Say No" Anti-Drug Slogan). The one president I remember feeling personal dislike for was George W. Bush.

Truthfully, I'm not sure if I could even name one instance where I thought he acted in a less than favorable manner. Maybe it was when he was given the news that terrorists had just struck the Twin Towers while he was reading to a bunch of elementary school children, and he sat there in shock for a few minutes... But the 20s-something me just didn't like the guy.

I thought Republicans were strong in the Darkside, and that George W. Bush's presidency was a result of a miscount in his brother's state of Florida which he presided over as governor.

But how much did I truly know about this president? Were my feelings about him solely based on what I observed from mainstream media; thus, how he was presented to us, or were they based on his track record, which I knew next to nothing about? More to the point, was it his administration that directly impacted me, or was it the man himself whose personality I found to be disagreeable?

I think the truth of the matter is I was part of that one half of Americans, who, for whatever reasons, just didn't like him. And by that, I mean, I didn't like his presentation. Much the same as we say "I don't like this or that actor or actress," meaning we don't care for their performance on screen; having never met these people in real life.

NOTE: Now, I've watched countless interviews of him, (the 2nd Bush) and I can't help but love his attitude on life and the current state of our Union. He paints, really well, and has added these paintings (of veterans if I'm not mistaken) into a book he published. He is quoted as saying, apart from the Towers, the worst moment in his Presidency was when Kanye West said he (Bush) didn't like Black people.

Apart from the 3 Strikes Law that was first instituted by my home state of Washington, and later federally adopted by a guy who I thought was the best President of our time, Bill Clinton, most criminals are rarely impacted by the policies or administrations from one president to the next; more so if we don't pay taxes, and barely notice whether gas is two or four dollars a gallon.

Most presidents, as a matter of policy and ensuring a second term, all take a hard-nosed stance on crime and the so-called War on Drugs in particular, because this is the popular thing to do. And the popular thing to do will always ensure more votes.

NOTE: As I transcribe this chapter from paper to laptop, it is now 05/06/2024, and there is more political division between what was considered Democrat or Republican than ever before. The last substantial law affecting criminals was the Bi-Partisan Federal Prison Reform Bill signed into effect by then President Trump. Despite his being perhaps the most polarizing president we've ever had, I got into the practice of fact-checking and reviewing our leaders' track records rather than reacting to what's being presented to me by mainstream media outlets. To date, former president Trump has done the following: First president in the history of our nation to provide funding in perpetuity for traditionally all-Black colleges. First president in history to create a federal law enforcement branch dedicated solely to investigating missing and murdered Original American women. (There are so many missing/murdered both on and off Reservations and Pueblos that the exact count is unknown. They are seconded by Black women in America). *Executive Order 13898, signed by then-U.S. president Donald Trump, formed the Task Force on Missing and Murdered American Indians and Alaska Natives, otherwise known as*

Operation Lady Justice, in order to address concerns of these communities regarding missing and murdered women and girls in the United States. *

Lastly, president Trump in his first term signed the Animal Cruelty Bill into law, making it a felony to abuse animals.

What I do know is that a president's - and person's - agenda will always be their own, despite what they choose to share with the rest of the world. Also, no matter how much good a person does, there will always be people who are negatively impacted by the end results of that goodwill.

The one exception which seems to run contrary to many of my beliefs about certain governmental policies is the amount of money that is now being allocated in order to help those who have been to prison get back on their feet.

We will examine what our government is currently doing to convert returning citizens into a different and more successful unit of measurable value.

I might point out that these programs only grew in popularity after the prison industrial complex became top-heavy to the point where it cost tax payers more than it benefitted the communities in which prisons were being built and operated. That a counterbalance to a costly prison system, with nominal effect, was the only practical solution to an otherwise paradoxical practice of gross imprisonment of a nation's citizenry, brought about by the industrialization and privatization of a segment of society that should always remain within the parameters of governmental administration, rather than falling under the discretion of private-for-profit businesses.

Many of these programs found much of their financial grounding during the presidency of George W. Bush. The practice of diverting criminals from crime through means of

---

* https://www.bop.gov/inmates/fsa/overview.
jsp#:~:text=The%20act%20was%20the%20culmination,mecha-
nisms%20to%20maintain%20public%20safety.

education, empowerment, and curb appeal, was in fact, originated and has been gaining momentum in his home state of Texas. This is one of the harder-nosed districts for punishment, but has since found that, as a result of these efforts, recidivism rates are down, as are the burdens imposed upon tax payers for the high cost of operating and opening new prison facilities.

Some like to opine that the origins of these programs were not created under the Bush Administration. Some also suggest that his contribution to anti-recidivism efforts is a topic which is also up for debate. The fact that these programs can help convicted felons pursue lives of legitimacy and success, as a result of their implementation, is not.

These initiatives come in the form of tax cuts for employers who hire felons or as bonding programs which insure ex-offenders for incidentals. Programs, in essence, that offer incentives to companies that hire felons by making felons that much more appealing to the potential employer, through no-cost insurance, and by providing extensive tax cuts for those that choose to take a chance at hiring someone who happens to possess a criminal past.

Money has also been set aside for programs such as financial aid and federal assistance measures which provide backing for those who wish to further their education, start a business, or who simply need more support when reentering society.

Fortunately, you don't have to be sent to prison in order to reap the benefits of these federally subsidized programs. In many cases, it isn't a requisite that you possess a criminal background either. These efforts were designed with the intention of providing an alternative means for people other than the option which got them into trouble in the first place. They are also intended for the purpose of keeping recidivism down by reeducation and providing assistance for those who have negatively impacted society and themselves through their criminality.

Of all the advice and information I've attempted to fill these pages with, I feel that this chapter provides the most concrete proof of support from outside sources that can actually improve one's chances of a successful transition. Most of what I've written is based upon self-motivation and finding the strength to succeed by one's own volition, because the ability to persevere, and to indeed advance, are traits that often times need only our own resolve to become reality.

To know that there are actually outside sources of aid and assistance is only part of the solution. Using these programs to your benefit can aid in affecting a positive change with the least number of difficulties. Effectively using these programs will also ensure that even more assets are devoted towards rehabilitation, and less towards building new prisons, if fewer among us are committing crimes.

The continuity of these programs is a matter of practicality, in that they were created for the sole purpose of reducing costs, as a result of the privatized prison industry boom, which inadvertently became more of a drain on tax payers than it ever was an advantage. And while I'm grateful that these programs do indeed exist, it's important to recognize that their existence is only one of common sense rather than philanthropy.

The numbers game is always at play. The amount of assets and people that are being focused on reducing recidivism and bolstering criminal rehabilitation will remain devoted to solving these problems in so far as their efforts continue to bear fruit.

If and when the return on this investment turns out to be a poor one, and if recipients choose not to use these programs to their advantage, the efforts put towards attacking this particular dilemma will cease to exist. And the administration in place will revert back to what has always worked in the past, even if only on a subsistence level.

This reversion will be manifest in more prisons, and more

investment in the complex as opposed to more effective and humane efforts for remedial action.

I focus heavily on a path of self-motivation because external supports feel impermanent, and at times, unstable fixtures in the unpredictable environment of government administration. And to rely upon self, and the inner strength we all possess, is a surer guarantee than to depend on something as fleeting and as temporary as a government subsidized program. But be that as it may, they are here for the time being, and our ability to thrive and advance off of these initiatives is something that should be taken advantage of, before the proverbial well runs dry.

BONDING OUT

The Federal Bonding Program or FBP is a program that provides benefits to both employer and employee alike. Its design is basically one of additional protection by insuring employers, and also one of adulation, in that it bonds the individual who makes use of its intended purpose by making them less of a liability to the employer.

Funded and administered by the US Department of Labor, fidelity insurance bonds are available to "indemnify employers for the loss of money or property sustained through the dishonest acts of their employees." i.e., theft, forgery, larceny, and embezzlement.

I really can't conceive of someone being hired – with the employer's full knowledge of their criminal past – and then robbing the person or company who hired them, as the aforementioned knowledge concerning their criminal history would only place them at the top of the list of suspects. But it is noteworthy to consider the stigma that often accompanies a person with a criminal record, and to recognize that the bonding program is the counterbalance to a stereotype often applied to ex-offenders due to their criminal past.

I've been hired, on more than one occasion, by employers who were well aware of my criminal history. The fact that they chose me in lieu of all those legitimate people that applied for the same position only further instilled in me a sense of loyalty to these individuals and their businesses.

Aside from the stigma that plagues ex-offenders, it's also significant that people consider the amount of devotion employers can experience as a result of hiring ex-offenders, and that that commitment can be a much better incentive than an insurance policy, for incidentals, should an employee choose to act in an unlawful manner.

Statistics show the amount of dedication most ex-offenders attach to the hand that feeds them, or in this case, the company that hires them, is much higher than the level of devotion most normal citizens apply to the companies they're employed by. In addition, employers that take a chance with people possessing a criminal past are finding those hires to be harder working, and more dedicated to the team than ones who view their jobs as merely a means of income, rather than a means of survival, albeit the two are synonymous.

In short, the FBP incentivizes employers, and provides a proverbial foot-in-the-door of an otherwise hard-to-access area of employment for many ex-offenders.

We as returning citizens can mention the FBP to a prospective employer, should you choose to, as an additional benefit of considering us for employment. But I feel this is a program that should only be mentioned if an employer is uncertain of hiring the likes of us; not because we lack the applicable skillsets, but because of the risk that our criminal record might represent.

Perhaps the greatest incentive of this program is that it costs the employer, as well as the job seeker, absolutely nothing. The reimbursement that an employer would receive, in the event of an unlawful act committed by an employee, is provided by way of zero deductible compensation.

The FBP bond insurance initiative has proven to be extremely successful. Since its inception, only 1% of the bonds issued have resulted in a claim. This speaks volumes, not only for the success of this program, but for the eligibility and competency of the individuals being bonded in hopes of becoming successful, legitimate members of America's work-force. For more information you can access the Federal Bonding program website by going to www.bonds4jobs.com.

CUTS

The Work Opportunity Tax Credit or WOTC is another program that kills two birds with one stone: it provides a substantial incentive to the employer while enhancing the job seeker's eligibility for employment.

The WOTC functions via providing employers tax breaks on their federal income taxes by hiring targeted groups that have historically faced significant barriers to employment, among these of course are returning citizens.

Although this program is also tailored to benefit other groups of job-seekers who have had difficulty securing employment, it is fundamentally a catalyst for increasing the appeal of job seekers that possess criminal histories. Business impact analysis is showing that it also aides in reducing the amount of companies who do not hire felons, as the tax breaks for reintegrating us into the work force is becoming quite the policy changer.

"An ex-felon under the WOTC is an individual who has been convicted of a felony under any statute of the United States or any State, and has a hiring date which is within one year from the date of conviction or release from prison."

The main objective of this program is to enable certified employees to gradually move from economic dependency to self-sufficiency as they earn a steady income and become contributing taxpayers. Simultaneously, participating employers are compensated by being able to reduce their federal income tax liability. For each new ex-felon hired, the credit is 25% of qualified first-year wages for those employed at least 120 hours, or $1,500; and 40% for those employed 400 hours or more, or $2,400.

The WOTC is a federal tax credit used to reduce the federal tax liability of private-for-profit employers.

There's no limit to the number of "new" ex-felons an employer can hire to benefit from these tax savings. This is one of the reasons why proactive anti-recidivism efforts are gaining so much momentum; that and the fact that employees being hired with the aid of these programs are proving themselves to be assets rather than liabilities.

It's important that we come to recognize the paradigm shift that is taking place with regards to our Nation's perceptions about Her returning citizens; and, the resulting effects these initiatives are providing. For one, it financially benefits the employer and gives them an incentive to take a chance on what some may consider a "risky" hire. Also, it functions as a mechanism to safely bring a return on an investment with limited liability. Lastly, the economic significance combined with the uplifting sense of self-worth provided to both employers and employees are hardly beneath notice.

Employers can apply for and receive a WOTC certification for each new hire from their State Workforce Agencies. There's minimal paperwork needed to qualify and claim the tax credit. For more information you can visit the government website at www.doleta.gov/wotc or www.irs.gov.

CONTINUED EDUCATION

The qualifications for financial aid seem to be a bit trickier in understanding, as certain extenuating factors have been included in the text which tends to confuse even the best of applicants. I think the chief disparity that I have with this is that federal financial aid seems to be practically nonexistent for people who are already incarcerated. Rather, the benefits and aid take place only after one is free to pursue their education once released from custody.

Decades ago, you could obtain a college degree in most any penitentiary, but tax payers, and/or the powers that be decided that they were already spending too much time and money coddling felons when funds should have been spent on keeping them safely secluded from the rest of society.

While this may be true, it's also true that money being applied towards educating felons actually reduces the rate of recidivism dramatically, and saves tax payers money in the long run. Funds devoted to building stronger and more secure prisons only do just that. They do not reduce recidivism the way empowerment and education are guaranteed to do.

Individuals who are incarcerated in a federal, state, or local correctional institution have some *limited* eligibility for federal student aid. In general, restriction on federal student aid eligibility is removed for formerly incarcerated individuals, including those on probation, parole, or residing in a halfway house.

"An individual incarcerated in a federal or state institution is ineligible to receive a Federal Pell Grant or federal student loans. Although an individual incarcerated in a federal or state prison is eligible to receive a Federal Supplemental Educational Opportunity Grant (FSEOG) and Federal Work Study (FWS), he or she is unlikely to receive either of these because due to the FSEOG award priority, which is that the grant must be given to those students who also will receive a Federal Pell Grant, and also duties of performing an FWS job while incarcerated."

"Also, those incarcerated in correctional institutions other than federal or state institutions are eligible for a Federal Pell Grant, FSEOG, and FWS but not for federal student loans. But it is also unlikely that individuals in correctional institutes other than federal or state institutions will receive these due to school funding limitations and to the logistical difficulties of performing an FWS job while incarcerated."

The way this translates to me is that practically every inmate is indeed eligible for financial aid, yet almost nobody is likely to receive it due to the manner in which policy dictates eligibility. Until we are free from incarceration it is highly unlikely that any of us would receive consideration for federal student aid.

NOTE: Upon my release on February 9th, 2015, I immediately enrolled at the Santa Fe Community College and began classes in their Criminal Justice program to receive an Associates in Paralegal Studies. I graduated in December of 2018. Prior to the beginning of each semester, I applied for the Federal Pell Grant via FAFSA. A student aid would direct me to a computer, they would key in the website where one applies, after which I would populate the necessary information and await my approval. I was approved every semester. The Free Application for Federal Student Aid (FAFSA) paid for my tuition and paid for my books until I earned my degree in Criminal Justice. I never needed to apply for a student loan, as I worked full-time in State government. I was also on probation while working and going to school full-time. There were moments of extreme difficulty and fatigue, but this was such a key component of my reintegration plan. I applied myself to the lesson's intent and succeeded. I also concede that I could not have done this without the Federal Pell Grant, and thank the federal government for their assistance... in this matter.

I'm currently enrolled in a college program in the federal prison system. Instructors come from Pueblo Community College to teach our class which consists of about 15 student inmates. These 15 students, including myself, are from a pool of about 1,200 inmates. The main reason for such a small class size is the lack of funding for educational purposes. Also, out of those 1,200 inmates, only about 50 of us applied for the program. Those are pretty low numbers but bear in mind most of us already knew that less than 20 students are selected for the class once every 18 months, as this is the limit of funding the government has for educational purposes.

The program normally takes about a year to complete, (give or take an additional 3 months for incidents such as lockdowns due to violence, etc.), and it takes us about two thirds of the way to an Associate's in Business Administration, but that's where the funding runs out.

Although I'm going to try my best to acquire a degree sometime after my release, I think it's going to prove quite difficult to complete school while I attempt to live up to the rest of my obligations, and I feel that it would be much more beneficial to myself, as well as to society, if I were given the opportunity to complete my education while still incarcerated.

I would be more than willing to pay the rest of the way myself but the amount of money I make through my job in prison, about 69 dollars a month, is hardly sufficient to cover my supplemental food costs, stamps, envelopes, and money for phone calls; let alone to cover the expenses for correspondence courses through one of the colleges located throughout Colorado.

Most of the information I've supplied pertaining to federal student aid thus far may seem pretty bleak, but that's only because the amount of aid one would receive while incarcerated is quite minimal, if not nonexistent. The amount that one is eligible to receive once that person is no longer incarcerated is sufficient, in most cases, to carry much of the financial responsibility students are saddled with until completion of their educational program.

The aid *only* comes once we are no longer in the custody of a federal, state, or local detention facility. And while the prospect of transitioning from prison to the streets is a hard enough feat to accomplish – without trying to obtain a degree at the same time – just know that there are many avereage citizens out there who have made their ascension through life by these same means, i.e., working hard and studying just as hard during their free time.

I feel I should convey just how demanding it can be to study and go to school while trying to maintain some semblance of balance in the environs of prison; but for lack of a better explanation, it is what it is.

The one benefit of furthering your education while incarcerated is that we don't have any of the normal responsibilities such as working, paying bills, taking kids to school, and a real life with real problems that would otherwise make attending college an added difficulty.

We do, however, have tons of extra time on our hands to better ourselves. If you don't have the money to pay for school while incarcerated, or if your family doesn't and is unwilling to pay for correspondence courses, I fear much of those years will be spent indulging in other pursuits.

NOTE: Thankfully, once we obtain our long-sought after freedom, there are complete curriculums that can be learned through community colleges as well as through online courses that have been improved upon since the Pandemic (COVID).

Correspondence courses drastically reduce the scheduling difficulties that arise from, say, leaving work and heading straight to school thereafter.

Also, recognize the positive reinforcement that furthering your education will provide, as opposed to possibly succumbing to the negative ones that extra time and empty pockets will surely entice us with.

To learn more about applying for federal student aid you can visit the federal government's website at www.studentaid.ed.gov/pubs.

SAVE HAVEN

I don't think there is anything more elemental, or more innate to one's existence and sense of well-being than having a home or place to live that is safe, comfortable and a sanctuary where we can lay head to pillow, cook food, relax, and decompress.

No matter how great the advances of today's society, no matter how convenient it is to acquire things instantly with a phone call or online order, the necessity for shelter is, and remains, the most fundamental aspect crucial - not merely for survival – but *living*.

Without it we have no foundation, no firm establishment, and no base point from which to launch ourselves into the world and at our intended ambitions.

We have no beginning, no centrality, and certainly not a sanctuary that protects, nourishes, and shields us from the bombardments life hurls at us on a daily basis. Without a place to call home, what we do have is a nomadic disposition which leaves no room for a firm and constant bearing in an other-wise tremulous existence.

Housing and shelter are, for me, the number one priority upon my release. It is the first step in liberating myself from the state of institutionalism I will be subjected to for over a decade. It was the thing that I strived for as soon as I was able to comprehend its significance. And it was, quite possibly, the thing that caused me to pursue my criminal career with such over-zealous enthusiasm to the point where it placed me where I am today.

I have a piddling amount of funds that were not seized along with everything else when I was arrested. But after putting them towards a deposit, and first and last month's rent, there won't be much left in the war chest.

The amount of worry that plagues me because of my lack of financial security is quite overbearing to say the least. I practically kick myself every time I think about the money I squandered that otherwise could have gone towards securing my future.

Thankfully, the assets that go towards providing housing for folks is something we can look forward to without that impending sense of doom. While I don't intend on seeking assistance for housing unless I have no other options, I thought it was of great importance that I familiarize myself with every aspect of housing programs.

NOTE: Upon my release, I moved into a shoebox of a rental unit connected with a main house that dad had found. The family that rented to us were nice, albeit you could hear arguments through the thin uninsulated sheetrock that separated their side of the house from ours. Massive desert centipedes abounded during the spring and summer. After saving up enough for a down payment and working a decent-paying job for over a year, I purchased a home in Santa Fe.

HUD or Housing and Urban Development is a nation-wide federally funded program whose purpose is to provide housing for those that are currently unable to afford it. Its mission is not to allow people to continue in a state of lethargy while under the wing of HUD, but to relieve some of the financial burdens that many people face, as a result of the high cost of housing, so that they may pursue educations and careers that will enable them to sufficiently provide for themselves and their families once they are in a position to do so.

Federal public housing authorities have great discretion in determining their admissions and occupancy policies for ex-offenders. While PHAs can choose to ban ex-offenders from participating in public housing and Section 8 programs, it is not HUD's policy to do so. In fact, in many circumstances, formerly incarcerated people should not be denied access.

On January 5th, 2011 during an Interagency Reentry Council Meeting, HUD Secretary Shaun Donovan reminded council member that "this is an administration that believes in second chances." He further stated, "And at HUD, part of that support means helping ex-offenders gain access to one of the most fundamental building blocks of a stable life- a place to live."

There are really only two convictions for which a PHA must prohibit admission- those are: If any member of the household is subject to a lifetime registration requirement under state sex offender registration program(s); and, if any household member has ever been convicted of drug-related criminal activity for manufacture or production of methamphetamine on the premises of federally assisted housing.

NOTE: I imagine fentanyl will be added to this list, as merely touching it can cause some people to overdose and die from its potency.

"Additionally, PHAS must prohibit admission of an applicant for three years from the date of eviction if a household member has been evicted from federally assisted housing for drug-related criminal activity. PHAs must also establish standards which prohibit admission if the PHA determines that any household member is currently engaged in an illegal use of a drug of the PHA determines that it has reasonable cause to believe that a household member's illegal drug use or a pattern of illegal drug use may threaten the health, safety, or right to peaceful enjoyment of the premises by other residents. PHAs must also formally allow all applicants to appeal a denial for housing giving the applicant an opportunity to present evidence of positive change since the time of incarceration."

Working within the parameters of the above regulations, many PHAs have established admissions and occupancy policies that have promoted reuniting families in supportive communities using stable housing as a platform for improving the quality of life.

Essentially, the public housing authorities are one of the more proactive departments dedicated to assisting felons. The only prohibitions which seemed to exist are good ones, as they're intended to keep sexual predators and harmful chemicals away from areas that are more than likely to house and have children nearby.

If housing is a concern for you, as it was for me, know that it is not as much of a cause for distress as some of our other obligations will be. To learn more about assistance and benefits through public housing, you can visit the HUD website at www.hud.gov. Housing applications can be mailed directly to the facility an individual is incarcerated at to further expedite the application process.

SUSTENANCE

I'm not overly familiar with the complexities of the welfare system, but I am acquainted with most of its basic workings to know there are some aspects of its makeup that have received far more criticism than others. Among these is the Food Stamp program.

Critics argued that "stamps" were being used as currency to purchase drugs and other commodities when they should have been going towards food. And in fact, they were being used to purchase food, but it was being purchased and consumed by the wrong people, namely drug dealers.

Drug dealers would accept food stamps for 50% of their original value by justifying to the drug users that they were only worth half their value because the only thing that could be purchased with them is food. Whereas money can purchase virtually anything that is for sale, food stamps became devalued due to their one-dimensional purchasing power. Also, when one craves illegal drugs more than food, one tends to overlook the 50% markdown on the only currency available.

Enter the era of the Food Card. This essentially looks and functions like a debit or credit card. A monetary amount is placed on the account (sometimes for food only, and in other cases for financial assistance). This dramatically reduced the amount of misuse of the food card, unless of course drug dealers were interested in buying food; in which case the card and its pin number would be provided to someone not on the account.

In 1996, convicted drug felons were banned from SNAP benefits. I believe the reason for this targeting and expulsion of drug offenders from the program were for two reasons: one, if you're selling drugs – unless you're selling them to support your own habit – you can afford to purchase food without government assistance. And two, officials realized that the main drain on this program were drug dealers accepting payment in the form of food stamps for their goods.

Taking into account the amount of revenue generated by local drug sales in a particular area, overtime the accrual can have a cumulative and staggering effect. And when some of that money is generated from government assistance programs, the efforts of every drug trafficker- operating in every town, every city and in every state, can drastically overtax a program that was initially designed to help alleviate impoverished areas.

Add to that the ever-increasing rate of addiction amongst the impoverished and you can begin to see the magnitude at which the Federal Food Program is being taken advantage of.

I think states realized, to some extent, that you can't completely ban people from this program simply because they have a felony drug conviction, or because they practice capitalism in the only fashion they're accustomed to, albeit illegally, without banning over half the people in the country that benefit from such programs.

Consequentially, many states have completely abolished the ban, while most have lessened the severity of its restrictions.

Instead, assets are going towards treatment programs that tend to have a more positive effect on individuals who are suffering from chemical dependencies, rather than to deprive people of food simply because they have an addiction, and possible drug convictions.

As I write this in 2013, only thirteen states have kept the ban in place in its entirety. Most states have modified or completely eliminated the ban. The states that have kept the ban entirely in place are Alabama, Alaska, Arizona, Arkansas, Florida, Georgia, Indiana, Mississippi, Missouri, North Dakota, South Carolina, Texas, and West Virginia. All other states have modified or eliminated it completely.

The following 18 states and the District of Columbia have completely eliminated the ban: Iowa, Kansas, Maine, Massachusetts, New Hampshire, New Jersey, New Mexico, New York, Ohio, Oklahoma, Oregon, Pennsylvania, Rhode Island, South Dakota, Utah, Vermont, Washington, and Wyoming.

The remaining 19 states have amended the ban to allow some applicants to regain eligibility by meeting certain criteria, like receiving or completing drug or alcohol treatment.

The SNAP program is fundamentally different from many of the federally funded programs available, (with the exception of HUD), because, like HUD, its purpose is more one that supplements needs of base survival, rather than assisting with things such as financial aid or programs that derive from sociological necessity. Earning a college degree, or perhaps acquiring a social security check after working the majority of your life should only supplement your retirement rather than being the basis of it. This represents a secondary requirement when compared to the needs that nutrition and shelter provide.

For more information, visit www.fns.usda.gov/snap/government/policy/htm

SOCIALLY SECURE

Crime is quite the paradox. It has the ability to generate myriad amounts of money, while at the same time relieving you of those gains as a result of being caught. What's more is that for the entirety we were committing crimes, we're not contributing anything to the whole. Bear in mind that that lack of contribution also means a lack of endowments earned through legitimate employment such as Social Security, pensions, 401k and other retirement plans and investments.

I fear that as criminals the majority of us never grasped the concept of investing for retirement beyond squirreling away as much money as possible, never realizing that those funds would be seized, or spent, instead, on lawyers that may or may not minimize the amount of damage the prosecutors and courts will inflict upon us to lay waste our flawed aspirations of success and subsequent enjoyment of the same.

Granted, the fear and projections abound as to SS funds becoming exhausted. But as I have alleged time and again, these programs are still here for the time being. I might also add that utilizing programs – as opposed to abusing them – by putting our fair share into sustaining initiatives, will also help to guarantee their continuity should we ever need to avail ourselves of their beneficence.

Generally, SS benefits are not payable if you've been convicted of a criminal offense and are currently incarcerated. However, monthly benefits are usually reinstated after a period of incarceration by contacting Social Security and providing proof of release.

Upon release, benefits can be reinstated without filing a new application. But you must first request reinstatement and provide proof of release to a Social Security office. Upon provision of the necessary proof, the Social Security office is required to reinstate benefits expeditiously.

If you never received SS benefits, but would like to; or,

more accurately, if you *need* to, you must file a claim and be approved before benefits can be applied to your case. For these individuals SS offers a prerelease application procedure which enables a claim to be filed several months *before* the scheduled release date. This process allows benefits to start shortly after release.

There are many misconceptions in prisons about people being able to receive SS benefits if they've been incarcerated for a period of 5 years or longer. It is believed by some that this amount of time renders ex-offenders disabled, as well as subjects of behavioral health disorders such as Post Traumatic Stress Disorder (PTSD) due to the traumatic experiences one endures while incarcerated. Not to mention, the side effects a life of captivity itself can produce.

Many believe in this misconception and use it to motivate themselves into attempting to acquire SS benefits simply because they were convicted of a crime and spent time in prison. And while it may be true that many inmates suffer from some mental or physical illness, it by no means makes us eligible to receive SS benefits simply because we acquired those illnesses while incarcerated; rather, it is the illnesses themselves that would make an individual SSI eligible.

A good example is a veteran who served their country in a combat zone, and came home suffering mental or physical illnesses that can be readily identified as an acceptable malady for which the VA provides treatment and compensation. Say a soldier was exposed to Agent Orange in Vietnam, or handled depleted uranium shells in Desert Storm.

Exposure to both of these doesn't qualify a veteran for VA benefits and compensation; rather, it is the subsequent illnesses associated to said exposure that would make a veteran applicable, i.e., Bladder Cancer, Chronic B-cell Leukemias, Hypertension, Hodgkin's Disease, etc.

By the time I was released, I had spent well over 5 years in the can. And although I'm sure there will be symptoms as a result of said incarceration, I hope that my level of PTSD or health-related issues for drinking water at FCI Florence – built in close proximity to a uranium mine – won't be at a level that would require me to apply for some form of assistance.

I think a reasonable conclusion is that it was the life I led while still free that had a stronger and more negative impact on me than the environs of prison. And that people who are in actual need of SSI would be the ones who receive its benefits, rather than those who are more than capable of supporting themselves.

This isn't to say that others who have experienced prison have done so with much more adverse effects as a result of their time behind bars.

I have noticed a growing trend in the prison system that is quite disturbing to witness. More and more people are entering jails and prisons who have mental and physical handicaps. Some of these individuals were born with difficulties while others incurred them through accidents or through intentional harm inflicted upon their person- both in the world and while in custody.

State-run mental hospitals saw a drastic decrease in funding. As such, their ability to house those for which they were constructed also diminished. Closure of state mental health hospitals began in 1967. The promise was that we would get smaller, community-based facilities... they were never built.

Purportedly, prisons have every resource at their disposal that psychiatric hospitals in years past have had, e.g., physiatrists, medical units, counselors, medications, etc. Thus, it is argued that it is unnecessary for two separate facilities to exist when one could serve the same purpose.

As a result of this pragmatic view, more and more people with mental illnesses and behavioral health disorders are finding their way into prison rather than to a hospital or treatment facility. The problem with this, as I'm sure you've guessed by now, is that these people have to be classified as offenders or convicted of breaking laws in order to receive "treatment" in one of our nation's penitentiaries.

I would argue that prison is by no means the appropriate place for someone suffering from mental and/or behavioral health disorders to receive help simply because treatments happen to be available there. Prison, in effect, seems to only worsen many of the disparaging side effects people exemplify as a result of their illnesses.

It seems hardly necessary to point out the obvious fact that prison is prison, it is not a hospital.

It would also pose more of an administrative and financial burden on the PIC due to these individuals' increased level of treatment, as the treatment they are likely to receive from some of their fellow inmates is by no means beneficial.

For those who truly need the benefits Social Security provides, or for those who need assistance in reinstating their status after being freed from custody, you can contact Social Security at www.ssa.gov.

For those of us who have a moderately clean bill of health in terms of mind, body, and soul, as well as a strong determination to advance, I suggest that we do just that, as the time for resigning ourselves to seeking financial assistance from Social Security has not yet arrived, and hopefully never will.

VETS

The VA or Veteran's Administration is quite like that of Social Security, with the exception that it provides services strictly for those who have served in the military. There are very few factors that would make a Veteran ineligible to receive his or her benefits, e.g., certain circumstances pertaining to a dishonorable discharge, or a particularly heinous crime committed while still in active service.

Statistics demonstrate that more and more Veterans are coming home from active duty only to find reintegration difficult. Interestingly, mental health professionals are noticing a correlation between experiences shared by inmates and Veterans. Both subsets display similar sentiments of frustration, incompatibility, and feelings of displacement upon reentry to society.

It was a reality at one point for Veterans to come home from serving only to find that the job they once held was no longer waiting for them. Thankfully, the law now asserts that if a member of the military is called into active service – while employed with a business – that that employer must reserve their position of employment until the service man or woman returns home from active duty.

Many veterans are returning home to find that the companies they were once employed with are no longer in business; thus, the search for work in an already emaciated job market ensues. Add to this disparaging reality PTSD and other health-related issues. And the combination of a difficult reentry can often lead to self-medicating and even committing criminal acts.

Regrettably, this is one of the many pitfalls that draws a growing number of Vets to the much-traveled route of criminality, either as a means to support their habit or as a means to supplement the income they no longer have; or simply as a way of venting the frustration of coming home to a world that has trouble acknowledging their efforts towards making it a better place.

I happen to be imprisoned alongside more Veterans than I ever thought possible; many of whom have trouble believing that their inability to find work, and their damaging modes of self-medication led them to where they are today. Thankfully, the Veteran's Administration works closely with veterans and their families, as well as communities and other branches of government, to ensure that veterans receive assistance upon their *second* attempt to reenter society, which is when they leave prison.

Because Veterans with criminal histories face additional barriers to employment and other services in their communities, and may be at increased risk for homelessness, the VA has two programs designed specifically to reach Veterans involved with criminal justice system. They are the Health Care for Reentry Veterans Program and the Veterans Justice Outreach.

The HCRV provides direct outreach to Veterans nearing release from state and federal prisons, emphasizing rapid association to needed health care and other VA community services. The VJO connects Veterans in contact with the "front end" of the system (police, courts, and jails), to mental health, substance abuse, and other treatment resources. Every VA medical center has a Veteran Justice Outreach Specialist who serves as the VA's liaison with the local criminal justice system.

Fortunately, Veterans can inform the VA to have their benefits resumed within 30 days or less of their anticipated release date based on evidence from a parole board or other official prison sources verifying the Veteran's scheduled release date.

An eligible Veteran, who is not currently incarcerated, can use VA care regardless of *any criminal history*, including incarceration. Only when an otherwise eligible Veteran is currently incarcerated, or in fugitive felon status, is he or she not able to use VA health care.

Because jails and prisons must provide health care for their inmates, the VA cannot treat Veterans while they are incarcerated. For Veterans who are not currently incarcerated and are otherwise eligible for VA healthcare, past involvement with the criminal justice system has no impact on their ability to enrol for or to receive health care. The only exception applies to veterans with an open warrant for a felony offence (fugitive felons), whom VA is prohibited from treating by a separate federal law.

The growing number of Veterans that are entering the

prison system, as a result of the many challenges they face upon returning home, is hardly a matter of a few men and women with adjustment problems. Rather, this is a dilemma whose epidemic proportions have now become recognized by virtually every community that has loved ones returning from combat zones.

Fortunately, the VA is not the only source of support available. There are now community initiatives that work in direct correlation with the VA in an effort to provide a greater amount of support for our Veterans.

For more information on the VA, as well as community initiatives you can contact the VA at www.va.gov or call 1-800-827-1000

NOTE: Upon returning home in 2015, I discovered that my dad had been trying to get his VA benefits for the past 50 years. While stationed in Pleiku, in the Central Highlands of Vietnam, dad witnessed several atrocities against the Vietnamese people by American servicemen, as well as acts of cowardice by his often-drunk commanding officers. I won't go into details except to say that for his actions, and the refusal to follow unlawful orders given by commanders, my father and several of his fellow soldiers were court martialed and given the option of prison time, or Other than Honorable Discharge and sent home. Dad chose the ladder. I immediately began filing for an overturn of his Other than Honorable Discharge. I can remember looking at his savings account one day (a couple years after I had applied on his behalf) and saw that a sizable sum of money had been deposited as back compensation from the VA. He also receives 100% medical coverage, additional compensation for other physical and mental health related issues incurred while serving in Vietnam, and a place of burial at the National Cemetary in Santa Fe, NM.

We try to thank him for his service at every opportunity.

THE BALLOT

One of the most impactful rights a citizen can practice – even if the pickings are slim – is the right to vote in the complex maze that is American politics.

As I previously pointed out, many criminals don't pay much heed to political elections, because the impact that a Republican, or Democrat, or Independent would have on us is relatively comparable, despite their insistence that their views are completely singular and unique from those of their political rivals.

The rather dismal turnout of votes from those who often find themselves on the wrong side of the law is for a number of reasons, many of those being fallacies about the rights, or lack thereof, of people who have felony convictions.

It is common knowledge amongst most criminals that the right to vote is permanently stripped from a person once they've been convicted of a crime, if that offense is classified as a felony or being more severe than that of a misdemeanor. I often joke with people that come to visit me here in sunny Florence Colorado, when the discussion of politics arises, that I no longer have to trouble myself with voting or jury duty, as my felony status mercifully relieves me of what seems like meaningless civil obligations.

Fortunately, my assertions concerning civil obligations were false, and my dull-witted jokes about being mercifully "relieved" from civic duty seem even more foolish now that I realize I hadn't the slightest idea what I was talking about; not to mention the fact that those rights should never be taken for granted, even if only in jest.

The only thing that kept me from feeling further shame at my ignorance of the law was that, ironically, each inmate I had this discussion with believed the same as I did.

The majority of people, in general, are of the mind that, once a person has been convicted of a felony crime they are permanently barred from voting in any political electoral process, be it of town, city, state, or federal appointment.

I can't say for certain if this mass disillusionment came from a voting agenda aimed at steering folks in an intended direction, and away from the ballots. But I will say that this misconception is quite common among criminals and civilians alike.

Even the guards and the prison administration believe this though it is within this very prison that I found irrefutable proof suggesting otherwise. I wanted to make sure said proof be substantiated by outside sources. Before I wrote about it, I contacted a friend of mine who in fact, found the same pages I had read in the prison law library on a federal government website.

"It is a common misconception that states permanently disenfranchise a person on the basis of a felony conviction. Every state is different with respect to disenfranchisement and restoring one's right to vote, but there is no federal law disqualifying people with convictions to vote."

Voting rights can be restored to people who have felony conviction, and in the States of Vermont and Maine, a person is *never* disenfranchised from their voting rights, even while incarcerated.

Only a few states do not allow re-enfranchisement, and those restrictions only apply to a few specific offenses. Generally, it is not a matter of whether one can vote, but how and *when* one can vote.

While many states do temporarily take away a citizen's right to vote for a criminal conviction, most states automatically restore that right once a person is no longer incarcerated or once they have completed probation or parole. Thus, in the real sense, most incarcerated individuals have their voting rights suspended, rather than stripped from them completely.

23 states suspend a person's right to vote until certain post-incarceration sentences and obligations are satisfied, including

probation and parole, and often times the payment of fees and restitution associated with such. 12 states require an additional waiting period, ranging from two to seven years and/or additional requirements such as applying for clemency or pardon from a governor, parole board, or judge, or even convincing a state legislature to pass a bill specifically designed to re-enfranchise an individual.

Some states do permanently disallow the restoration of one's voting rights but only for certain criminal convictions. These include Alabama, Tennessee, Ohio, and Maryland. In these states, even pardons, expunged records, or other such restoration methods can be prohibited.

Some sources incorrectly cite Virginia, Kentucky, Iowa and Florida as states that permanently disenfranchise individuals for criminal offenses. But all of these states provide restoration processes for all disqualifying criminal conviction, albeit some are lengthy.

If maintaining or reacquiring your right to vote is a necessary factor of your life, as it should be, you can visit the Sentencing Project at www.sentencingproject.org or you can also visit the National Conference of State Legislatures at www.ncls.org for information on enfranchisement rights.

The right to vote, and indeed, the very act of voting by more people whose liberal pursuits of capitalism are defined by law as illegal, is the very thing needed in order to reduce the amount of time that many of us are serving as a result of strict mandatory sentences for drug convictions and other non-violent offenses.

Criminals who pursue non-violent crime for financial gain, and who provide services for clientele knowing full well what they are paying for, are a far cry from criminals that commit crime for satisfying a sadistic urge, and more often than not, we are treated with more intolerance than offenders that criminals themselves feel should be punished with far more severity, e.g., rapists, child molesters, and other violent offenders whose victims are not criminals themselves.

Many of us tend to believe that this is one area of lax control and punishment that needs a closer examination, as sexual predators seem to receive far less punishment, only to be released and resume a vile form of predatory criminality once more.

I might add that this is also the reason criminals tend to deal with this subset with more finality than the legal system does, thus guaranteeing that they will no longer continue their abuse of targeted victims via revolving door catch-and-release policies.

These are just some of the reasons why voting is so crucial to every person who falls under the jurisdiction of law, which is to say, *everybody*. I can state with all certainty, that every capitalistic criminal who exchanges a product or service for a fee would vote on and take a harder stance on issues such as domestic violence, and rape and murder as compared to your average law-abiding citizen.

It is also reasonably feasible to surmise that most ex-offenders would take a more proactive approach to supporting lesser sentences for non-violent offenses, that otherwise burden tax payers and the PIC.

These are just a few examples why it is necessary to reinstate our right to vote as soon as humanly possible. Those of us who are still able to vote should practice this right whenever we are able, as the ability to change and help resolve systemic issues is within sphere of influence.

NOTE: After being terminated from probation early, I contacted the Santa Fe County Clerk's office. They instructed me to pull my records from each court I had been prosecuted in, i.e., municipal, district, and federal courts. Once they reviewed my early termination letter and verified that I had satisfied all other obligations from lesser courts, my right to vote was reinstated. I requested an absentee ballot this year as opposed to dealing with the political circus act that is fast metastasizing into an all-out shit show.

FOUNDATION

While the amount of support offered by both federal and state governments can be substantial, it's important that we come to recognize just how that support is obtained, and also, just how fragile these systems can be. But most importantly, we must recognize that that support could not be a reality without the honest, hard-working taxpayer.

Budgeting and prioritizing funds that are to be directed towards specific uses are not so much premised upon what issues are deemed important; but rather, which issues take political precedence over others, i.e., what generates revenue, what issues are politically correct to support or are argued against. And what produces the most results with the least amount of angst for taxpayers.

That angst, when continually fueled by disappointment and frustration in failed policies can lead to a less than favorable number of votes for the politician whose career lies in the balance.

Corporations and those whose interests are in direct relation to certain matters of importance usually have more at stake, at least financially, then they believe the average citizen does. It is for this reason that politicians can be obligated to two constituencies: those citizens that voted for them, and those corporations whose contributions and greater financial gain is hard to ignore.

There also exists, however, a rudimentary amount of core values and principles that accompany a political career which also cannot be ignored. Because of this, the majority of politicians are apt to feel the pull between several choices. First, the ethically correct choice that would benefit their constituents. Second, the pragmatically correct choice for the sake of a grander scale of prosperity as compared to the impact on a targeted minority of people. And finally, the decision that will guarantee the continuity of their own career.

Unfortunately, for the politicians, as well as their constituency, one cannot assure their own career without fully supporting only *one* of the three options. This reality leaves either a very large group of people feeling as if the politician they supported does not have their interests in mind, or a smaller group wielding far more influence placated by the decision of those politicians who make policy in their favor.

This paradox and the decisions made by ones who operate within its parameters is the fundamental truth that governs politics in America. It is a truth in which political pressure, numbers, and finances play a larger role as to how our laws and policies are formed than most would care to admit.

Most politicians focus more of their public debates on the moral aspects of life that people concern themselves with, or are subject to. Because politics or affairs of state are in fact, affairs of people; and ethics should never be excluded from any decision which affects the people. But numbers are also part of the equation which cannot go unnoticed unless disregard for one necessary element over another ruin the formula in its entirety.

Think about the amount of money – Gross Domestic

Product (GDP) – this country generates. Think about how much of that money goes towards maintaining relations with other countries in the form of aid, military commitments, agriculture, healthcare, education, and simply for the expectation that those receiving aid will keep our collective interests in mind.

Now consider how much funding our recent wars have cost us over the past 20 years. Consider how much other nation's wars have cost us. Think on how much money has been thrown at the War on Drugs and other efforts within our borders.

Try to imagine the amount of funding it takes to maintain the basic infrastructure of federal government and each administrative agency. There are 24 total ranging from the Department of Agriculture, Civil Rights, and everything in between.

Know that as of 2012 our National Deficit equaled our Gross Domestic Product, and has long since surpassed it. Basically, what this means is that our country now owes more money than it generates through the production of goods, services, etc.

It becomes easy to deduce that funds that were once squandered on failed policies – or policies in which the public and the people they were intended never received any benefit – will now be diverted towards merely maintaining administrative agencies at a subsistence level, i.e., stimulus packages to reinvigorate corporations, lending institutions, and other high-impact industries such as the car manufacturing business.

It is at this point that the buck stops: when folks who need federal, state, or local support should no longer expect it because the government, at all levels, will be too busy focusing on sustaining itself, lest it should fail in that regard as well.

The initial compulsory solution is to throw money at these problems in hopes that they will no longer be issues once the economy finds its proper balance. But nothing, including our economy, ever fixes itself, nor does it find its equilibrium via printing money and blindly investing it in systems and policies that have failed at the outset.

It is at this point, or shortly passed it, that we begin to lose the foundation of support that we so often take for granted.

I never saw myself as someone who felt a sense of patriotism. It would be safe to say that my arrest and punishment left me with a somewhat bitter experience with our federal government, and the manner in which it prosecuted my case.

Programs such as the ones mentioned in this chapter are things that would make even the least patriotic person feel inclined to be grateful for the efforts made on their behalf.

If your sense of patriotism does not fully extend towards government – as mine did not – at least let it extend towards the working-class taxpayers that constitute the bulk of our citizenry, without which, we would have no support to speak of.

Until recently, I gave little thought to these programs, nor for the amount of money taken through taxation from others in order to keep these programs alive. But I imagine those being taxed are well aware of just how much these programs are taking from them and their families, so that others may have a fighting chance as well.

By volunteering, working, and making selfless contributions upon my release, I will have devoted at least *something* to people that I have, thus far, given nothing- people and a construct I have only further burdened via my criminality and imprisonment.

I grasp now that although I may not be the most patriotic citizen, my sentiment can be manifested in lawful behavior, and by contributing, rather than taking, so that by carrying some of the weight others may feel less burdened.

This is the solution to ensuring the stability of programs that are already on the brink. The level of involvement with our contributions and our government should be a high priority for all returning citizens. My guess is that our participation will be appreciated by our fellow citizens as opposed to being met with skepticism and higher taxation.

When I think in terms of people rather than in terms of governing bodies, it becomes easier to feel the sensation that is defined by the word *patriotism*. And it becomes that much simpler to devote myself to a foundation of support based on people, and their efforts, rather than on government and its policies; in hopes that when the time comes, I may garner some support from that system as well.

PRIDE

Some of the aforementioned programs are not solely for felons. In fact, they're not even intended for people with criminal records. But the reality of falling on hard financial times is closely paralleled with criminal activity in an effort to supplement one's income; thus, given enough time, providing that person with a criminal background.

But to always associate people who are underprivileged with those whose behavior is of a criminal nature would be a false observation on my part. It's just that I see how easily the two can go hand-in-hand, more so when I reflect on my own choices and the destitution which motivated me. The significance of making the distinction between the honest underprivileged, and the criminal, is necessary to ensure that we don't mistake them as one and the same.

Know that there is an abundance of people who choose poverty over crime; who would rather live in a state of indigence than to break the law to rise above their precarious condition. I speak of those who make their way to the labor pools in the morning, who door-knock and offer cleaning or landscaping services, and even those who choose to politely ask for money rather than to take that which does not belong to them.

It is for these people that charitable support programs

were designed, and not for those who wish to make use of something that will enable their complacency, or what they deem to be an acceptable standard of living.

This gross manipulation of systemic support is a classic example of the abuse of something that was intended for another whose desperation may supersede our own.

It is rather disconcerting to see a person who has worked and successfully supported themselves their entire lives suddenly fall on hard times. It's even more troubling to see that same person's pride prevent them from taking part in programs that were designed to assist them now that the chips are down. Instead, they choose to survive by the same means they've always known, which unfortunately may not be enough to relieve them of their current state. Or even more distressing, by immersion in illegal activity which eventually reclassifies them as criminal; hence, a substandard citizen.

These programs are designed to help those who have worked most, if not all of their lives, and who may need to see the law of reciprocity take effect. Or for a teenager who suddenly finds themselves a parent with no education or means to further themselves while raising a child. Or even for the felon or ex-offender who is now ready to lead a life that constitutes more than just taking and earning for their own sake, without thought as how this impacts the rest of society. These programs are *not* in place for applicants to live off of in a state of perpetual welfare.

Someone whose very nature suggests idleness towards their own advancement could never be of assistance to those who take progress seriously. It is that very contentment to remain fixed in their current station in life that would also cause us to remain rooted, right along with them, should we choose to associate with those that possess such an inert disposition.

We must, as a matter of pride, and indeed, as a matter of survival, strive for advancement and continuance of success upon success, so that even if we do fail nine times out of 10, we are sure to hit the mark at least once.

At various intervals, we must also serve as a support for others, be they friends, family or complete strangers; thus, we too facilitate the cycle of foundational support, rather than being the mechanism which precipitates systemic failure.

I have a mind, that when focused on a goal, can be quite successful at achieving that goal. I have a body, one that easily runs five miles a day, and that can lift an amount of weight that the average person's body would find difficult to support. I have an insatiable curiosity and positive outlook on life that empowers me to view the most intimidating situations from a logical and calculating point of view; a point of view that informs me of my possibilities, challenges, and solutions.

If I am in possession of a strong mind, body, and spirit, I think it would be damaging to me, my self-esteem, and my very composition, to seek assistance from programs that I would otherwise be able to do without. This is one of those rare instances where pride does not come before the fall. Instead, it keeps the fall from coming to us, by not surrendering simply because there are programs that would enable us to do so.

I wrote this chapter so that others may see that there exists help from places we least expect it. I wanted to convey the need to explore every option available before succumbing to, or relapsing back into a state of criminality. It is for the criminal who no longer wishes to advance or retreat through crime that I write this. But for those who have no intention of changing their lives for the better, and contributing to the whole... I write nothing.

SUCCESSFUL REENTRIES, RECOVERIES AND TRANSITIONS

Fernando Ruiz

Born on August 26, 1977, Chef Fernando Ruiz began a life of crime at an early age. By the time he was 13, he was involved with a street gang, carrying firearms and delivering drugs in Phoenix, Arizona. He spent his 21st birthday in one of former Maricopa County Sheriff Joe Arpaio's tent cities, where he first learned to cook and obtained his GED.

After his release from prison, Chef Ruiz hit the ground running and never looked back. He attended culinary school in Scottsdale, where he excelled in his studies. He later moved to New Mexico, working as a private chef and cooking at various restaurants in Santa Fe and northern New Mexico. Encouraged by his wife, Michelle Romero, Chef Ruiz participated in and won several culinary competitions, including Guy's Grocery Games and Chopped. Notably, he gained attention on the Food Network when he beat Bobby Flay with his chiles en nogada dish.

In 2024, Chef Ruiz opened his first restaurant, Escondido, in Santa Fe, NM. He has since been featured in numerous news broadcasts, magazines, and other media highlighting his culinary talents and his community service efforts.

Chef Ruiz's passion extends beyond cooking; it is also deeply rooted in his past. He founded the Entrepreneurial Institute of Northern New Mexico and pioneered the Culinary Reentry Program, which started with inmates at the state prison in Santa Fe, NM.

Recently, Chef Ruiz celebrated the success of his first

graduating student from the New Mexico state prison. Since his return home, Chef Ruiz has helped him secure a restaurant job, find housing, open a debit and savings account, and enroll in a local gym. The success story has been featured on KOBTV Channel 4's "Hometown Heroes" series.*

Chef Ruiz credits his wife, Michelle Romero, as the driving force behind his success. He states, "It is true that behind every great man is an even greater woman."

---

* https://www.kob.com/community-stories/true-heroes-fernando-ruiz/

Ralph Martinez

Ralph Martinez was born on February 22, 1978, and raised in Espanola, NM. At a young age, he began trafficking and later experimenting with illegal drugs. Ralph has several felony convictions and has been incarcerated in detention centers across the southern United States.

He eventually became addicted to heroin, alcohol, and crack cocaine, living under a bridge in his hometown for several years while his health deteriorated.

In 2012, Ralph began to observe life, including his own, through a different lens. Watching his children grow older without him motivated him to choose recovery. Now, he has been sober for over 13 years.

Since his recovery, Ralph has dedicated his life to educating, training, and helping others break the cycles of addiction, recidivism, and homelessness. He has raised over $4 million for various causes, including the Espanola Pathways Shelter, Pathways Village Recovery Living Facility, and the Entrepreneurial Institute of Northern New Mexico. Ralph is also a co-founder of many of these nonprofits.

Defying the stigma often associated with being a convicted felon, Ralph secured his career pathway as a Government Relations Manager at Los Alamos National Laboratory. He continues his volunteer and philanthropic efforts through the EINNM, where he and Chef Fernando Ruiz developed the Culinary Reentry Program, teaching inmates cooking skills and job placement in restaurants in New Mexico upon release.

In 2018, Ralph had his felony record expunged and received a pardon from the governor of New Mexico in 2019. He now lives in the home he built for him and his family.

Jimmy Santiago Baca

Born on January 2, 1952, Jimmy Santiago Baca is an American poet, memoirist, and screenwriter from New Mexico.

Baca was born in Santa Fe, and was abandoned by his parents at the age of two. He lived with one of his grandmothers for several years before being placed in an orphanage. At the age of 13, he ran away and ended up living on the streets. When he was 21, he was convicted on drug possession charges and incarcerated. He served five years in prison, three of them in isolation. During this time, having expressed a desire to pursue education, he was placed in the same area of the prison as the Death Row inmates for a period before his eventual release.

While in prison, Jimmy taught himself to read and write, and he began composing poetry. He wrote an essay titled "Coming Into Language," which reflects on his upbringing and the challenges he faced. Baca wrote about his struggles in prison and how he discovered the beauty of literature through reading. He even sold his poems to fellow inmates in exchange for cigarettes. A fellow inmate encouraged him to submit some of his poems to the magazine Mother Jones, which was then edited by Denise Levertov. Levertov published Baca's poems and began corresponding with him, ultimately helping him find a publisher for his first book.

Santiago Baca also wrote the screenplay for the Hollywood film Blood In, Blood Out. He not only worked as a screenwriter but also appeared as an actor in the film and served as one of its producers.

He is the recipient of the prestigious International Award for his memoir, A Place to Stand, which is also the title of a documentary based on his story.

Jimmy continues to work closely with various communities

and the New Mexico Corrections Department to reduce recidivism and promote successful reintegration for returning citizens.*

Isaac Vallie-Flagg

Born on April 8, 1978, Isaac Vallie-Flagg is an American mixed martial artist who formerly competed in the Lightweight division of the Ultimate Fighting Championship (UFC). A professional competitor since 2003, he has also fought in Strikeforce, Titan FC, and King of the Cage.

Isaac has been open about his struggles with drug addiction, which began during his teenage years. He has faced challenges with heroin, methamphetamine, alcohol, and prescription pills. In 2018, he was arrested on suspicion of burglary in Albuquerque, New Mexico, while in possession of drugs and multiple weapons. After being released from jail, he sought help and has remained sober since that time.

Throughout his journey, Isaac attended various treatment centers but had difficulty finding success until he made the commitment to change. In 2016, he married Yvette Rojas.

In 2024, Isaac became the New Mexico General Manager for Interstate Roofing. Under his leadership, the New Mexico branch generated over $2.6 million in revenue during its first eight months of operation, providing roofing services to residents of the state. Isaac promotes Interstate Roofing as a company that understands criminal histories and offers second chances to returning citizens.

In addition to his professional achievements, Isaac

---

* https://www.jimmysantiagobaca.com/

continues to train at Atos Jiu-Jitsu. He recently participated in the Bare-Knuckle Fighting Championship and enjoys being a father to his stepdaughter, Maddy.

INTERMISSION

If you have read up to this point, then you are halfway through. And I can only hope that those of you who have made it this far are willing to go a little further.

After reviewing the chapters I've drafted thus far I can see that I have rather unintentionally used a few different writing styles. I don't have an editor, or even anyone resembling a constructive critic besides my fellow inmates. As such, I'm hoping that it will be acceptable if my approach concerning certain subjects alters and shifts with each passing page.

When I express my concerns about this, I'm told that I'm being overly critical, and that it is being written exactly the way it should be, or the only way it *could* be. They justify their advice by pointing out that although this work essentially covers one main topic, the many complexities involved in the delineation of that one topic call for a broader spectrum of clarification, as opposed to a simple monologue of instruction and advice.

Another uncertainty I have is the use of strong language, namely in the first couple chapters. While I'm rather fond of cursing, I don't think overuse of it would complement this manuscript the way I intended.

Someone once told me that those who curse do so because they lack the intelligence to properly express their thoughts without the use of expletives. And while this may be true, I think it's also true that using expletives, to some degree, only amplifies one's intent, and the seriousness they mean to convey through the spoken or written word.

Subsequently, in order to counter the effects of writing a thoroughly unentertaining and insipid manuscript, I elected to

include some earnest arguments that may at times be punctuated with a curse word or two... or three.

Above, all, I wanted to impress upon people whose lives
are impacted by the choices they make the seriousness of the
resulting consequences, without using obvious scare tactics
that would undermine, or diminish the practical rationale
society employs when dealing with those who use crime as a
means to further themselves.

STEPS

After outlying in detail, the many drawbacks that accompany
the criminal lifestyle, I wanted also to impress upon the reader
the need to recognize what motivates one to commit crime for
profit... a part from the profit. I also felt it necessary to
communicate the need for diversions, hobbies, and the slow
yet steady regression from our criminal activities to ones that
are more productive, and above all, legal.

It's also important that we learn where our criminality
originated so that we're not justifying the continuance of the
same for the wrong reasons, as I was.

As we discover in Chapter 2, Fear Itself, I believed, and
still do, that my own criminality didn't begin at the moment in
time where I first thought it did. But much earlier than that.

Using the excuse that I was underprivileged in order to
justify selling drugs was just that- an excuse. I truly feel that
had I not endured hard financial times that I would have
found some other justification for my involvement in illegal
activity, such as wanting to supplement my income or the like.

I implore each of us to look at our own situations and see
if you can determine the exact moment, or moments, where
you began to think outside the parameters of what is legally
acceptable; either by our own volition or capitulation, or by
someone or some circumstance that caused you to travel a
somewhat darker path than most.

I believe you'll come to find, as I did, that your choices were not steeped in reason, but in impulsiveness, intimidation, or even fear.

Next, I felt it was necessary to compare you, as well as your fears, to those of legitimate people in hopes that you would see that they are just as uneasy as we are when it comes to searching for and obtaining employment. And that the fear or anxiety one experiences when trying to divert their life from the path it is on, to a better one, is a universal angst experienced by all.

Many of us, legitimate and criminal alike, will at one point or another have employment history that is either non-existent or seriously lacking in one regard or another. But allowing this to handicap us can be a deprecating act, as opposed to improving yourself through education and experience; thus, potential employers will see a progressive advancement in someone who may have had a slow start, but is now building momentum and skillsets through working, volunteering, furthering their education, or all three.

Fear can be such an influential part of life – if we allow it to – which can often lead to bad decisions. Or it can be an instrument, that when controlled, becomes the very motivation which drives us to advance in the face of fear; to harness and use it as a means of conquering any adversity, no matter what its size or dimension.

Legitimate employment on one hand is simply a means of income, but so too is crime. And I felt it necessary to devote no small amount of attention to this subject, because I feel that many of us regard good jobs as things that are only obtainable by people who've been working most of their lives, or by those that don't have any criminal history to speak of that would otherwise damage their prospects of landing a decent entry-level position.

Fortunately, this theory holds no value in the real world. The reality is that good jobs are out there just waiting to be filled. And how we choose to market ourselves – and the skills we garner through education, through experience, and through previous employment – are the abilities which capture the interest of prospective employers.

On the other hand, it's important to remain positive and know that a good job or career can also come by way of other means, i.e., networking, knowing the right people, and sometimes simply being in the right place at the right time.

In truth, many people obtain employment via an association with a friend or colleague already employed with the company in question. Success or advancement by association should always be practiced by the fostering of meaningful relationships. To not do so is to impair ourselves in a way that most would never freely choose to.

If we're not exactly computer savvy and the prospect of creating a resume seems daunting to you, I would suggest getting help from FFC or contacting a career counselor at a community college. As stated previously, feel free to copy/paste the examples I've included in this manuscript.

Mastering the basics of computers is a relatively easy and intuitive feat to accomplish these days. And it usually begins with getting that first smart phone whose software and system platform often resembles that of its big brother, i.e., a tablet, laptop or desktop computer. If you haven't done so yet, now would be a good time to level up.

If we are the type that exhibits a reluctance to immerse ourselves in some but not all things technical, I implore you to disregard that particular aversion, as this will make it much more difficult to become a part of something that the majority of the world has already embraced.

Enrolling in a computer literacy course, or learning from others are perhaps the best jump-off points for immersion in this particular skillset.

The next step I wanted to impress upon the reader is the importance of being able to blend, and to not do things, nor to behave in a manner, or to dress in a way that would identify you as a criminal. When speaking in terms of damage control, I think this is perhaps the most important chapter of this book (Incognito).

The need to blend and to stay under the radar, while we're still criminals, is something that hardly needs justifying. But the knack for avoiding detection and arrest, while trying to change your life around, is much more important to the soon-to-be retired criminal than it could ever be to the one that still practices crime.

Getting arrested while you're still doing dirt is just par for the course. It's just one of the many cons that come with the Life, and most criminals accept it as such. But getting arrested, and convicted, while you're trying to transition is tantamount to ruining your chances at a new existence before it even moves beyond its beginning stages. "Killing it in its cradle" would be the most apt expression.

Sadly, many of us have lost, thrown away, or simply traded our camouflage for something as vain and as self-deprecating as the need to be recognized as someone greater than what we currently are. When I think of this mass event, I also think there are still issues to be discussed where using an expletive or two would not be uncalled for.

While my hope is that we all come to retire our criminal pursuits, I would never expect any of us to relinquish our ability to protect ourselves by blending with the rest of the herd. And I hope this trend of seeking validation will soon only be practiced by criminals who deserve the negative outcomes that their crimes will afford; thus, effectively killing the ability to blend – for the wrong reasons – definitively in its crib.

"Out of the Frying Pan" is essentially a guide which instructs the reader on how to successfully survive probation and parole. But there are many pieces of advice within that chapter than can be applied to virtually every other aspect of social compatibility. The talent to be flexible when dealing with others, and with personalities that don't mesh well with our own is a skill that is practiced by virtually every competent and successful business person.

To master the art of dealing with people – through compliance, placation, assertiveness, circumvention, or cordiality – are skills that will greatly improve every aspect of our lives.

"Foundation" is a chapter whose contents can either be used to great benefit or great detriment. I found it difficult to write about, as we can either avail ourselves of its support, or it can serve as an enabler that hastens the process of corroding one's independence; thus, we succumb to the ideology of victimization that so many are readily embracing.

I would much rather stand on my own two, if I am able, than to lean upon others for no other reason other than because they allow me to. And knowing that I tried my damndest would make it easier for me to feel gratitude as opposed to shame when I humbly and graciously accept assistance from programs whose very design is aimed at helping those who have, at one point or another, contributed to supporting the system itself.

If you're thinking, as many do, that if it's there why not make use of it? You might also consider that that train of thought can lead to justifying other actions that could be considered lazy or fraudulent. And also, quite similar to the very practices and lifestyles which we are, at present, trying to escape.

In essence, I feel that to use these programs when they are not needed is to further indulge in behavior that is more reminiscent of complacent criminality, and less demonstrative of one who wishes to advance via self-motivation and independence.

REGRESS

The first half of this manuscript is dedicated to identifying one's criminality for the damaging and reprehensible thing that it is. It also is designed to show that a gradual and systematic weaning from this lifestyle can be a more favorable approach, for some, than to go cold turkey, as this leaves loose ends and criminal clutter that almost always causes a reversion back to crime time-and-again. Under the pretext that we weren't quite ready, or we needed more time, or we still have obligations to others, to ourselves, and to our families, that otherwise could not be fulfilled unless our criminal obligations are satisfied as well.

And while I feel that a gradual declination of criminal acts can also leave us open to liabilities, I'm convinced that the harm that comes to us through a constant cycle of recidivism would be more damaging than the effects that a measured and steady withdraw would present.

This is the reason why I chose to promote a gradual adaptation to change, because the finality that accompanies brash decision making is often irreversible. Case in point- I'm writing this from prison. But with steady and calculated movements we can guide ourselves in the right direction, with as few deviations from that pathway as possible.

The choice that I have elected on has also proven to be a sort of mental training ground for me and my fellow inmates whom are now practicing it. We've all began to notice that we find ourselves talking less about who owes us money on the streets. Who ratted and how best to go about exacting revenge, and how we're going to get back to business under the guise of legitimacy while committing crimes on probation. And other negative thought processes similar to these.

Sure, I'm still in prison, and survival here often runs contrary to methods of survival in the world. But bear in mind we are talking about transitioning from survival on the

Inside, to succeeding and actually *living* on the outside... and not merely on a subsisting plane.

We're finding that we focus more and more on genuine positive planning for the future, such as what job markets, commodities, stocks, real estate and other ventures will look like upon returning home. I'm not holding these discussions with white-collar criminals. But with prison and street gang members, drug dealers, bank robbers, and those of every stripe, color and creed.

And also, how to avoid harmful settings and other gravitational allures that might bring trouble our way, i.e., clubs, dope houses (think the kids are calling them trap houses these days, and it fits), and old haunts in the neighborhood. How to substitute those places for activities and venues that can provide the same sense of entertainment and diversion without compromising our safety and freedom, such as vacationing, MMA training or the like.

Going cold turkey often leaves a void in our life that – unless replaced with activities as equally satisfying as those we're trying to forego – will leave us unfulfilled in our new existence, an inadequacy no longer having a role of significance in our current vocation. This sentiment is what leads us back towards what we practice best; that and the fact that our legitimate careers are never, initially, as financially satisfying as our criminal careers were.

EQUILIBRIUM

People's success is often measured by the amount of money they're able to generate, and we as criminals apply this form of measurement to our own worth as well. But many are finding that equating money with success, and even contentment, can be a flawed formula for the measurement of each. And that money fulfills many needs with the exception of certain emotional gratifications.

Studies are showing that careers that are intrinsically rewarding are proving more satisfying than merely striving for financial success through jobs that provide no reward with the exception of significant monetary compensation. Interestingly enough, financial success seems to come easier; almost effortlessly, when we're living lives and working jobs that we love as opposed to pursuing a career with the end goal of generating the most revenue for our efforts.

This doesn't imply that jobs that are agreeable are ones that are more than likely going to pay less. It simply means that doing something you enjoy over something that pays more money is going to provide more satisfaction across the board.

I would never have anyone believe that money doesn't buy happiness; because, to an extent, it most definitely can, more so for those of us that measure happiness via material gain and financial security.

In this sense, money brought me tons of happiness, and I didn't feel in the least deprived or lacking in anything. But a person's needs and wants change over the course of time. And the things money *can* buy quickly become dissatisfying and lackluster once they're obtained.

I found myself searching for other things that were to me, unattainable, more so when I consider they were of a nature that couldn't be purchased.

"Money isn't everything." That statement usually garnered whoever was saying it to me a harsh reproach; or, at the very least, a request to hand over to me whatever money they had on their person seeing how it wasn't "everything" to them. I often expressed this point to people with more anger and assertiveness than they thought their statement permitted.

While I'll agree that the response I usually gave was by no means appropriate, I think the initial lack of truth with which that statement is often given is quite an unnecessary notion to have me or anyone else lacking money believe. Money is the very thing which makes it possible to have or acquire literally *anything* in the modern world, at least when we speak in terms of material goods and services, which is to say practically *everything.*

Most people who have voiced that belief already had more than a fair amount of money and success, or they were born with it or inherited it. And working in order to put food in their mouths, or to pay bills and keep their children clothed has *never* been something they had to consider. I pointed these facts out to them in no delicate way.

Those who have had to work hard to be in a position of financial security will tell you just how important the role that money plays in their lives, and they will just as passionately try to convince people that it is indeed, *everything-* just as fervently as I voiced my opinion to those who've never been in a position to grasp the significance of their own security.

But these people, too, are on the extreme side of the spectrum, rather than being harmoniously balanced somewhere in the middle. I know because I was one of these people, and my life experiences, or lack thereof, suffered heavily, as I never enjoyed the things that money could have afforded me, because I was too damned busy worrying about making more money.

So where does the balance come from? I think for me, it comes from striving to reach financial security while focusing raw ambition into something more tempered; and then balancing the two with taking the time to enjoy life, instead of seeing daily living as a triviality that only slows our pursuits of financial success.

I promised myself that when I'm free I'm going to use a more well-rounded approach to life. I'm going to stop and smell the roses, or listen to a track that someone sends me rather than letting it be buried in the text string. And I hope that those of you who are already out there attempt to do this as well. Because it is so vital to make that conscious decision of placing the same amount of importance on things of an aesthetic nature, as it is on those of material significance.

If we prefer one over the other, we are in discord, and will find ourselves in a constant state of struggle or angst without truly knowing *why*. If we cannot enjoy the fruits of our struggles, we missed the point of the struggle in the first place. Or we may end up one of those people whose justification of an unfulfilling life will manifest in the form of witty phrases such as, "money isn't everything."

Balance is the key to every aspect of life. To earn our bread and butter through crime is to drastically upset that balance, as the forces that move to prevent our criminal success are a much heavier offset than the those that oppose conventional methods of making it in the world.

I understand – with no small measure of certainty – that this never would've occurred to me when I was out there chasing after success in an illegal fashion. It is for this reason that my life is as horribly skewed and offset as it is at present: the very reason I write to you, not from the confines of my house, or during lunch-breaks at the office, but from prison, where the Unbalanced got to either find their equilibrium or to become further unhinged by allowing the experience of prison to prevail over them, rather than being the instrument which provides us with the equanimity we've sought after much of our lives.

I encourage those who read this to find that ever-crucial balance in life. To seek after and enjoy the things that bring balance to the imperfection that a constant pursuit of wealth will afford. For to seek wealth without seeking emotional and spiritual stability is to become unbalanced. And to search for happiness or spiritual contentment, without the practicality of monetary support, is to have contentment that is not complete, but rather, temporary and inconsistent, and over-shadowed by thoughts of financial insecurity.

ADVERSITY

Each time I was arrested, or defeated (if you will), it only made me want to try harder to win, to overcome, to persevere; or more accurately, to attempt to vanquish an adversary that can never be conquered. It only made me determined to devote more of myself and my focus towards crime, while simultaneously avoiding arrest for longer periods of time, if not indefinitely. Of course this is an absurd impossibility, particularly when you consider that the more crime one commits, the more likely it is that that person is eventually going to get caught.

For those whose job it is to fight or curb the effects of crime, to them it is simply a social sickness that must be cured or managed using the tools available, i.e., arrest, confinement, a criminal record established, followed by limitations on that person's freedoms or abilities to continue down an incorrect path.

The efficiency demanded from those who are tasked to fight crime do not leave much room for managing people first and problems second. To them, they, we, are one and the same.

Because of this, and because of our own emotional investments, the personal aspects of punishment that accompany our arrests have an amplifying factor on our psyche, more so than the actual punishment itself.

Have we ever given any thought as to how it must feel to law enforcement to constantly arrest people, only to have other willing individuals spring up in their place? While I'm sure this provides for good job security, I imagine it also feels like an uphill battle that likewise pulls several psychological strings in the minds of law enforcement officers; thus, lending a personal nature to their jobs in kind.

Law enforcement often has open cases on suspects that

never amount to anything. All the while their suspects are free for the time being, and operating with impunity and complete disregard for the law these individuals represent. This also tends to make matters more personal for law enforcement; thus, generating feelings of incompetence and frustration, or worse... reprisal.

I suspect, also, that those who are employed through law enforcement are often overcome with feelings that started off as dedication, earnestness, and devotion to an intrinsically rewarding career, but have since metastasized into bitterness, frustration, or overzealous tendencies with respect to certain targeted subjects.

Such feelings can then be expressed during arrests by gloating over those whom they just placed the cuffs on, sometimes in a rough and physical fashion, with brutality occurring before, during and after. Exhibiting "victories" such as these over the public, and criminals, can instill within those arrested the need to further dedicate one's self to crime, rather than allowing themselves to be "scared straight" or to acquiesce to an adversary whose joy over our downfall can hardly go unanswered.

The adversarial cycle – once formed between criminal and law enforcement – creates an environment of fervent and personal dedication in people, on both sides, as opposed to the professional indifference with which both occupations should be practiced.

Resulting from this overdose of human emotion, and other factors, stems the urgent need to succeed by both parties; further perpetuating the job security of law enforcement, while simultaneously invigorating the spirit of determination in people who commit crime.

By shedding light on the criminal's factual role in this tragic play – not by disillusioning one's self or by taking our profession and its drawbacks personal – my hope is that we will begin to see the futility in combating a system and going after an enemy that has no centrality, no head to cut off, and no beginning nor end.

To also identify ourselves as the enemy, and to understand the adversarial role that our criminality plays in defeating us, is to identify a threat that is much more damaging, personal, and in your safety bubble than law enforcement will ever be.

OVERVIEW

The second part of this manuscript will focus primarily on the personal and social issues that are nuanced and affected by crime; how to identify and help others make positive transitions in their lives, and also, how to effectively and permanently conclude a life of social, moral, and spiritual ineptitude.

The goal is to examine the many different types of criminality, why they exist, and how best to steer those who are still involved to pursue other courses in life that will benefit them – while at the same time –filling and or replacing the great material void for which the fruits of crime are so often responsible for perpetuating.

I don't think it's realistic to suppose that anyone, myself included, will ever fully grasp the "how" or the "why" of crimes such as the ones described in this work. But be that as it may, the side effects themselves have greatly impacted my own life; to such an extent, that I felt I should make some effort at deterring others from practicing, and then being influenced by the same.

I hope, too, that others will take up the torch and perhaps discover more effective solutions than the ones I have thus far provided.

I wholeheartedly agree with *most* of the measures society has developed to combat certain aspects of crime, and I will go into a bit more detail on these arguments as they align with context in each chapter.

I especially want to shed light on sentencing guidelines that require the offender to serve mandatory minimum sentences for drug convictions and non-violent offenses, as opposed to the often-lenient forms of punishment for offenders that operate on the far opposite of the criminal spectrum. In many instances, there are no mandatory minimum sentences, and far less severity for crimes such as rape, molestation, and violence.

We as a society – as purportedly the freest society in existence – have the ability to implement treatment and punishment that is much more effective and far less damaging than the policies currently in place.

New ideas and more efficient measures can very well become reality if people choose to take a more hands-on approach to moving them from theoretical to practice. The reality of progressive change first begins with the individual either affected, or aware of the problem at hand. It is correct to assume that if certain changes made by us, the individuals, prove successful that others with similar intentions albeit different processes might then follow suit. And bring about additional changes in policy and procedure that are universally beneficial for everyone.

I hope that you, the reader, will take time to study, consider, and indeed believe in the reoccurring theme that is woven into this work. The significance that awareness and self-motivation affords is very real, and is just as self-perpetuating as the negative aspects of criminality, if not more so, as it provides a transition that begins with and benefits you, but will by no means end with you.

While crime may seem worth pursuing in the beginning, know that it is in complete and utter discord with every single institution, society, practice, observance, religion, theory, belief system, principle, credence, and law known to mankind. And because of this, our labors and criminal pursuits will be twice as difficult, twice as perilous, and twice as likely to fail, because of the imbalance and lack of conformity which accompanies the criminal lifestyle.

Positive action causes a ripple effect that is contagious, conducive, and in harmony with all legitimate efforts of progression.

With focus, determination, and sometimes even with ease, it will extend to every aspect of your life, and it will substitute parts of your life that were once fraught with negativity and hardship, with simplistic yet positive proficiency. Bleak outlooks towards a bleak future gradually begin to dissipate, and are exchanged for realistic obtainable goals, that in kind will lead towards even greater challenges and subsequent accomplishments.

Accomplishments, when taken into account collectively, will eventually provide a life of sound structure whose firm and unshakable foundation was built by your own resolve and ability to change.

Remember that like attracts like. People within your sphere of influence will be affected by this change; and, as a result, we will be surrounded by others, and by a tangible reality that no longer reflects the uncertainty and negativity that permeates a fearful existence.

I don't make these statements because I have faith in their validity. I make these statements based on the results of practicing positive self-motivation in my own life, in prison no less, and under such grating duress as to leave no doubt as to the results' origins. And yet, it is the minority of positive thinkers who persevere, who multiply, and who begin to outweigh the number of negative thinkers that were once prevalent among us.

There are men and women within the PIC that have no likelihood of going home, no chance of ever receiving a visit from a friend or family member, and no hope for a life beyond the one in which they live. And yet the manner in which they arise each morning and tidy up their cells, the jobs they go to, the exercises they perform, the arts they practice be it painting or cutting hair, drawing or studying a profession they may never have the opportunity to practice... the sheer moral strength they exude keeps them not merely treading water with their heads barely above the surface, but thrashing forward and achieving advancement and near perfection in everything they set their minds to.

I implore the rest of us who have the good fortune of second chances to learn from the example of those who have no hope of getting a do-over. And yet they fight with every fiber of their being to live as fulfilled as they possibly can. Such is the nature of the human spirit.

I implore the reader to consider the steps outlined in this manuscript as if your life depended on it, because it most certainly does.

I urge each of us to deny the allure of crime and the seemingly endless number of benefits that it will *initially* promise; to recognize it for the harmful and reprehensible thing it represents to us and our interests. For to pursue it and to utilize it, is to abuse it, and have it eventually consume you entirely without you even knowing it was there; that it was real, containing substance, seduction, and consequence... and promises of dreams that were already broken before you even conceived of them being possible.

The hypnotic magnetism of crime was something that disillusioned me from the time I was a child until not long before I decided to undertake this work. For two decades and counting I have been a slave to the prestige, social status, and monetary benefits that crime provided me with. For over two decades I have been living in bondage to a notion of success that made it impossible for me to conceive that other, better routes were even an option.

The course that I am now on is not one that we should all have to experience before seeing the truth of things. It is not necessary for each of us to spend time behind bars, lose the ones we love, and lose our freedoms over something as obtainable as financial security or social status. It is for these reasons that I write to you now.

7

THE DISTINGUISHED CRIMINAL

 "It is better to be hated for what you are than to be hated for what you are not."

— ANDRE GIDE

WHEN I FIRST STARTED THIS project, one of the beliefs in the back of my mind – insisting and pushing itself ever forward – was the need to enlighten readers as to the two types of criminals and why it is necessary to make a distinction between the two. The more I shared this concept with my fellow inmates, the more they supported and wanted to enforce that this narrative be added into drafts and hopefully a final print.

What's the point of distinguishing one criminal from the other, you ask? Well, for starters, I don't care to be associated with those who practice criminality which runs contrary to the Criminal Code of Conduct (CCC). And 99.99% of criminals who abide by the Code do not like being associated with this subset either.

There are practical reasons for us wanting to be disassociated from those who are not like-minded; who, from our perspective, often receive unjust and lenient sentences for crimes of a sexual or violent nature, and for which the victims are innocents, civilians, women, and children who should therefore be exempt from being marked or targeted by *anyone* for any reason.

We also believe that crimes of a capitalistic and bilateral nature – where one party sells a service or product, and another party inspects, approves and purchases said service or product – without double-crossing the other side are a far cry from criminals who commit murder, rape, mass-shootings or other reprehensible acts simply because they are compelled to do so.

But how does this distinction benefit society? How does it benefit you, the reader, whose civilian designation may preclude you from knowing the difference, or even caring? I can assure you that knowing the difference between the two – particularly if you have dealings with them, or, if you are one of them – can be of great advantage for obvious and not so obvious reasons.

Most of us who follow the Code see ourselves, rightfully so, as people whose business is deemed illegal by law, but whose morality when it comes to violent and or sadistic acts is manifested in an immovable set of values which prohibits us from engaging in such acts; and, even more to the point, it prevails upon us to punish the criminals that do, as we feel that the punishment afforded them by the law is in no way reflective of the severity with which these people prey upon their victims.

Knowing which is which can often be the difference between life and death, more freedom for violent offenders or less, or merely the outcome of a discussion whose finer points can either be argued by us, or by the more informed person next to us.

The one defining quality that separates the "good" criminals from the bad is strict adherence to the Code that all good criminals practice. This code, in essence, provides structure, order, and guidelines to an otherwise lawless form of existence.

Without regulation of crime by criminals, lawlessness would never align with policy that would allow it to function within parameters tolerable to society and its subsets. A lack of a CCC would also make it difficult to have any measure of control or stability resulting in profit and best practices in an otherwise tumultuous market.

We must consider that most crime merely consists of providing products and services that happen to be illegal or unregulated; thus, it isn't so much a matter of those products and services being *harmful* as it is a matter of non-regulation and taxation of the same.

NOTE: Fentanyl has changed the drug market for the absolute worse. It is not regulated, nor buffered to prevent those ingesting it from experiencing harmful side-effects including death. No matter what your poison, be it cocaine, opioids, THC oil, ecstasy, ketamine, methamphetamines, you name it... it can be laced with fentanyl. Therefore, you may not be addicted to your drug of choice, but to fentanyl, and all that comes with it. It's an interesting thing to hear law enforcement dismiss cocaine (or even heroin) as sideshows compared to the newest enemy that fentanyl represents. It feels demonstrative of the crack epidemic in the 80s, then crank, the resurgence of heroine, and now this. Not long ago, I was looking at about an ounce of coke someone was proudly showing me (an ounce is about the size of a medium-sized onion or a large clove of garlic. For nostalgia purposes, (I promise) I analyzed it by smelling the chunks of powder rocks that were in there (it smelled like coke). Much to the dismay of my friend, using my thumbs and forefingers, and the bag as insulation, I broke one of the rocks up and noticed the "fish scale" stratified quality, another indication that it was "good" cocaine and not overly reconstituted, or "Recon." But then, I noticed something I had never seen before. There were little, barely perceptible chunks of blue within the powdered rock, not in great quantity, but here and there. They looked like pieces of blue laundry detergent or "microbeads" that you often see in laundry pods. My friend immediately purchased some fentanyl test strips and sure enough, his bag of what he thought was high-grade coke was laced with fentanyl... beware.

If said service or product is an enjoyable thing to partake in, most people, (civilians included), see no harm in pursuing it, nor in marginally adjusting their moral compasses a bit in order to override prudence. If they are implicated or caught in the act of doing it, whatever that "doing" may consist of, be it engaging in sex for money, illicit drugs, illegal gambling or other vices that can be harder to define as lawful or unlawful, it is normally plead down in court to the proverbial slap on the wrist. Or simply dismissed in lieu of more pressing criminal cases.

Any person that participates in crime not categorized as a bilateral, contractual agreement; but who preys upon, and victimizes targeted individuals who are either duped, (this includes selling fentanyl in the guise of another drug) coerced, forced, or accosted in some way, shape or form by their aggressor- be it tele scams targeting seniors, to human trafficking, rape, murder, etc., are Bad Criminals. And ones that deserve little if any compassion, and only the severest of punishments.

These bad criminals and their actions are the reason criminals who practice crime of a higher standing vehemently deny the generalization and grouping together with those who engage in criminality of a deplorable nature; thus, it is the intent of this chapter to identify and separate the two – both ideologically and lawfully – in hopes that these distinctions will provide a better understanding. And perhaps more favorable and effective methods of correction for those who commit crime for profit, without harming others; versus those who indulge in violence for reasons inconceivable to the rest of us.

It is believed by the majority of those behind bars that if society focused more of its efforts upon punishing and curtailing the spread of the sadistic criminal, as thoroughly as inmates do while incarcerated, the world would be a much safer place than it is today. Because it is more often than not the individual infected with behavioral health disorders and sociopathy – that exploits the mercy of society and earnest efforts at rehabilitation – who continues carrying out unlawful acts via a pattern that intensifies with each crime successfully committed.

When dealing with criminals, being able to tell the difference between the two is similar to the distinctions between venomous and non-venomous snakes. There are garter snakes and there are rattle snakes... but they are all snakes.

WAY BACK WHEN

One of my favorite past times (now that I have ample time to practice it) is to relive events that have long been in the rearview. I think about practically every decision made that inevitably placed me where I am today. The ability to think back on events and decisions with clarity is the one concession that prison seems able to provide better than any other environment. And it has afforded me, literally, years of reflection.

I can remember my first criminal act with more specificity than my last. It was in 1984, just before my 4th birthday. That same day an old Black gentleman put his hands on his knees, peered down at me with a wrinkled smile and asked in a deep voice, "how old are you, young man?" To which I responded, "I'm free, I'm free years old!"

I was at the local 7-Eleven less than a block from our house with my mom. This was as far as my knowledge of the local geography extended but it seemed like the end of the world.

There were these little chocolates wrapped in foil printed like footballs, basketballs, and baseballs that the store sold for 3 cents a chocolate piece in a bottom bin. I remember counting the pennies I had and taking more chocolate balls than I could afford. I put these in my pocket and paid for the rest by putting them, and my coins, on the counter.

Legal ramifications were never something I considered. I doubt I could even tell you what the word *illegal* meant at the time. But I *knew* that what I was doing was wrong... even without four rotations around the sun, I knew.

Although this particular form of criminality was at best petty, it taught me a valuable lesson, and it also later instilled within me the chief form of criminality that I would practice for the whole of my criminal career, which was, "buy it for a dollar and sell it for two." Or steal it and make 100% profit.

Fast forward about ten years from that moment in the 7-Eleven: I'm now thirteen years of age and my criminality is blossoming and progressing at a rate as fast as the opportunities present themselves.

In 1992 we had moved from Tacoma Washington to Espanola New Mexico. The area of Northern New Mexico is a setting of such natural beauty and sunsets that countless photographers and painters flock to this region to capture the landscape, sunsets, and people. Santa Fe, in particular, is a city known for its celebration of art, its quaint picturesque atmosphere, and its elitist allure for the affluent. This also made it the perfect place to sell cocaine, as many Santa Feans were clients with inexhaustible resources. It would later be the City of Santa Fe and much of Northern NM that I concentrated most of my trafficking efforts.

The majority of Northern New Mexico is rural, and good paying jobs are scarce unless one works for the national labs, or owns their own business, or works for a business or company that is well-established.

This makes living in these picturesque communities not as harmonious as one would think, and the deadly mixture of poverty, poor educational systems, and high availability of narcotics only fuel notions of success through methods that were anything but legitimate.

I think it's interesting to note that one of the reasons my parents elected to move to NM was to escape the drugs and gangs of the late 80s and early 90s that were sweeping up the West Coast from California.

Had they done a little more research on the area they were moving to, they would have discovered that Española (and the village of Chimayo) were known not only for their quaintness, but for being the heroin trafficking hubs of the Southwest.

The town of Española was once referred to as the "Lowrider Capital of the World," a declaration that is not necessarily synonymous with drug trafficking.

Prior to larger cities allowing for open-market heroin and fentanyl practices, Española and Chimayo topped the nation's cities and towns with the highest rate of opioid-related deaths per capita.

Española would become my business incubator, my school of criminality, and my stepping stone from which I would leap to pursue and direct no small amount of trafficking in the key cities and towns that straddled I-25, the I-40 Corridor, and other highways throughout Northern NM.

Some, such as the federal prosecutor that tried my case, suggested that such success required of me a level of violence and ruthlessness needed to "take over" the areas I effectively monopolized. But that sort of aggression was rarely necessary. In fact, it is probably better demonstrated in corporate settings than it would be in the streets.

Most dealers are hooked on their own product, and they will only perceive you as a threat so long as you operate in the same market share, or if you are tentative and unable to manage something as commonplace as another human being. Usually, because of their need to shine, or because of bad business practices coupled by impaired judgment, the competition removes itself from the equation that it only nominally contributed to in the first place.

The most effective way to take over *anything* is with a sure and steady approach that guarantees the most profit with the least amount of risk. As far as drug trafficking goes, it basically entails supplying at a price that undercuts the rest of the market so that the rest of the market eventually ends up buying their wares from you.

Once local market dominance occurs, we can effectively curtail drug-related violence by not supplying those who prefer to have their guns blazing continuously. And by keeping the product cheap and affordable – so as to stymie drug-related thefts, the most prevalent form of collateral damage from high-traffic drug areas – but I digress...

For better or worse, we moved to Española. In hindsight, it was for the worse. But at the time, we were determined to make the best of it, and for a while, we did. I think it's also worth stating that the majority of people who hail from Española are good, hardworking people, and that it was/is the minority consisting of people like myself – whose moral constitutions do not suffer from restraints that would prevent them from practicing free enterprise of an illegal nature – that give the City of Española and towns like it, a bad reputation.

It is also to the detriment of that city that its geographical location makes it the hub and distribution point for narcotics in much of Northern New Mexico.

Be that as it may, the 12-year-old me suddenly found myself in an environment whose criminal element was far more active and aggressive than the one I left, and I quickly had to adjust to my new settings lest it became the thing that turned me into a victim of circumstance.

Most of the crimes committed by me and my friends were ones that were viewed by us as crimes of necessity, meaning that if we didn't commit them, we wouldn't survive. Selling enough cheap brick-pack weed to have enough money to purchase clothes and food was definitely the main source of income for youngsters who had yet to reach the stage of criminality that would reap any real profit.

The other crime of choice was theft (usually for the same clothes and food we didn't have money to purchase). Private property, and people's homes and vehicles were bypassed as much as possible. Not so much out of a code of conduct, but because most homes and vehicles were owned by lower-middle class citizens with not much in the way of valuables.

I viewed most corporate stores and businesses as entities that practiced usury – by marking up products and selling them at a profit to consumers – as fair game, and I justified stealing from them by that same rationale.

As my greed increased, so too did my ingenuity. One of my favorite modes of entry into steel-framed or stucco structures was through skylights in the ceiling. In the early 90s, most skylights weren't wired with magnetic breakers the way windows were, and motion detectors weren't as commonplace as they are today.

The only violence that ever took place was the typical street-gang violence that so many youths are prone to participate in – from the ghettos, to the sticks – and in our case, we defended ourselves against older teenagers and adults whose greater numbers and legitimate status as hardened criminals far exceeded our own... at least initially.

It's necessary for my own conscience to impress upon the reader that during my entire tenure as a criminal, I practiced these same methods of crime over and over: buying something for a dollar and selling it for two. Or stealing, first from corporate entities, and then from other drug dealers.

These two acts may have been refined and perfected over

the course of time, but they were never practiced with sadistic or violent intent. Violence was only committed; or rather, I thoroughly committed myself to violence, if it was absolutely necessary.

There were certain criminals, thugs, gangbangers, drug dealers, etc., that differed from me; that were different from most people, criminals included, as their criminality was often times accompanied by some violent act that was hardly warranted. In fact, their criminality *was* the violent act.

I had an associate in my early teens who I later came to realize was one of these people. We'll call him "Eduardo."

He was a decent enough kid, or as indecent as the rest of us. He smoked weed, partied when the rest of us partied, but wasn't addicted to any heavy drugs. I think he was on par with the normal amount of experimenting that any teenager does. He didn't strike me as short-tempered or anything. Just... average.

Eduardo linked up with a girlfriend whose mother encouraged the relationship, and he moved from affordable housing to affordable housing with the mother and daughter.

One day, myself and another guy were ditching school and hanging out at Eduardo's. He decided to pop in one of those death videos which contained footage of people dying in accidents, gangsters in South America walking up to their targets with cameras recording in one hand and shooting them with a gun in the other; beheadings and other appendages being sawed off in middle-eastern countries, and all kinds of abhorred shit.

Since then, I have witnessed, first-hand, many reprehensible acts, i.e., killings, stabbings, shootings, horrible accidents, etc. To this day, I don't think I've ever witnessed anything as awful as what was shown on that video, probably because someone recorded these acts and compiled them for the sake of viewing "pleasure." But more to the point, the look of excitement on Eduardo's face as he watched the various scenes of death and torture play out on the TV screen was the most disturbing thing of all.

Despite the fact that I barely kept down my revulsion from watching that shit, stoned no less. And despite a growing anger mixed with sadness when it began to occur to me just how many people watch this sort of material for the sake of amusement – else why would there be a market for such things? - I promised myself that I would see it through to the end so I might have a better understanding of what sort of people I might encounter out there in the world.

Nonetheless, that experience left me numb, and with a sense of dread in my heart I had never known before. And with the knowledge that people kill other people... all the time.

I know for certain that the other kid watching that video with us was just as troubled as I was, because he fled to the adjacent bathroom to vomit, blaming his upset stomach on the weed we had just smoked. This too, was an immense source of humor for Eduardo.

The only other time I witnessed his abnormal behavior was also the last time I ever hung out with him.

One day we were hanging outside of yet another one of Eduardo's girlfriend's mother's impermanent residences. (They seemed to revolve around the same area of Española where many of our friends lived on the Westside of town).

Several of us were outside drinking, smoking, shooting dice (with no clue on how to play craps) and in various poses and attitudes of fabricated toughness; basically promoting our own delinquency and ruin before our lives really began.

I was on the sidewalk with Eduardo and another individual when a cute little mixed-breed German Shepherd puppy came sauntering down the street towards us. He was probably about 3 months old. I can recall one of his ears was in the classic shepherd upright position while the other was bent in the middle and sort of flopped up-and-down as he approached us with his tongue hanging out.

I was just kneeling down to give him a pet and scoop him up in my arms when Eduardo's foot came from nowhere and gave him a medium strength kick, causing the puppy to yelp and skitter off back down the street from whence he came.

I do not remember staring at Eduardo for what my friends later recounted was about a good half a minute after he kicked that puppy. I do remember using his shoulder and head to push off of him and stand up after savagely beating him.

In hindsight, it wasn't that one instance that caused me to physically attack, and thereby punish Eduardo. But rather, all the little instances culminating where he exhibited some manner of behavior that was less than becoming of a good criminal, or even a decent kid, or just a normal human being.

I could mention countless other instances that should have been warning signs that Eduardo was fast becoming a coward and promising sociopath, i.e., his girlfriend acting more non-communicative than usual with a bruise under her heavy "chola" makeup, supposedly from some kind of "accident." Or the time he stated to us he was going to beat and rob the old lady living next door for asking him to turn down the music before she called the cops.

We eventually stopped hanging out with him. I heard he was later arrested for dog-fighting, battery on a household member, and statutory rape of a minor. I also heard he received his due punishment while in jail, but what became of him, or where he is today, I couldn't say.

What I *can* say is that he is the perfect example of the type of substandard human that participated in actions and crimes that had little or no monetary value compared to the violence and sadism they provided him with. Although Eduardo was and is considered by me to be a fairly minor and inactive "Bad Criminal," the amount of pain and suffering he inflicted was quite considerable. And to truly *know* this type of person for who and what he really is, is to avoid a potentially dangerous encounter with the same.

The story of Eduardo is perhaps one of the least appalling accounts that I could regale you with, but I wanted to tell it because its inception happened at such an early stage in my life. I thought it better to paint a picture using adolescents as its main characters, as opposed to telling one of the many stories of the villains who were a part of my adulthood, whose unfathomable cruelty was usually counterbalanced by my indifference to acts that ceased to shock me after being exposed to them countless times over.

Although some of the crimes that were committed by me where by no means civil or harmless in nature, I take pride in knowing that acts of violence were *only* committed out of necessity or defense, and never once were they acts that I took pleasure in doing. I will also admit that there were many instances where I intervened and punished those similar to Eduardo who were committing violence against innocents.

Those few who truly know me – perhaps better than I know myself – know that although I am viewed by some, including law enforcement, as a dangerous criminal; I am also more than willing to forfeit my own safety to ensure the safety of others.

This is the deep-seated truth that separates me and those like me from bad criminals. The ability to maintain and exercise a sense of right and wrong – while enmeshed in the criminal lifestyle – is the very principle that could one day provide us with some mercy of our own when it comes time to face judgment.

Know when our actions are affecting people who do not voluntarily take part in what we're involved in, and understand that these are the actions of a bad criminal. Intervene by any means necessary when witnessing an act committed (not by a criminal) but a sociopath, whose criminality is never questioned nor analyzed by their inner-voice; but encouraged, and fueled by each subsequent act committed.

These are the qualities that make us Good Criminals, and

worthy of a higher classification than those who forget their humanity when committing crime.

CREED

In this day and age most people are aware of the very basics of the CCC which, thankfully, furnishes only a few simple rules to follow. It may be just as amusing to you, the reader, as it is to us to think of an obeisance to any kind of law as counterintuitive to the idea of criminality, but I assure you it isn't.

Without rules, regulations, and indeed laws, there can never be a stability whose permanence is needed in order to bring about anything resembling a well-functioning economy, albeit an illegal one.

Criminal enterprises and their employees must adhere to conduct that is considered acceptable and reflective of the business itself, lest that business lose its trust capital or reputation as an entity that conducts its affairs with a measure of professionalism.

A bad reputation doesn't make for good business. It just makes those who might have been willing to use your services seek out more reputable product/service providers with better outcomes than you and yours could ever provide.

Although I do adhere to a set of principles that align with the Code, I also suspect that same code is, more often than not, for the sake of profit. Be that as it may, practicing business without compromising ethics is also a characteristic of a Distinguished Criminal. This of course is worthy of recognition, even if that recognition is from yourself and no other.

Snitching to save one's own skin is prohibited by the Code, and by every criminal in existence with the exception, of course, of those who snitch. While this may not be an act that directly affects society, it most certainly affects those who are being told on. Even more so, it impacts those who are doing the telling. They could very well find themselves in a position where they are no longer informing for profit or to safeguard their freedom... but snitching in an effort to save their very lives.

We will explore the phenomena of snitching/cooperating and all of its side effects in the following chapter. Needless to say, it is by far the one cardinal rule in the Code that is most prevalent, the most strictly enforced; and also, the one that is most often broken.

Anyone who practices the reprehensible act of rape, upon anyone else, is in violation of the Code, and deserving of whatever punishment comes their way, from the justice system, their victim, family members and friends of the victim, criminals, and otherwise. This particular act ranks among the worst for strict and immediate reprisal. Most of us have children of our own; not to mention wives, mothers, sisters, etc., and to be forced to live with an individual who rapes is to basically force us into receiving a felony assault charge, or the killing of another inmate.

Most corrections officers are also family-based men and women. I believe it is for this reason that rapists are sometimes put in general population with the rest of us in hopes that a more severe form of punishment will occur than that which was prescribed by law.

However, strides for advancement in more humane forms of punishment have resulted in entire prison complexes, units, and yards to be built strictly for this type of criminal. These prisons are also ones that have far less security restrictions than most, and the amenities available for the inmate are far superior to the ones that the rest of us are provided.

If it doesn't make dollars, it doesn't make sense. And if we are committing crime without the obvious expectation of seeing a monetary return for our risk, then there is something wrong with us... with you.

Believe it or not, most criminals are weary of these types,

as is the rest of society. Although our "wariness" often manifests in aggression rather than avoidance or circumspection.

There also exists certain criminal acts that provide one with profit, but whose disagreeable means of doing so merits no praise, nor place among distinguished criminals. These acts include but are not limited to such things as indifferent or targeted drug dealing, which is the act of encouraging the sale of drugs to people who otherwise should not be doing drugs or who have limited resistance to the addiction itself, e.g., pregnant women, minors, or someone who has an obvious physical or mental challenge that would increase their susceptibility to becoming addicted.

Much like alcohol and cigarettes, drugs need no sales pitch, and people who choose to use them hardly need a dope dealer convincing them that their product is the "thing" to do. Aggressive drug dealing is akin to the marketing strategies of products in the 1980s, which practically guaranteed middle-aged men and women mortality, heightened sex appeal, and more success if they drank alcohol and smoked cigarettes.

Of all the drug trafficking campaigns I undertook, I can state with all honesty that I *never* once attempted to blanket advertise, nor specifically target and then peddle my poison to someone that wasn't looking to buy it. And to sell it to someone who is obviously abusing it and harming themselves, or perhaps others, was something I would prudently forego.

Some may argue that this doesn't preclude me from being a shit-bag drug dealer, and it doesn't, but at least I can retain some moral fiber in knowing that I didn't try to intentionally ruin some unwitting person's life through persuasion and by my indifference to their welfare; not so much the case with other dealers.

Strong-arming is also one of those criminal acts that one can either choose to utilize with discretion or with great indifference.

A Strong Arm is anyone who receives monetary compensation for inflicting body injury, property damage, or the threat of both to an individual, property or business, in hopes that that harm or threat of harm persuades a targeted entity to comply with whatever demands the person paying for the services of the Strong Arm is making.

I've done this kind of "work" on occasion and can assure you that the line between good and bad will not become hazy if one adheres to the CCC while performing their duties in this capacity.

Strong-arming is primarily used for the purpose of attempting to extract payment from people who don't live up to their end of the bargain.

For extortion purposes, strong arms are used to extort payments from working-class citizens in return for protection or "insurance" purposes; i.e., forcing one to pay money to the same individuals that would inflict property damage or inflict bodily harm to the person and place of business being extorted.

Such tactics smack of an antiquated form of making money employed by criminal organizations whose ethnicity often reflects that of the neighborhood in which they operate. And is most certainly demonstrative of a bad criminal act.

Apart from this one discrepancy, bear in mind that most people victimized by strong-arm tactics are criminals themselves, who at one point or another, defaulted on a loan, a gambling or drug debt; or who did something that merited some form of street justice.

Legitimate citizens hardly need to be persuaded via strong-arm tactics, as it is rare that they would find themselves a target of criminal coercion or punishment.

The exception to the decline in crimes such as extortion can often be found in minority populations whose origin countries and governments often practiced corruption at several levels; thus, civilians would rather pay an extortion tax to a local gang than to involve "untrustworthy" authorities that might be quicker to question one's legitimate status than they would be to investigate a crime against them.

An act of strong-arming that does in fact victimize an innocent civilian for the sake of capital gain or personal pleasure, or both, would most assuredly be a deplorable performance, committed by one whose lack of principles would classify them as a bad criminal.

Pimping, or the forced "management" of prostitutes is also an occupation whose economic upside seems to be overshadowed by the amount of exploitation and abuse heaped upon those whose illegal actions are no longer governed by themselves. But by the direction of their pimps, who often care more about maximizing revenue from an inexhaustible resource than they do the welfare of that resource... prostitutes and sex slaves.

NOTE: In speaking with sex industry workers since coming home, ranging from massage parlor staff, to escorts and street prostitutes, there exists managers, pimps, etc., that practice a mutual contractual agreement between themselves and those that peddle their flesh to strangers. This agreement often comes in the form of protection, transportation, and other services for a percentage of the profit as opposed to *all* of the profit. But the countless pimps I was in prison with, as well as those I interviewed on the streets have all informed me that those they manage do not receive one dollar for their services. Rather, it is the pimp who collects all the money and feeds, clothes, and provides a level of care for the prostitute in whatever way he deems appropriate. I say *he* because more often than not, this form of bad criminality is practiced by males.

This, to me, is an act of greed coupled with an amount of sadism and cruelty necessary for perpetuating the victimization of people who, once ensnared, are unable to break away from such ruthless overseers as the pimp so effectively embodies.

In today's pop culture a pimp is also someone who has a way with the ladies and whose joviality and charisma is something to be admired. I have applied this term to friends of mine whose prowess with the opposite sex was something I found to be quite impressive, and those same friends (when I merited it) have applied that term to me.

I have even used this term affectionately with women when I witnessed them working a crowd at an event or charming an individual with something as harmless as a smile. But I assure you the act of pimping is nothing short of breaking a person's spirit in order to profit from the use of their body.

In most cases, pimping involves the rape – not necessarily of one's body – but of one's soul. And once such a fierce assault on the soul has been committed, there is rarely a need to rape the body, as the constitution of one who has been raped and decimated spiritually is more often than not compromised. They're susceptibility and acquiescence to the constant presence and suggestion of the rapist is now assured.

To be a successful pimp it is necessary to administer a form of psychological manipulation towards an individual whose vulnerability is often the trait pimps search out and fixate upon- much the same way as predator's search out sick, old, and weak prey. If this description doesn't resemble a complete and utter sadist, I don't know what does.

Arson too, is one of those crimes which require some other, harder-to-identify gratification other than monetary whose very nature suggests a distorted form of criminality, expressed in acts by an individual who is driven by something other than what motivates the rest of us.

Lighting a thing on fire simply to take pleasure in the burning of it is as incomprehensible to the good criminal as it is to the average citizen. Acts of violence or destruction committed because of the pleasure they bring the perpetrator are deplorable and abnormal; thus, unbecoming of morally sound and distinguished criminals.

Whether these crimes affect people physically, emotionally, or financially pales in comparison to the reward they provide for the criminal who practices them. Making the distinction between that which is an innovative yet illegal form of capitalism, versus satisfying an unnatural urge, is to make the distinction between which type of criminal you are either dealing with, or being victimized by.

All of the crimes I've described, and more, are what separates the Eduardos of the world, i.e., (rapists, murderers, wife beaters, child abusers, animal abusers, sadists, sociopaths, arsonists, etc.) from the distinguished criminal who sees his or her own behavior for what it is: and unlawful means to a favorably financial end. But *not* an immoral and harmful act that runs contrary to the Code.

In short, there should be a clear and concise separation between these two pathways. There should exist the urge to rehabilitate for those of us who are aware of who and what we are, and the reasons we pursue our criminality, <u>as opposed to those whose criminality can never be cured.</u>

Being distinguished criminals lies not so much in taking pride in the fact that we can abide by the Code. But in knowing that what we do is unlawful; thus wrong, regardless of whether it harms and compromises others besides ourselves. And making a conscious effort to change for the better is to aspire to be more than just a criminal, good, distinguished, or otherwise.

WHY A CRIMINAL?

crim i ·nal
/ˈkrimənl,ˈkrimn(ə)l/

noun

- A person who has committed a crime. convict, crook,
culprit, felon, fugitive, gangster, hoodlum, hooligan,
lawbreaker, mobster, offender, thug.

I thought long and hard about the different terms and
expressions I would use to classify Us, those who employ
unlawful acts for a living. I thought about using all the many
different words synonymous with *criminal* because I feel that
that particular description is one that often times is associated
with many unpromising stereotypes. I considered using words
such as ex-offender, ex-felon, legally-challenged, thug, gangster, etc., etc.

But the word *criminal* itself seemed to represent and
encompass more of what I felt my life constituted. It didn't
feel immoral, even though I know that many of the things I
did *were* immoral. When taken into consideration that this was
a form of employment, rather than a voluntary choice to
commit acts that were in conflict with my personal values, it
became acceptable to view what I was participating in as
merely a trade or profession. And like any trade or profession,
there were pros and cons that accompany it. I also knew that it
would never grant any form of pleasure or satisfaction other
than the intended economic relief I hoped for.

I also believe that some degree of justification is necessary,
not to make light of my actions, but to distinguish them from
those whose motives vastly differ from my own.

As we make distinctions between ourselves and others, and
as we separate or disassociate ourselves from those whose
behavior we find to be reprehensible, we inadvertently, or
sometimes consciously and willingly, create an atmosphere of

prejudice and dislike for those who are different. After all the interviews and analysis into the various forms of criminality people employ, I can see that my own prejudice towards bad criminals is apparent.

And yet, this is a case of discrimination that does not cause me to feel in the wrong, nor biased as a result of this self-examination. But rather, I feel trepidation for society's inability to tell the difference between the two.

Failure to identify an incurable form of criminality, practiced by those who have no misgivings about harming others for profit or pleasure, only further enhances my distaste for this type of criminal. Because of my inevitable connection to them, in that we have *all* broken the law, I will forever be judged and classified by the same standard so long as I have criminal history to define me.

Criminal, in my view, is an expression whose definition is used to describe people, such as myself, that practice capitalism in a manner that conflicts with the law. But that is *not* in contradiction to our knowledge of that which is unjust to provide, or to seek, or to indulge in according to human nature and the freedoms we should be allowed to exercise without constraint or legality hindering those pursuits.

Bad criminals only fit this description because what they do is illegal. The rest of what they are comprised of and the acts they commit call for a much more comprehensive analysis other than labeling them as criminal.

It is for this reason that I take that word and apply it as something that defines us, the good criminals, and which separates us from those who are classified as the same. And yet they are different; those who should be aptly referred to by whatever various names and vulgarities reflect their acts, their character, and their soul.

For they most assuredly are not criminals. Their actions do not reflect the need to advance by way of enterprise or a bilateral agreement; but rather, they embody cruelty and inflict pain by way of a win-lose situation in that the people receiving consideration from these so-called criminals are in no way benefitted by their attention. Instead, they are harmed, abused, robbed, raped, and murdered. They are deprived of what made them of notice in the first place.

In the end, the common knowledge that some people are bad while others are good is a sentiment that can be readily accepted by all. With that acceptance though, comes a much more complex situation that cannot easily be governed by the black and white of Right and Wrong, good or evil. Of course, there are good people that have done bad things. And let us not forget that there are plenty of bad people out there, who despite their inherent wickedness, are known for their impulsive acts of kindness and benignity.

Shall we agree that the distinction, then, is more a case of our acknowledgment, pursuit, and attraction to that which is good, and our instinctual avoidance and aversion to that which is not? And also, the perception of the clear defining line between acts by people that can easily be classified as evil, and that provide no benefit whatsoever, versus acts that are illegal though not necessarily evil, and that are practiced for mutual consent for mutual benefit?

I can't say for certain if the illnesses that afflict bad criminals are things that are beyond curing (I believe they are).

I know without a doubt that my own criminality, even though I distinguish it from the bad, is nothing short of a variation of similar illnesses that affect bad criminals, and that is just as debilitating as any virus that infects its host.

Criminality, no matter how many different variations it becomes manifest, is a malady that can never provide a standard of living and level of security as it fosters despondency and suffering; not only for those who are victimized by it, but by those who practice it. To make that jump from criminal > to distinguished criminal > to normal citizen is the objective that we should all be aiming for.

CHOICE

When I observe my condition as objectively as possible, I can't help but feel that my own period of recovery is perhaps as bad as the illness itself, if not worse. I say this because the healing is never guaranteed, and the time it takes to convalesce is often fraught with the same measurement of fear, doubt and uncertainty as when we were dependent upon such a life-threating disease as our criminality.

Although I am, on a daily basis, surrounded on many sides by criminality, I don't feel susceptible to its gravitational pull. And the amount of empathy I feel for those who are still subject to its call; and, who are quite obviously still enchanted by their infirmity, is the measurement I use to determine my convalescence and hopeful state of remission.

The healing process one endures – and is likely to analyze at regular intervals to ensure a continued remission – can be likened to someone surviving cancer. The only options for fighting it is to either carve the bad out of you in hopes that there is enough healthy tissue (or presence of mind) remaining. Or to subject yourself to a form of chemotherapy/prison that will course through your mind, body, and soul, effectively dampening the criminal inclination, much like smoke slows the autonomy of bees... only to have them awaken once they are no longer subdued.

Bear in mind that we only want to kill the disease, not the host it has affixed itself to.

To thoroughly sever all connection from criminality is to rid ourselves of a sickness whose potency has yet to become terminal within us. To endure the healing process that arrest and imprisonment affords is to experience a form of treatment that is far more arduous than a voluntary transition, and whose success rate is relatively low.

In many instances, forced treatment only further weakens the resolve of those afflicted to resist the allure of crime. For how difficult is it to resist one's self, and something as intrinsic as our own thoughts and feelings?

It is not estimated, but proven, that more than 75% of people who have spent time in prison will eventually return for similar crimes, or crimes of a more severe nature than those that initially placed them behind bars.

These numbers don't leave much hope for me and those like me. And yet, I choose to place my hopes, not upon statistics, but upon the same entity that fostered criminality in the first place... myself. I continue to endure the baptism by fire that is prison, with the expectation that that fire will course through me with enough intensity to burn every diseased cell, thought, and inclination from conscience.

The ability to choose and to make decisions, and to contemplate those decisions both before and after they transition from thought to action, is the one liberty that can never be stripped by another. It can never be taken away, no matter the style of government or society we exist within. Just as we have the option to choose pathways that lead us to our current circumstance, we also possess the ability to reverse those patterns and thought processes... so long as we remain aware that it is our *choice* that inevitably manifests our fortune or demise.

Once stripped of the philosophical and moral arguments I've made thus far, what ultimately remains is pure unabated choice: choice that, for good or bad, results and consequences must now be endured.

I chose to be where I am today. Perhaps it wasn't a choice of mine to spend the better part of a decade behind bars. And yet, I opted to make those decisions knowing full well the risks and rewards, if a distinction could even be made between the two.

The televisions run in this place day and night. News programs describe in detail, events that unfold in the world.

But more importantly, they document choices being made, and the results of those choices.

Unless we are viewing natural occurrences in which we have no control over, all the news really covers are the outcomes of choices made by people like us, and nothing more.

We are, to a very high degree, defined by the choices of humanity, our own and others.

When I detail the dissimilarity between good criminals and bad, I'm really making the distinction between good and bad decisions. I'm describing the outcomes, best, and worse practices, as well as the mentality and nature of criminality.

I'm attempting to convey what we do out of necessity; what people do out of desperation, and what people do to bring about satisfaction for themselves with little or no regard for the negative impact their decisions bring upon others.

I describe people that consider the ramifications of their choices, and then elect to perform them anyway. I describe those who, despite the harm they may cause, stay the course they've charted because what drives them is the advancement of their own interests.

This is crime in its purest form- an act or choice that is deemed illegal, either because of the disproportionate amount of benefit it provides for the perpetrator, or the lack of consideration for those who are victimized by it.

Even a good criminal is a distortion of the true meaning of crime and criminality, for to hold to a set of values that precludes you from practicing certain crimes is hypocrisy, and a watered-down version of pure criminality.

Should we not then assume that if we possess a conscience that hinders our ability to commit crime to the fullest extent, that we would be better off pursuing another form of advancement that does not contradict the values we adhere to?

If this were the case, that would be an indication that the bad criminals are actually the good ones; or to put it more accurately, the True Criminals, as their lack of compunction or remorse distinguishes them as purely criminal, in every sense of the word.

Perhaps we as good criminals are nothing but frauds, counterfeits whose diluted ideas of criminality are the reason why there is not a sharper distinction between crime of a harmful nature and crime of a capitalistic one. Perhaps it is Us who have essentially saturated society's collective conscience with so many different facets of crime, petty and severe, that it has simply become a matter of convenience to classify the lot of us as one in the same.

While I remain affected by this classification, and while I remain a subject, or subjected to my own choices, I will maintain with conviction that there is a fundamental difference between the frauds (good criminals) and the bona fide bad criminals... who are as distinguishable from Us as night is from day.

CLOSING

It was Friday the 20th of June 2012 when I first began writing this chapter. The horrible events of that day which took place in a movie theater in Aurora CO was evidence of one who practiced crime for no benefit and no outcome beyond personal gratification.

During the aftermath that ensued, there was also the usually questions posed by criminal experts and the media as to how this could have been prevented; what caused it to occur, what preempted his decision to act. What could have been done to check his downward spiral into a depression or frame of thought that would ultimately manifest itself in the manner in which it did? Did we as a society fail this person to such an extent that he felt he had no other option besides the one that he chose? I'd like to respond with a resounding "Bullshit."

While I agree that the dissection of such a horrific event is necessary so that we may better prepare or even thwart the next, I believe that a closer inspection of these types of criminals is not. And to focus on this person, rather than on those who either perished or survived the ordeal, would only lend credence to those who least deserve it, while undermining the voices of those we should be listening to; and of course, allowing survivors to speak for those who no longer have a voice.

Why should we presume that this was an individual who *wanted* help? And, if he had received help in time would he have committed the same murderous act? The fact of the matter is that he *did* commit this act rather than electing not to. He consciously planned it out for months, possibly even longer. And because of his actions, numerous lives have been affected, and indeed ended, due to this criminal's unwillingness to seek help, or to attempt to change the thought processes he indulged.

I maintain that no matter what manners of constraint are placed upon us, either via society, by circumstances, or by our own volition, there remains the choice to accept those constraints, to balk at being harnessed by them, or to change a manner of thinking that proves destructive.

He could have opted to take his own life; thus, curing an incurable disease that he, instead, allowed to spread and cause as much affliction as it eventually did. But he *chose* not to.

I don't believe that he sought help, nor even wanted it. Even if he saw a professional, it's quite possible that he only did so to further imbue himself with the resolve needed to convert thought into action. Conventional thought and rationale were only influences that ran counter to fulfilling his intentions that were, above all, purely criminal.

Such an individual as this has proven beyond doubt that

his criminality is absolute in nature. Only after do we see society's reactionary response confirm this, rather than a preemptive law preventing it. His sentence to Life in prison will be paid for by the survivors that live in Colorado and that pay taxes to ensure his existence continues unabated while behind bars.

At one point or another, I have felt the urge to kill everyone around me, to lash out at everyone and everything when frustration, depression and despair reaches an unendurable level. I'm sure most of us have entertained this thought while stuck in gridlock traffic, in a long line at the grocery store, or dare I say at the beginning of a long stint in prison, surrounded by inhospitable and unwelcoming forms of crass humanity.

But I have never acted upon this urge, nor will I ever. <u>Nor have the rest of you.</u> It is most often alleviated by secluding myself in my own home, or, as is now the case, my own cell, with a good book or a little down time so that I may recharge and face the world yet again. With optimism, rather than with the cynicism that an overexposure to humanity and a malnourished spirit are sure to provide.

Whether they are outright murderers and rapists, or the lowest form of scam artist attempting to deprive the elderly of a comfortable and secure retirement, I implore each of us to recognize the bad criminals for what they truly are.

If we make our way in this world via committing crime, knowing the difference between these criminals and people like ourselves is to acknowledge that we are *nothing* like them; that we are deserving and capable of manifesting a better life, if we would only choose to pursue it.

8

INFORMATION AGE

I HAD an incident occur with a guy, we'll call him "Kevin," asking me if he could make a purchase. I knew him fairly well and had done business with him on occasion, so it wasn't like this was some random request out of the blue.

But prior to Kevin calling me I had another colleague reach out and inform me that Kevin was seen, moments ago, being placed in cuffs by the local narcotics team.

So when my phone started ringing and I saw Kevin's name, I was more than a little apprehensive. Rather than play stupid or attempt to bade for time, I asked, "Didn't you just get arrested?" Rather than say yes or no he responded by asking me how I knew that. I asked him if the narcotics detectives were next to him and to put them on the phone.

I roundly cursed out the two detectives (Sgt. Altunji, and Det. Ramirez) for trying to set me up, and possibly getting Kevin killed in the process of setting up other dealers. When I finished berating them for being crooked cops and first-rate fuckups, I told them to put Kevin back on the phone. Surprisingly they did.[*]

I knew Kevin didn't buy much – mostly for personal use – and that this was probably his first pinch. I told him I was going to call my lawyer and inform him of a new client, to walk in there, set up a guilty plea; after which, Kevin would be placed on a year of unsupervised probation.

I also told him I just saved his life, and to tell those cops that busted him with a misdemeanor or Fourth Degree Felony amount of coke to go fuck themselves, and he would be rid of this particular life-altering event after a year and my attorney's motion to dismiss the conviction subsequent his clear conduct.

Kevin never made it to my attorney's office. He instead gave up a few of his friends, further isolating himself from support and confirming him as an informant. Later, when the two detectives deemed he had served his purpose, they pulled his protection. He was re-arrested for some violation or another of his conditional release, and the shit got even deeper.

I heard he was severely beaten in the dorm unit (D-Block) of county jail, and later performed various cries-for-help such as wrist cutting and attempted hangings with his jumpsuit, boxers, etc.

Sometimes when you're on suicide watch, you are provided a "pickle suit," a green Velcro contraption that is

---

[*] https://www.justice.gov/archive/usao/nm/press-releases/2007/2007-05-10_arrest_warrant_danny_ramirez_070508.pdf

similar to a tunic or skirt that is impossible to tear or mutilate in any way.

When corrections officers were not making their assigned rounds through the protective custody or segregation units, the inmate orderlies definitely make theirs. And they used this opportunity to throw dirty mop buckets of water into informants' cells, including urine, feces, blood, and any other fluids they can fit under a cell door.

A couple years after our phone call, and just prior to my arrest which preempted this work, I encountered Kevin at a local gym. He apparently waited for me by the doors to whisper and murmur his apologies to me for what he had done. He also confirmed what I had heard as to his treatment by the police while he was informing, as well as his treatment in jail subsequent his re-arrest.

After opting not to indulge my compulsiveness to beat him to death (also not knowing if he was still working with one branch of law enforcement or another), a number of emotions coursed through me; pity, contempt, disgust, and so forth.

Kevin knew I was on probation for another charge (felony assault, I believe). He knew had I been successfully setup and arrested while on probation that my resulting sentence would have been compounded in severity. And yet he elected to set me up. He chose to forego my advice and set up other people that considered him their friend.

I told him all of this, and I told him the pity I felt for him. I explained to him that he had become as much of a victim as anyone could ever be, and that the catalyst for his victimization was his own choice, coupled with the very people who promised him protection in exchange for his cooperation.

Had Kevin refused to cooperate he never would have been accused of misconduct while cooperating; thus, giving the police the excuse to pull his protection and throw him to the wolves. He never would have endured such a downward spiral as the one he was subjected to when he was coerced into cooperating.

Since being in prison, I have witnessed time and again the ill effects that cooperating affords people. I have participated in this form of punishment meted out upon other inmates if they hailed from the same area and groups located in northern New Mexico as the rest of us. And I always pose the question in my head either before or after administering or witnessing this form of street/prison justice: Why not do two years of easy prison time if that's what the courts sentenced you to rather than one year of absolute hell in an effort to shave time off your conviction?

Why endure punishment of the sort that might leave you permanently scarred and your life forever altered, if you have any life left to speak of?

In the previous chapter I made mention that snitching is not necessarily an act that directly affects society. But if it is your son or daughter, or a loved one, or any dependent, or *yourself* who is placed in such a weighty matter of choice-choosing to cooperate is often times the difference between doing time or doing hard time; putting your life on a brief hold, or no longer having any life left in your body.

It wasn't long after I saw Kevin that I was successfully set up by another person/persons, whose actions and intent, coupled by my own choices, culminated in events that brought about what I know was to be my final arrest.

And still, years after my May 5th, 2008 arrest, I feel the same pity towards those individuals as I did towards Kevin... and disgust if I'm being honest.

I know that they have to live with themselves and their choices. I know that cowards die every day, a thousand times over. I know they can hardly look at their reflection without perceiving a substandard individual staring back at them, growing older without the level of success and acknowledgment they hoped to attain.

I know what awaits them if they haven't used the extra time given them to make something out of their lives. I know that their cooperation will pale in comparison to the indifference of law enforcement, and punishment at the hands of others if the Life catches up to them.

While snitching may not have any foreseeable benefits to society, choosing *not* to snitch certainly provides benefit to those who find themselves at the precipice of Choice.

It is primarily for those who take their arrest on the chin that I write this chapter; who value their ability to look at their reflection in the mirror and recognize what they see as principle-driven. And for those of us who have opted the other way... perhaps, imbued with this knowledge, you will elect for a different course.

MAKES AND MODELS

Generally speaking, there are three different types of informants that cooperate with law enforcement. Knowing them, or knowing which category they aspire to; or worse, knowing which category police may wish to assign to you is essential to understanding how best to resist that categorization, and to deny cooperation in its entirety.

The **First** is the informant or snitch who is, to one degree or another, a criminal themselves, and who cooperates with the intention of lessening the severity of their own charges and subsequent sentencing.

The **Second** is the person who fits less into the criminal categorization and is more demonstrative of a drug addict or alcoholic who suddenly finds themselves caught in the act of breaking some law or another, usually theft to support their habit, DWI, etc. And who are rather easily coerced or bullied by law enforcement into cooperating to keep from withdrawing in jail, and/or to simply continue living life as they are accustomed to.

The **Third**, and most dangerous – to themselves and others – is the one who cooperates with no leverage to affect their choice, but who does so for the purpose of monetary gain, or simply because snitching is a part of their business model- a part of their character. It can be gratifying to wield the sort of power that trades information for imprisoning people, more so if the snitch in question has very little power and influence in the streets or elsewhere. I assure you, this type of informant is the greatest liability and threat to your operations, to your freedom, and possibly your life.

The exception to the threats that informants pose is our choices, which inject so many variables and liabilities into our sphere of influence.

The First is by far the most prevalent of informants. This is the type of person who has been involved in crime for much of their lives. The type of person who knows the stakes, and yet they choose to break the CCC, despite what they and everyone around them has been preaching for much of their criminal "career." These individuals have a scarcity complex, and as such, are always broke; selfish in what little gains they make, and often brazen in their displays of nominal success, i.e., flashy cars (if they're too broke, flashy clothes, etc.)

This is also One of the Three who is probably most aware of the end results, and yet they choose to snitch anyway, justifying their actions in the interest of self-preservation, which, is an irony unto itself if they are ever discovered.

I imagine Number One manifests itself after they reach a certain level of complacency through crime, and imprisonment is no longer an acceptable setback that comes with the job. What few or great possessions and freedoms they think they have are more important than the freedom of people they are now compromising.

Initially, snitch Number One may not reach the decision to cooperate lightly, given that their neighborhood has probably fostered them, as well as those they snitch on in very close proximity. They may be friends of the family, or even family members. They may also be growing older and have already endured arrest and prison time. Prison is a young man's game, and the older we get the less time most are apt to commit to.

The more time passes, the more they realize their prospects for a successful retirement through crime are drastically diminishing.

Law enforcement being the opportunists they are understand the criminal life cycle, and play upon what snitch Number One already knows, even if on a subconscious level. The police will either subtly, or not so subtly stir these thoughts to the surface- that the majority of us are not likely to experience "retirement" outside of a body bag or cage... and they'll be right.

Law enforcement will sell snitch Number One on a Second Chance at Life. But beyond *possibly* lessening the severity of their sentence (no guarantees), and *definitely* placing their informants in harm's way, providing a new life is something that is reserved for either the utmost elite of informants, or it means something entirely different to law enforcement compared to what they would have the informant believe.

Snitch Number Two is the unwitting pawn in a larger game who is motivated, and often times blinded, by their own addiction. They are usually unaware that they are being used or placed in extreme danger by law enforcement, more so if their judgment and awareness is impaired by self-medication, and/or their failure to perceive other's exploitive nature for what it truly is.

Number Two often has no clue as to what they're participating in, nor the villains they are associating with on both sides of the legal spectrum, and just who it is they are going to be victimized by. There is no written policy and procedure that police use to safeguard and properly manage the interests of the informant. They are essentially offering snitches a *Quid*

Pro Quo, or this-for-that, meaning "do as we say, and you will walk away."

Number Two's nearsightedness and craving for self-medication allows them to see only so far down the trail. And what they see is obscured by a number of influences. Unfortunately, ignorance in this case is not bliss; but instead, a hell constructed by their own uncertainty, and by individuals whose crafting and exploitation is most often exemplified by their willingness to use and control others to make the case.

Number Three is the real anomaly, as it is completely beyond comprehension *why* someone would choose to earn off such a dangerous method of employment. I was told by a friend of mine in law enforcement that the amount of pay is "sometimes commensurate with the results," meaning that if you're setting people up for buy busts on a scale of say, an ounce of coke, heroin, or a "boat" of fentanyl (a boat equals one thousand pills), you might make five hundred bucks per buy. But if the amount of narcotics is a kilo, there's no way your local law enforcement is going to afford paying you tens of thousands of dollars. And with no pension nor benefits to speak of, the motivation becomes even harder to define.

Of even more concern is that Number Three's willingness to provide information is sometimes performed *not* for pay... but for free.

I would argue that Number Three does not offer free information to the police with the belief that they're making some positive contribution to society. Rather, this is usually a bi-product of some malicious or jealous sentiment, or an act of vengeance upon another. Because snitch Number Three is an individual that utilizes subterfuge and deceit to defeat their enemies rather than to combat them head on.

As is the case with bad criminals, I ceased trying to figure out certain aspects of human nature long ago, and I simply see some folks for what they are: dangerous and unpredictable to all those within their sphere of influence, seeking gratification through the harm of others in hopes that self-worth can be obtained in an otherwise worthless existence.

Needless to say, I apply this same sentiment to those that fall within the categorization of snitch Number Three. It is for them that my want for understanding or consideration for what they are will never extend. We know what they are.

To steer clear of these types is to avoid danger, either because they are the danger's genesis or because we don't want to be in proximity to them when danger inevitably searches them out, which it most assuredly will.

PERDITION

When someone decides to cooperate, there usually takes place within them a dialogue or one-on-one talk where they justify what they are about to do for the sake of themselves, their significant other, family, freedom, for king and country- you name it.

Attachment to materialism can be stronger than our integrity, more so if our integrity is defined by our material-ism. It becomes easy to take the route touted as having the least resistance.

Being that the person(s) they snitch on will more than likely be an associate, friend, or family member, informants – with the encouragement of law enforcement – will then distort their opinions about their intended target. This distortion then paints a picture of someone who is much worse than they appear in order for the informant to come to terms with their betrayal.

Once an individual has committed to the act of cooperat-ing, a shift has taken place in their value system where consid-eration for others is no longer a priority, nor an afterthought, nor even a golden rule far back in the recesses of memory. Prioritizing the preservation of one's self now takes prece-dence over All.

What's interesting to observe, and what most tend to overlook, is that it is often our most basic instinct to survive; that feeling of self-preservation that triggers our fight-or-flight response which inevitably results in a successful "flip," much like tossing a coin in the air and determining a pathway via heads-or-tails.

Unfortunately, these instincts are not in tune with today's world, and were more apt to save our skin in an environment when we were still hunting and gathering in order to survive. Regrettably, law enforcement uses shock and terror tactics that are designed to trigger our fight/flight response, which then forces most to make decisions rather quickly and foolishly.

These tactics are similar to the rather transparent strategies used by aggressive salespersons the world over, in that when they suggest you purchase their wares *now!* as opposed to later – that purchase – or failure to do so, is going to mean the difference between instance gratification or buyer's guilt.

When this practice is applied to your freedom, rather than a new vacuum, it isn't hard to see just how many of us will be sold on the offer. However, it's not until the deal is closed that we begin to have that feeling of cognitive dissonance, which often describes the amount of misgiving and regret one experiences after being coerced into an expensive purchase.

NOTE: Aggressive sales tactics can include a variety of techniques that may be considered high-pressure or manipulative. Review the methods below, and determine if any of these have ever parallelled a conversation, interrogation, or discussion between you and law enforcement, or anyone for that matter. I have been interrogated by police before, in fact several times as a minor (which was illegal). The parallels between those conversations and the sales tactics listed below are shocking:

- Hard sell: A direct, forceful, and insistent sales approach that may include abrupt language, cold calls, unwanted pitches, or misinforming the consumer. Hard sells can also involve directly challenging a prospect's objections.
- Upselling: A common technique where a salesperson tries to convince a customer to buy a more expensive version of a product or add extra features. Aggressive upselling involves using pressure and manipulation to persuade customers to spend more than they intended.
- Scare tactics: Using fear to convince a customer that they need a product.
- Guilt: Using guilt to force a customer to make a purchase.
- Refusing to leave: A salesperson refusing to leave a customer until they make a purchase.
- Pestering: Constantly contacting a customer to make a purchase.
- Appealing to children: Persuading parents to buy a product for their children, or for the sake of their loved ones.

We begin to question the actual value of what we purchased- if it was dearly sold, at what cost, and if its perceived utility was even worth our money, or in this instance, our freedom.

In addition to this philosophical perspective, there isn't any fine print to read that would outline a unilateral contract's less-than-favorable conditions. And to make matters worse, there was never anyone present to explain the terms and conditions – besides the sales rep – that will do and say anything they can in order to close the deal.

Once an agreement through coercion has been struck, this

also makes us more pliable and easier to manipulate than previous.

This freshly tapped susceptibility also allows for decision making which reflects the thinking of one who lets others make decisions for them. As a result, the end product of those decisions probably will not have your best interests in mind.

The police would have the informant believe that the best thing they could do for themselves is cooperate, because it not only helps *you*, but it helps a society that desperately needs another hand in the fight against all that is unlawful. By cooperating, you are supposedly making the transition from someone that was bad and criminal, into someone that is good and worthy of society's consideration.

This is of course, bullshit, or just another sales pitch. And all you really are is a criminal. One who will probably *never* transition, at least not on your own, as your lack of fortitude and commitment is demonstrated in your ability to be manipulated by something as commonplace as the threat of imprisonment, which is what you are facing anyways (or so say the police).

Because of this unflattering self-portrait the informant inexorably painted, he/she/they have made of themselves nothing more than a tool that is to be used with caution lest it hurt its operator, and then quickly discarded once it no longer serves its intended purpose.

Law enforcement distrusts cooperating informants, and has a greater mistrust and dislike for them than the hardened criminal from whom they know what to expect. This is because the informant is a volatile and unpredictable element in the criminal world.

The only way to control such volatility is to instill a level of control through fear that supersedes the informant's inclination towards self-preservation, in the most reckless and puzzling of ways... snitching.

Ultimately, what forms is a relationship of constant chastisement followed by proverbial pats on the head, i.e., "Good job bud." "Here's your check for 500 bucks Number Three." Or, "Name three, and you're free." "Don't lose sight of what's important to you and your family..."

This particular method of tit-for-tat reinforcement closely resembles the way some humans train dogs; e.g., rubbing the dog's nose in its own feces when it has accidentally defecated in the "master's" house. And then tossing the dog a scrap from the master's table when it does something commendable.

This is comparable to the police talking to you, and treating you like shit, only to reinforce their abusive verbalizations with head-pats and ear-scratches for risking your very life to ruin another's. Let that sink in for a moment...

Although law enforcement has an obligation to protect its cooperating "witnesses," those witnesses must realize that that obligation ends the same time as their usefulness does. The police are well aware that no matter what type of The Three an informant is, their contributions have nothing to do with the greater good, and everything to do with furthering their own ends.

Mutual aid between two opposing parties creates an environment of abhorrence and dissension among those involved. Once this allegiance has ended, so too will any consideration from one party to another.

The informant is a secret weapon to the police, and most effective in its purpose. It is an infiltration unit that looks, talks, and interacts with others as if it were a criminal itself (think Terminator film franchise).

What informants must realize, however, is that they are an expendable tool with an inexhaustible number of replacements for which it can be substituted. And federal, state, and local law enforcement use and discard informants much like the rest of us use and discard toilet paper.

It is only the person targeted by law enforcement, and for whom the informant is intent on setting up, that places any consideration or value on the informant themselves. The greater this target's criminal status is, the greater the worth police place upon the informant tasked with gathering evidence on the target objective. Never forget this... <u>you informants out there are only worth the value law enforcement places on their next arrest.</u>

If we are involved in criminal activity of any kind, it is practically guaranteed that we will be arrested. If said arrest did not include people more desirable to law enforcement than ourselves, rest assured that we will be at a crossroads of a very important juncture on our pathway as criminals.

If you have already been arrested know that the path to freedom and a better life *must* derive from your own ability to make the correct choices, and by plotting a course for a conscientious future via ensuring each step was made with your transition in sight; and not by taking the easiest route, thereby leaving the most collateral damage in your wake.

We must never attempt to safeguard ourselves and our freedom by compromising others while serving the interests of those whose lives and job security are still defined by criminality, i.e, law enforcement and criminals alike.

It is often said that to take the path of least resistance is to travel a road that provides an easier route to where we are going– and parallels another adage, "work smarter, not harder." But the path of least resistance, in this case, is an illusion; or a deception rather, which provides the traveler with more barriers, pitfalls, and detours than they would've thought possible.

To walk a higher path, or the road less traveled, is to set a course that may seem harder at the outset, but will prove worth traveling in the long run. And, at the end of which we will find our integrity and principles still intact, if not stronger and more plentiful than they were before.

Some would argue that our involvement in criminal activity would be indicative of those lacking integrity in the first place. I would counter by saying that finding it, or strengthening it through accepting responsibility – and resolving *not* to forfeit something as quickly as it was discovered – would seem preferable to discarding integrity via subservience to materialism, persuasion, or even intimidation and fear instilled within us by others.

The route others would have you take is easily discerned by the benefits it provides them. The path mapped out by others whose interests are in opposition to your own is the road to perdition. Granted, the paths we choose may inevitably lead to challenges. But I prefer an approach designed by my choices as opposed to someone shoving me onto a trajectory that would most certainly lead to a disastrous outcome.

IS THE JUICE WORTH THE SQUEEZE?

The thinly disguised threats posed as questions or scenarios one is presented with when being flipped are designed to prevent us from having time to think about the predicament we've found themselves in.

Threats, scenarios and assertions that strongly hint at impending doom are the hallmark of police around the world whose intent is to flip you and have you on the streets that very same day, cultivating information for their investigations.

If we have time to think, we also have time to consider the proposition being offered as a shallow one- single-dimensional in purpose and scope. The art of the flip is one of expediency, and relies heavily upon coercion through misdirection and subterfuge, with just enough truth to keep you hoping you'll walk out a "free" person, rather than being shackled and entering a county, city, or federal lockup.

The more time they spend in jail or missing appointments, or not answering the phone, the harder it is for that person to come up with a viable excuse as to why they weren't available.

When you disappear, the street gets antsy and She begins to wonder why you were absent when you should've been more considerate of Her feelings, Her time... and Her needs.

A swiftly executed bust or arrest is done with as much speed as possible. Sometimes a careful inspection of your personal belongings, texts sent by people, etc., provide more insight into the person they intend on flipping. And anything from religious symbols around your rearview mirror, or who you're dating, or the type of music you favor, may provide some indication as to how best they can relate before they manipulate.

It is not until after the celebration of your arrest – replete with high-fives, handshakes, circle jerks and back-slapping – and after they've had a chance to calm down from the coffee, energy drinks and other stimulants they consume do the police begin to initiate the flip.

Flipping is most often practiced using the Good Cop/Bad Cop routine, the bad cop being the most boisterous and roughest during your arrest. The good cop, of course, counters the bad cop's bravado and abuse to gain your trust in a rather paternal fashion.

The flip begins by the bad cop storming into your interrogation room and informing you that he's got you now, and whether or not you want to make a deal means shit to him. Because he doesn't like you, doesn't give a fuck about you, and would rather you *not* cooperate, because he couldn't stand the thought of a piece of shit like you catching a lucky break... you motherfucker, you.

Then – almost as if on cue – strolls in the fatherly and caring police officer, (A.K.A, the Good Cop), who calmy tells his buddy to go find you a coffee and a cigarette, "Oh, that's right, you don't smoke, would you like some water, something from the vending machine?" Then he attempts to relate to you based on the personal items they rifled through in your car or your place of arrest; how very dire your situation is, but that it's good it's finally over because things could have gone a lot worse if Bad Cop was leading the operation. They received intelligence that you were armed and dangerous, etc., etc...

Several things have already occurred backstage and right in front of you. Your life and freedom were threatened by bad cop, and your life was also threatened (and saved) by good cop leading the arrest, and good cop coming to your rescue.

Now... depending on which role you're more receptive to – good cop's paternal kindness or bad cop's intimidation – or a combination of both, your amenability to either will be the determining factor as to which method will be used to flip you.

What makes this so unnerving, is that it is the police who are doing it. It isn't until after you've agreed and your freedom was won that most experience that feeling of cognitive dissonance, which is your sub-conscious warning you of a counterfeit freedom purchased at too high a cost.

Unless you were raised in a tightknit crime family, gang, or in a neighborhood that has been besieged by the police for generations, the likelihood of you being flipped by the Good Cop/Bad Cop scenario is pretty high.

The more aggressive flip is often used when time is of the essence, or when the attempt to kill you with kindness is not as effective as they had hoped. At this point, both cops drop the facade and good cop's face contorts into something much different than what first greeted you in the interrogation room.

NOTE: Myself and a friend were arrested for multiple felony assaults after being jumped at a party. I was White (still am), my friend was a large Hispanic who came from a well-known and rather tough family, full of uncles that had done time. When the Good Cop/Bad Cop routine failed, they cuffed me to a post in the center of an empty concrete room about two feet high off the floor. (I had to kneel on the ground. I could not stand). Two police with ski masks on then circled me while a third held a German Shepeard barking inches from me while they yelled things like, "You think

Daniel gives a fuck about you? His uncles are already waiting to take care of him in prison! (We were just with his uncles earlier that night. None of them were in prison.) "Your white ass is going to get fucked, ripped open, and left in the showers!" And on and on this went while their dog ripped at my shoes and spit from the cops' lips flew from their mouths onto my face. I was 17 years of age.

The aggressive flip is usually punctuated by the detectives telling you to stand up to be re-shackled, as they tell the uniform cops to get this piece of shit out of their site, and they'll see you in twenty years, fucker.

It is this coarse, highly unprofessional, and foul-mouthed dismissal that usually marks the moment of truth – when someone has been teetering on the edge of indecision and they are about to be introduced to jail – that causes them to cooperate.

Sometimes people make the decision after enduring a few days of booking and the experience is more than they can handle. Other times, people discover that jail isn't that bad; that your people bailed you out, or the judge released you as a first-time offender, and your freedom is won through the normal course of the justice system, and no flip was necessary.

NOTE: I had a friend of Korean lineage, who was a small, thin, and well-mannered guy that was arrested for trafficking. As fate would have it, he was snitched on by an individual with the same surname as his own. The snitch that set him up was the most dangerous, belonging to the third category, and was known for routinely ratting on people by having them come to his father's car dealership where the police waited among the many vehicles for sale. Fate determined that he would die last year of a drug overdose.

Everyone thought "The Korean" had flipped. To the contrary. He stayed in county jail for several months until our attorney got his bail reduced from $100k to $10k. He got out, he pled guilty, and he went on with his life. He now manages a highly-popular restaurant, and is straight as an arrow.

The threat of an abrupt end to life as you know it is quite often the thing that brings about a successful flip. There are also many loose ends the police point out that cannot, that must not, go unattended, i.e., your children, your job, mortgage, fiancé, girlfriend/boyfriend, etc.

God forbid they point out they need you to keep up your criminal practices to maintain the illusion. God forbid the police even encourage you to continue committing crime so long as it is of a non-violent nature. Once your obligation to them is over, they still have one more unreformed criminal they can rearrest and charge... You.

What most folks who are arrested don't realize is that in states where bonding out via a bail/bond company still exists (New Mexico transitioned to Criminal Alternative Dispute Resolution or ADR some years ago) is that only ten percent of your bail amount is needed to secure your release, i.e., bail is ordered at $100k Cash or Surety X .10 = ten thousand dollars.

A bail of 100 grand cash only is usually set for people who have criminal pasts, such as mine, that are characteristic of a career criminal, i.e., multiple past charges for the same current offense, violence, etc.

The argument then is that despite how scary or expensive your arrest may seem, it is by no means the apocalyptic end of your world, as some would have you believe. It might be the end of your month, or summer, or your twenties, (as it was the end of my twenties, and half of my thirties). But more importantly, if we're smart, and we choose correctly, it *will* be the end of our criminal career.

THE INSIDE

"He has sent me to bind up the brokenhearted, to proclaim freedom for the captives and release from darkness for the prisoners."

— JESUS CHRIST

I can honestly state that my own opinions about prison have changed drastically from those I harbored before coming here.

I never once witnessed someone on the receiving end of violence who didn't deserve it. Being an informant, a child molester, a rapist, or not paying your gambling or drug debts are, by far, the most prevalent of offenses one is guilty of committing; hence, subject to punishment for.

Even if an inmate is generally viewed as overly timid compared to the average convict – as long as their jacket is clean – they are often left to their own designs, in their cell, yard, handball court, library, art studio, or wherever else they choose to do their time.

I never witnessed or was subjected to the random acts of extreme sexual or physical violence the police so fastidiously depicted for me when I was a minor, and promised I would fall victim to when I got to prison. My arrest, and the shock and impact that federal agents and their tactics had on me were by far the most stressful moments of my life as compared to the rather tranquil, if not boring years I have thus far experienced in prison.

It takes a strong-willed person to tell the cops they would rather take it on the chin than to cooperate and secure their instant yet temporary freedom by informing on others.

But an uncooperative witness can also experience years of subjugation and harassment from police since childhood, which then trains them, reflexively, to never speak to the police under any circumstances. Prisons are often filled with this type of convict; unwavering in their belief system, their loyalty to the neighborhood which fostered and cared for them, and the criminal enterprise which advanced them to a point.

Squeezing an orange to yield the juice it contains is a common enough practice. It is also common practice to dispose of the orange peel once it no longer contains what made it of value. This same act will be performed on you should you ever choose or be coerced into cooperating in a criminal investigation.

COUNTERMEASURES

"Non-cooperation with evil is as much a duty as cooperation with good."

— MAHATMA GANDHI

In regards to combating the flip, as with anything in life, being prepared for it is key. Arming ourselves with the necessary knowledge to resist terror tactics is essential to coming out of this particular battle unscathed; or, if not unscathed, stronger and less damaged as a result of accepting punishment on our terms rather than theirs.

Granted, any arrest or criminal history can be harmful, but only insofar as it remains current, instead of slipping further into the recesses of history. The prolonged mental and financial strain of enduring legal difficulties are perhaps the most damaging in nature. Just think how much more we would endanger ourselves, our families, and our futures when cooperation occurs and becomes common knowledge.

We must acknowledge our existence within a country whose laws, at first, minimize the amount of damage sustained by committing illegal acts. And that punishment compounds and worsens as we demonstrate a continued propensity for crime, as well as further indifference towards a lawful state of being.

In order to flip someone, the law must have you believe otherwise- that the judge will throw the proverbial book at you for your first arrest and conviction. That you will be cast into a lawless prison where violence is far more erratic and indifferent to those targeted by it.

The truth is convicts subscribe to a form of justice, and a justice system, that is far more humane than the one which places us behind bars.

In order to be flipped, you must be made to believe that your situation is a dire one, one that no lawyer or amount of money could possibly rectify. The only way to relieve ourselves of this circumstance is to have a friend on the inside of the system we have now found ourselves targeted by: the police.

What we really need to be mindful of is the law, our own criminal history, or lack thereof, and what that means after an initial arrest. Unless it's a federal case the chances of going to prison for a drug bust, possession, unarmed robbery, etc., are extremely low; and when I say extremely, I mean it.

There is not a State in our Union that has mandatory sentences for first time drug offenses. If there is, there also exists loopholes, probation, bootcamp, community service and other alternatives that would better serve the offender, and their community, as opposed to placing someone behind bars for a first-time non-violent offense.

We also need to be aware of what the maximum penalty is for the crime we are accused of; the sentence that accompanies the classification of drugs and the amount we were caught with, and other information relative to the level of punishment we *could* receive, as opposed to basing our decisions upon the amount of time law enforcement is assuring us we *will* receive.

Don't lose sight of the fact that if the chain of arrest stops with you, the police will have to actually investigate and draft a report, rather than have an informant do their job for them. This too ensures that their investigation of your activities is stymied instead of the snowball effect they hoped your cooperation would cause.

Knowing what laws we are governed and punished by, particularly for trafficking in narcotics, should also require of us to take preventative measures that would reduce the severity of our sentence when it comes time for us to fall; such as carrying guns with drugs, selling drugs near schools, dealing crack instead of coke, fentanyl instead of heroin, or cooking methamphetamine as opposed to consuming it.

Of course, it would be preferable if, after learning the possible penalties for our criminal actions, we would then have the prescience to discontinue these actions all together instead of using that information to avoid stricter sentencing while continuing to commit crimes.

It is my hope that those of us who are imbued with this knowledge use it as a deterrent to crime instead of simply minimizing its affects. But our lives are determined by our choices, and not by any hopes that I may have for us.

Listed below are a few of the more commonplace inquiries posed by law enforcement leading up to and during a flip. Also listed are a few of the more common threats, tactics, and ploys used by police in order to acquire information that is not so easily relinquished. In addition to the questions and tactics used by police, I have listed the countermeasures that can be utilized in order to deter further probing by the same.

NOTE: It is crucial that I point out the proper response to any unwarranted questioning or coercion is <u>silence, or a verbal invocation of your right to an attorney</u>. Also, if you have not been Mirandized, i.e., read your Miranda rights, this too could result in a dismissal of your case. *See* Miranda v. Arizona, 384 U.S. 436. This case was a landmark Supreme Court decision that requires people must be made aware of their rights before being questioned. Another requirement is that the suspect must be in custody when being mirandized.

Countermeasures are steps that we should be mentally walking ourselves through during their attempted flip. Also remember that to even *speak* or sign anything is to possibly incriminate yourself by the sound of your voice, the hand that you're using, or the signature you're providing. The answers to the questions posed by police are answers you should be working out in your head rather than verbalizing them to law enforcement.

Q&A

Q. Do you want to help yourself? This is perhaps the most blatant form of flipping in that it requires little imagination to figure out what making a deal consists of. This inquiry also comes in varying degrees of the same offer, i.e., "Do you want to make a deal? Do you want to help your family? Do you want to help others for a change?" and so forth.

Every question posed by law enforcement is a carefully and psychologically engineered query designed, not necessarily for you, but your personality type and disposition (don't go thinking you're unique or more intelligent than the next criminal when you're not). Unless you're being interrogated by a rookie, most police have dealt with all types of people; hence, it's safe to assume that they also know which style of questioning you will be most susceptible to.

A. When any member of law enforcement has you in an interrogation room, you are either under arrest or their hope is that you will be very soon, either by your own testimony or by evidence they already have for which they hope you will be kind or stupid enough to supplement.

When the police are asking you if you want to help yourself, we should be translating that in our heads to mean, "Yes, *I* want to help *Myself.*" That help can only come from within. There is not a deal out there that would entail *you* helping *yourself* by helping another. It doesn't work that way.

If our self-talk has time to continue, it should go along the lines of... "As a police officer whose job it is to make arrests, and not judge or prosecute a case, is this person even qualified to assume that I will be convicted and sent to prison; in which case, how valid is this so-called deal?" "When has a deal every been equally beneficial to both parties when one party is in a position of leverage over the other?"

The short Answer is, "At this time, on audio and video recording as documentation, I invoke my right to speak to an attorney." Even when the attorney comes, you still say nothing.

Q. Do you think any of the people that we want you to set up would take the rap for this if situations were reversed? How do you think we caught you? These are questions designed to help you come to the conclusion that it's a dog-eat-dog world out there, and it's ok for us to continue our downward spiral in an environment that lacks principles and values. And passing the buck by snitching on others is no more dishonorable than selling drugs or whatever you were arrested for. But we already know that don't we?

The problem with this rationale is that we *do* live in a world where values have eroded to the point where the lines between what is right and wrong have become a bit hazy. Although crime is by no means the right way to go about making a living, it doesn't mean that you have to subject yourself and your beliefs to further erosion via practicing new acts that we know to be less than honorable.

Just because someone did it to us does not mean we have *carte blanche* or complete freedom to burn someone else and continue the cycle.

By allowing ourselves to be flipped, this decision only further convinces law enforcement that our character is substandard; thus, it is of less concern to them what may happen to a substandard human being that they now have to manage and work with to set up and arrest other substandard human beings.

A. "I can't speak to what others would do in my place. How you caught me isn't my concern. If someone snitched me out to save their own ass that's on them, and I feel sorry for that person when their decisions catch up with them."

Again, these are statements you should be saying to yourself to prevent your being disadvantaged and threatened to cause you to cooperate or even opening channels of communication between yourself and those who are interrogating you.

If enough people refuse to cooperate, it may cause law enforcement to question their own dubious methods of fighting crime, and whether flipping informants is the most principled form of protecting the communities they are tasked with policing.

Q. Why risk losing all you've fought for when you can help us help yourself in the process, and start a new life or go back to living your old one as if this ever happened?

What this question is alluding to is the possibility that you won't take such a large hit as you would should you refuse to cooperate. It also alludes to the fact that the police are complacent, or indifferent, if not supportive of our continued criminality so long as it furthers their interests. They have no interest in our transition. In fact, our transition would be detrimental to their job security. You would of course continue to commit crimes under the guise of a criminal who has now flipped. But at some point, you will run out of information. You will run out of usefulness, and when they tidy up their multiple investigations, you will be re-arrested and sentenced along with all the others you informed against.

A. "Why don't I just help you destroy what others have worked for while I continue down the path of my own destruction? Because that's what you're offering me. At what time does my usefulness run out, and at what point does my inability to provide you with further arrests guarantee me a much deadlier prison experience than the probation or minimal amount of jail time I would've received had I refused to cooperate? Are you offering me a choice that's already mine to make or are you saying I can continue to commit crimes with impunity and the blessing of the police force so long as I feed you arrests in return?"

Trust that the person who offers you leniency in the form

of Question No. 3 is perhaps one of the more ruthless adversaries you will come across. This will be the same person who re-arrests you and goes out of their way to pull your protection when the time comes. For, surely this detective can't have a liability such as yourself running around committing crimes under the assumption that he *allowed* you to do so. You even know his name and could testify in court against him, costing him his pension and everything he's worked for. Why would he risk that when he can simply throw you to the wolves and site your violence or continued criminality as something that outweighed the benefits you were providing?

In truth, no matter how many questions you are asked or how many different formats they're packaged in, knowing the intent behind these questions is equal to knowing that any answer you give short of confessing or cooperating will never appease them. How many real interviews have you seen on cop shows where the police tell the suspect, "The more you tell me the more I can help you, and the more you can help yourself?" And after all that help was given, how many times have you seen the cops stand that person up and slap the cuffs on them before saying, "although we appreciate your honesty, we must also bring charges against you for incriminating testimony, but thanks for coming clean nonetheless."

The purpose of the investigation is to get information that will incriminate as many people as possible, including and/or especially the one being interrogated. Declining to answer any questions, and refusing to be goaded, threatened or intimidated is to exercise your rights under the law.

Refusing to cooperate also provides legal protection against an organization(s) whose sole purpose is not to judge or interpret the law, but to enforce it; and to make arrests based on the belief, suspicion, assumption, and concrete or circumstantial evidence provided that a crime was committed.

Remember that we belong to a nation of freedoms, with laws to counterbalance and protect those freedoms. Some of these laws protect us from incriminating ourselves by volunteering facts that should otherwise be discovered through investigative police work. And to offer these facts, gratis, and at the expense of our freedom, is to not practice the law as it was designed for safeguarding the citizens of this country; both from themselves and from others.

This next segment will cover a few of the statements that, like the questions, are meant for a sole purpose. If we bear in mind that it is most often voluntary or forced disclosure that places us in legal peril, and not due diligence of law enforcement, then we remain one step ahead of the flip.

FACT & FICTION

Statement: We've got you now. You're staring down the barrel at X-Amount of Time. How much you want to help yourself is entirely up to you.

Truer words have never been spoken! They do in fact have you. Although they seem to forget that "having" you is only a temporary thing, and that helping yourself consists of so much more than merely helping them.

If we've done our homework and know our local, state and federal sentencing guidelines, then we know that the only time we're "staring down the barrel" is when they had their firearms pointed at us while being placed under arrest. If they lied about staring down the barrel of 10, 20 years, or life in prison, then what else are they being untruthful about?

How much we help ourselves is comprised of how well we've prepared for the inevitable day of our arrest. Do you have money set aside that can be easily accessed by others to secure your freedom and the retainment of an attorney? Do we have a chunk we can come home to and/or rely on once our criminal careers are over and a forced transition requires of us to begin school or job hunting?

Response: You're right. How much I want to help

myself is entirely up to me; and my friends, family, and part-ners in crime that have helped me thus far. Why would I put them in harm's way when all they've ever done is help me?

If we've done our homework, then we know the circum-stances we've placed ourselves in are not good, though not as bad as they would have you believe. And that because we've prepared for this day, it isn't necessary that we take the hand they've offered us; which, I might add, is the same hand that pointed a gun at us, and slapped the cuffs on while we were being arrested.

Statement: Your boy is in the next room, telling the other detectives (over a cheeseburger lunch), everything we need to know. Now's the time to come clean before he buries both of you.

This statement can be translated to, "We are telling "your boy" that you are in the next room, over a cheeseburger lunch, ratting on him; and hopefully, one of you will be stupid enough to believe us. We've got bets on you, and bets on your buddy, (the winner gets a free cheeseburger lunch paid for by his fellow detectives)."

This particular situation can be a good indication that they have absolutely nothing, or very little, on both of you. And they're hoping that one of you will be gracious enough to provide them with *something* before they stand you up and walk you out of the precinct, and into the free world.

Response: If that's the case, then why aren't we both in jail?

Although I have been interrogated countless times, the only time I fell victim to this strategy was when I was about 10 years-of-age. The interrogation was performed illegally and the buddy I was with quickly folded. I think we were stealing candy bars or something. Usually you and your "buddy" will know what's at stake, as well as the tactics that the police use during dual interrogations. Thus, it would be safe to assume that as long as you said nothing and denied everything, so would your buddy.

It is crucial in criminal partnerships that each party is aware of the risks and both be willing to accept the consequences. The shyer out of the two of you, and the one with less criminal history will definitely be the one they will try to break. If your partner is a friend, it might also be to your respective benefits that you both take steps to move the partnership, or one like it, towards legitimate enterprises, and see if you can't work together, honestly and profitably.

Statement: You're not doing anything wrong by helping us. Or, there is no honor amongst thieves.

This can be translated to, "You yourself, as a shitbag criminal, have no honor, so what is it to a person such as you to betray another whose ideals, or lack thereof, are in conjunction with your own flawed sense of right and wrong?"

This is just one more act of coercion with the purpose of persuading you to disregard that gut feeling in your stomach that is telling you not to agree with a most disagreeable proposition. If there were no honor amongst criminals, there would be no such thing as successful criminal enterprise whose profits and influence could not have been achieved without some measure of trust, honesty, and loyalty among its members.

Response: "Perhaps there is no honor amongst thieves. But I am not being interrogated for theft. And the decision I'm making not to cooperate feels a whole hell of a lot more honorable than what you're suggesting I do."

There are countless statements that can be used as examples; or tricks and deceits fabricated to secure your cooperation to incriminate others, or to incriminate yourself.

To discover the true purpose of the interrogation or flip is to acknowledge that these processes have everything to do with arrests and nothing to do with providing those that are flipped with a clean slate, better life, or a chance to do some good. You-are-a-Criminal. Never forget it. I assure you, those who are not criminals never will.

DEFINING MOMENTS

The pincer-like scenario where one is caught between a rock and a hard place, or instant jail time versus temporary freedom – where neither alternative provides relief – but only a constant pressure which they are placed in the middle of, is the very thing that police hope will grind away at a person's resolve until they choose a path that is not their own.

I would argue that to *not* fold or flip is to be honorable. To not cooperate is to be courageous and upright in the face of adversity, and to accept sole responsibility for our plight. To not bend through intimidation or coercion is prudent and praiseworthy, not because it protects others but because it safeguards our integrity. To not provide cooperation is to demonstrate a steadfastness of character that is not readily identifiable in all criminals whom police interact with, and you will be remembered for it.

Voluntarily providing information for the purpose of preventing a harmful crime committed by a bad criminal – not for monetary gain or to lessen the severity of your own conviction – but for the safety and concern of a fellow human being, is to be what an informant was intended to be; one that protects others who are unable or unaware they need to protect themselves.

A situation where someone needs protection from unlawful and unwarranted harm from others – and where the informant is not at a vantage point or lacks the physical or mental fortitude to defend the targeted victim – should be the only scenario in which an informant functions.

ROUTING

Are the police not on the side of justice? Is "To Serve and To Protect" not quoted on the side of every marked police vehicle? Does the option they provide not pose a lesser threat being that you are now under the protection of the law and not lawlessness? Isn't it their job to protect *you*? Unfortunately, this is not entirely true.

Their idea of protecting and serving the public will always be at the criminal's expense, which, in this instance, happens to be ours.

In order to see yourself as someone who needs protection, you must first be victimized by some form of criminality – recognized by the police as an unlawful act – committed against an otherwise lawful citizen. If, however, you *are* the crime, how could you expect any protection from those whose mission it is to combat you? Is it really feasible then, that cooperating would be the safest and best practice? I think not.

If you have reached the point in your career where you are now under arrest or in an interrogation room and are being offered a deal in exchange for your cooperation, would it not be wiser to consider that *now* is the end of your criminal career? Why would you even entertain the possibility of further immersion in an enterprise that has, thus far, failed to such an extent that you now have to consider risking your life to save your freedom?

<u>Know that the choice to sever yourself from any further criminal acts does not and should not require more criminality on your part;</u> nor should it be encouraged on behalf of the police that arrested you.

NOTE: Our inevitable arrest (and possible imprisonment) may very well be a blessing in disguise, as mine was for me. Prison did not make me worse; it improved me to the extent that I was committed to survive, and to thrive legitimately upon returning home... and I did. There were no lasting effects from my time behind bars (apart from gaining weight after I was released and eating delicious food at every opportunity). Once in a while I'll awake from prison dreams where I'm in a place that is dramatically worse than the reality of prison, i.e., constant darkness pierced by thunder, castle-like dungeons, rats and other vermin crawling around. In fact, I used to have these dreams while I was still in prison, only to awake and say to myself, "Thank God I'm in *my* prison, and not the one I dreamt about!" My prison had a reputation for being one of the worst places to do time in the entire country... and it wasn't that bad, honestly.

"There is no honor amongst thieves." I would also argue that police who utilize snitches as their secret weapon are lacking honor themselves, or else why would they encourage and practice such dishonorable methods amongst our populace, civilian and criminal alike? To encourage someone to give up their enemies if they don't want to give up their friends is to demonstrate how little honor is involved on both sides of the spectrum.

Now that we have an idea of what the flip consists of, try to focus not so much on the questions being posed to you, but rather the questions and statements you should be asking yourself. 'What will be the end results for me and my family if I cooperate?' 'Prison is not what the police are making it out to be.' 'I'm only staring down the barrel at a year's worth of probation, and zero prison time!' My situation is not as bad as they are making it seem.' 'I can do this.' 'I'm stronger than this. I'm stronger than they realize...'

For every criminal that chooses to cooperate with law enforcement, know that there are countless others that choose not to. There are also countless civilians that have been witnesses to crimes who are attempted or forced into bearing witness. And yet, these people choose not to.

Pitting friend against friend, or family member against family member, or even enemy against enemy is not a new concept employed by those who are at odds with a foreign adversary. But utilizing informants in our communities, and in the fashion practiced by law enforcement seems to be demonstrable of hostility between neighnors, if not a state of civil conflict.

Is law enforcement through the use of informants utilizing one of the only effective methods available to combat drug trafficking, murder, and other crimes that have steadily increased over the years? I really can't say. Is the use of informants by police placing people in harm's way, and further eroding the ethics of our justice system, our neighborhoods, and people who operate on both sides of the spectrum? Absolutely.

It is the consequences of informing that cause me to believe that perhaps it would be better if covert cooperation with law enforcement should be outlawed entirely, not solely due to the violence and dissension it promotes among our citizenry and the relationship between police and communities. But because of the erosion of conscience and principle it breeds among all those who are party to its advent.

Any individual whose job description includes enforcing what is right should also be averse to encouraging behavior that is wrong, and that corrodes the values of those they are supposed to protect. Snitching to save your own ass would, in my opinion, run contrary to beliefs and best practices that law enforcement policies proclaim they instill. And yet, this is the preferred and most effective method of combating crime.

Informing against another to reduce the severity of one's own sentence ought to be prohibited. Or, if not made illegal, then no leniency other than consideration by the court (not the police) that the informant has saved a life, prevented a murder, or some other bad criminal act; thus, proving themselves worthy of a possible sentence reduction.

The legal requirements for cooperating should be rele-

<u>gated only for the purpose of protecting another individual as
opposed to advancing one's own interests.</u>

Because the act of cooperation, such as it is today, is not moral. Nor is it safe, nor reflective of a form of policing that trumpets its ability to protect as a virtue.

The only thing the informant has to offer the police was never theirs to begin with: incriminating information about others in exchange for lessening the impact of the information the police have concerning *you.*

Information in general has become a resource today; a form of currency whose value is determined by the worth of the information itself. A resource that has far out-performed its predecessors in its ability to afford us sustenance, affluence, and security. And yet, it is an intangible thing. It only exists insofar as its value or rate of exchange to others.

I find it unsettling to think that what people *know,* and what that knowledge can provide them with – in the form of both material and immaterial conciliation – and at the expense of others, is all it takes to minimize the measure of punishment resulting from what others know about *them.*

I find it disturbing that this resource or form of currency has drastically altered the way in which laws are enforced in this country. I find it reprehensible that this trading of information is an approved tactic of law enforcement; a tactic which is recklessly practiced, accepted, and endorsed by those who are supposed to stand for something more honorable than that which they are fighting.

I find it absolutely heartbreaking that our laws have made of our citizenry a nation of whistleblowers, tattle tails, snitches, rats, liars, and masters of deception who traffic in a more valuable currency than money and illegal drugs combined- who are taught that to save their own asses is the American Way.

To believe in this concept, and to believe in a sense of freedom that this mode of operation encourages, is to believe in a deception more criminal than the acts for which most of us are being arrested.

Contrary to this entire work's purpose, I would much rather us continue to commit crimes than to victimize, or allow ourselves to be victimized by something as abstract and indifferent as Information.

9
IN TIME

 On the streets is where I do my time... In prison
is where I'm free."

— DARIO

Prison. It's such an outlandish place for one to spend any
length of time, be it a year or several. Before I came here, to
hear of it, or to have friends come back from it was like
hearing about an unpopular war that somehow, I had
managed to avoid being drafted into... until now.

As with conflict, prison's survivors and veterans have their
war stories and battle scars. It was from these survivors that I
heard much of what prison entailed prior to experiencing it
first-hand.

Veterans of the prison system are quite comparable to
veterans having served in the military. Several of the inmates
in prison who were interviewed had also served in one military
branch or another, and experienced combat as far back as
Vietnam > Central American anti-drug conflicts in the 80s >
Desert Storm > Bosnia, and more current wars in the Middle
East.

There are also parallels in that time away from family, and

strife, both with the "enemy" and amongst those who band together to achieve a common goal are rather commonplace. Similarly, there exists a level of camaraderie and closeness with those that fight and survive together that can never be duplicated.

That familiarity or shared bond between us is often forged out of reliance upon someone as we've never relied on another person before. To know that the guy (or gal) watching your back holds your life in their hands, and vice versa, is to appreciate that person's vigil, if not their friendship, more so than you would an average friend or colleague on the street.

I can say with all candor, and no judgment, that some of the guys on the team in here, would not by any means be an associate on the streets. But because of the mutual benefit our strength in numbers provides, it forges allies with those who might otherwise be considered customers, rivals, and indeed enemies.

This circumstance, my imprisonment, has caused me to reevaluate my own ideas of what friendship consists of. And it brings to light my rather objectified and skewed perceptions concerning what people could *do* for me versus what those same people should have *meant* to me. I often overlooked significance in lieu of utility.

My current status as a prisoner has also allowed for plenty of reflection as to why we seek others out for friendship, for mutual benefit, for agency, and indeed for conflict.

In general terms, we seek that which we are attracted to, either because of the feelings invoked, the common interests that are easier to pursue as a collective, or some other need or sentiment that is satisfied through a relationship with another.

In prison, that shared sentiment is survival. And there is no substitute, no stand in that could possibly replace an alliance founded on the need to survive.

Long before my current reality, a friend who had been released after 5 years of prison on a retrial for murder told me he would forever be closer to his friends in prison than those on the street. He highly recommended prison time as a tool that would help us "put things in perspective," as the struggle, and the meaning behind it tends to get misinterpreted while on the streets.

He further related to me that the superficial makeup of the outside was something that made him long for the straightforwardness and easy-to-define lines in prison drawn between friend and foe, inmate and guard, and partnerships based on perseverance as opposed to those premised upon profit.

It is often this sentiment of "belonging" which segways to feeling more at home in an environment that most would see as hostile and uninhabitable.

Imagine if you will to what extent our needs have shifted – when we feel more at ease in an environment such as prison – than the one we dreamed about returning to for however many years our captivity lasts?

Imagine what the veteran feels like after returning home from serving one or more tours of duty, to be met by FFC who have not been changed by time and conflict. Consider if you will the veteran's mindset, and the eyes and other senses they use to perceive those they once knew as strangers in comparison to the men and women-at-arms they fought alongside of.

I had trouble believing that such a shift in thought and sentiment would be possible; that is, until I came here.

When I interviewed a repeat offender as to why he continued to spend more time behind bars than in the World, he stated to me that prison was simply a matter of comfort and convenience. When asked to elaborate, he told me that coming home to FFC that looked at him as if he were a stranger was more than he could handle. And with each homecoming, he felt more like a 5th wheel, or an uninvited guest, who was an intrusion upon an already whole and functioning family unit.

He further explained that his time at home felt like hard time in an uncomfortable place, and with people who were alienated by his presence- who viewed him as a potentially unstable element in an otherwise peaceful continuum.

'It was always like this,' he said to me. 'The first time I hit the streets, it was like heaven... after all those years.' 'Then, it was like we all saw this space between us, and the more time I spent with them, the bigger the space. It got to a point where we all cared less about rediscovering each other. It was easier for me to keep with the lifestyle I adopted in prison, and easier for them to continue living as if I never came back.'

The picture he painted was one I saw described by lots of people that either returned home from prison, or returned from the military after being "down range." The unfamiliarity with people that were once family can be the determining influence as to why so many returning citizens recidivate time and again.

While Chapter 5 deals with the immediate problem of familiarizing ourselves with social and legal aspects of reentry, i.e., probation and parole, here we will examine the damaging components of prison life, the side effects it has on those subjected to it, and how best to return home better-suited to once familiar conditions. In addition, we'll focus on mastering the ability to rediscover people we once knew; people who suffered due to our absence, who supported us while we were away. And who grew, matured, and saw personal progress while we were gone.

THE PROJECTS

 "You heard about the 'War On Drugs'
Now won't you tell me who you think winnin... Cuz it pay to play for a day up in my projects."

— COO COO CAL, MY PROJECTS

Whether it's jail, state, or a federal correctional center we may one day have the misfortune of calling home, know that they are all, more or less, designed with the same purpose in mind. Punishment via separation from the rest of the world and its freedoms.

Much like their criminal counterparts, *all* citizens eventually find themselves brushing against the law to one extent or the other.

For most, such chance encounters only further guide a trajectory towards the "straight and narrow," perhaps more so after they forgot to pay that traffic citation. But for others, this experience is perceived as par for the course, a minor setback. Unfortunately, this lack of concern or indifference towards a brief stint in county jail (rather than to give "the system" any money) is often the thing that precipitates a second, third, and fourth visit, either to the same place or eventually an institution designed to accommodate longer stays.

Jail is by no means prison; but on the flip-side of that coin, prison is a far better place than jail in many respects. Cramped and overcrowded conditions, lack of movement or recreation, a lack of respect by short-timers who don't know how to properly conduct themselves and must be taught one way or another- I believe I stayed in federal holding for well over a year before I finally threw in the towel, plead guilty, and was shipped off to Florence.

Being in the same one thousand square feet or so of real

estate, and going to an outside kennel maybe once a day in the warmer months will start to feel claustrophobic to anyone. It was a relief coming to prison and being able to "walk the line," lift weights, hit the yard, pick weeds, to feel dirt in my hands, music in my headphones, and a choice of television other than the same shit most inmates have the attention span to watch, i.e., music videos and reality TV.

But jail is just the tip of the iceberg. The ultimate destination - if your punishment is commensurate with the crime you committed – is prison. That word alone can be enough to cause some "bubble guts" in the stomach region.

Depending on the severity of the crime, the state you're located in, and most importantly, the temperament of other inmates, prison can either be a bad place to be... or a very bad place to be. In either case, it is by no means home, but rather, a form of communal purgatory that each of us resides within.

Have you ever lived in or visited the projects or a public housing community? Did you ever get the feeling that everyone residing there did so impermanently, and practically on top of one another? It's not really your front porch if twenty strangers are hanging out on the same entry stoop at the same time, is it?

That angst of feeling crowded by others, crowded by such a small amount of square footage; of having to share or possibly fight over the same broken washer machine or barbeque grill, in the same backyard, are just a few of the dynamics that make living in affordable housing projects difficult to bear.

When we take into consideration the criminal aspects that are prone to fester in public housing, those feelings of frustration and claustrophobia only begin to proliferate. For many people in our country, this is often what daily life consists of-enduring rather than living. And it is the very reason why no person or family lives in these communities for longer than is necessary.

Now take away from this mental picture of public housing the freedom to come and go as you please. Throw up gates and barbwire, not to keep trespassers out, but to keep those residing their within.

Remove the children, the senior citizens, and the opposite sex from the picture as well. Remove the sounds of youngsters playing and laughing, and people milling about or leaving to work and/or coming home. Remove the vegetation, scenery, and everything else needed to at least provide the facade and makings of a normal neighborhood.

Now... remember the small percentage of criminal element in this community? It is now 100% of the population. You now share the same kitchen facilities, bathrooms, showers, recreation area, and even your room/cell with that criminal element. Knock down all the walls so that we are living in the same crowded general space with maybe 5 televisions per one hundred or so inmates... I give you prison in a microcosm.

Is it starting to get a bit uncomfortable? Are we beginning to feel somewhat claustrophobic and invaded? Now change the property manager to prison guards who will make you strip, order you from one side of the projects to the other on the hour, every hour, and have no sense of appreciation for the job security our actions have provided them. We begin to have an idea of what prison consists of.

Last but certainly not least – as it will be at the forefront of our lives for however long we are there – place two bunks, and two men (or women), in a 6x8 foot cell, slightly larger than the size of an elevator. Prepare to share that space, or even fight, die, or kill for that space as you contend with another human being whose idea of hygiene and cleanliness may be far removed from your own.

Picture living this way for three-to-five, or ten-to-twenty years, or for the rest of your life, and we will begin to appreciate, or even welcome, living in the projects as opposed to life behind bars.

NOTE: While I was awaiting sentencing, I was housed at the Sandoval County Correction Center (federal side), just outside of Albuquerque, NM. While city crews were doing construction between the jail and the Wal-Mart next door, they broke a water main. Before we locked down, I told one of the guards to call the captain that was on duty. I advised him that there were old men in here, people with high blood pressure, and other illnesses that required running water and the ability to flush their toilets at night while locked in their cells. I asked him to call the Fire Department, bring an engine so we could fill up our mop buckets and force-flush our shit. I also thanked him if he gave us the opportunity to fill up our empty water bottles with excess Koolaid or whatever that dyed and flavored water stuff is they serve with meals. The captain thanked me for my foresight and ordered everything as we requested. He even had bottled drinking water brought from the adjacent Wal-Mart for each of the inmates. This went on for about 3 days before the water main was repaired.

About a year into my pre-prison incarceration the same issue occurred again. I informed the sergeant on-duty of what had occurred before and the resulting mitigation. This was several hours before our 10PM lockdown. He failed to take the initiative. We refused to lockdown, and prepared for a US Marshall-led incursion into our housing unit. At about 1AM, one of the telephones rang, and I spoke with a negotiator who informed me that I would be assigned an additional *assault on a peace officer* charge every time one of the Marshalls was struck by an inmate.

I informed the negotiator of the previous mitigation, to which there was a long pause before he asked me if this were to happen, would we then lockdown. I informed him that of course we would. Water was brought, we each filled up our mop buckets, and we each went into our cells and were locked in afterwards.

A week or so later (after I was already sentenced to 78

months in federal prison) a guard knocked on my door at 5AM and informed me I had court. I told him I didn't have any more court proceedings and was waiting to be shipped out. Nonetheless, he told me to dress for court. I remember my cellmate or "celly" telling me, 'Don't go, man, they're gonna arrest you, and take you somewhere else.' The irony of being rearrested while already imprisoned did not escape me.

Sure enough, they walked me about 50 yards down a long hallway where there were about 20 U.S. Marshalls waiting for me. They basically lifted me off my feet and threw me into a cell that had long been abandoned. It had about 3 inches of putrid shit water covering the floor, and a small raised level of concrete about an inch above the shit water. No window, and no light, and no shower. I stayed there barely sleeping, eating or drinking water for about 3 weeks – crouched over the concrete pad and smelling the stench of my own body contending with the smell of sewage – before I heard yelling further down the hall. The negotiator on the phone came to my door and told me he would keep his promise that none of us would be further persecuted if we locked down after receiving our water. Apparently, the inmates, not just the Hispanics I ran with, but the old Black guys, Whites, etc., began hunger striking when they took me.

I received a visit from the girlfriend I lost as a result of my arrest... A ray of sunshine during The Lowest Point of my life. I didn't care if she saw how emaciated I looked. I was thankful the safety glass and telephone kept her from noticing my body odor or bad breath from lack of brushing and showering. Or if the stress-induced alopecia had pushed my hairline back a decade or more. Or if the Bell's palsy had one side of my face sagging... I just wanted to bask in her femininity. I kept trying to take mental pictures of her and retain them, as I knew this would be the last woman I would see for a very long time. I know that blinding love causes most to think that their significant other is the most beatiful thing ever created. I can tell you truthfully that the modeling contracts she was offered, and the dozens of suitors that followed me (mostly rich guys or trust-fund babies) are testimony that this woman was, and is, one of the most beautiful creatures ever devised in our time.

When I left the visiting cell, I found my belongings from my old gen-pop cell in a rolling laundry bin. I was informed I would be going to segregation. I found that statement perplexing, as I thought where I had spent the last few weeks was segregation. It was just some dungeon they used to punish unruly inmates.

Segregation turned out to be like a regular housing unit where everyone stayed locked in single-man cells. About a week later I was brought to the captain's/warden's office, where he and the negotiator were waiting for me. I asked that a member of my car be brought to bear witness as my "Second" to confirm what was being discussed, and that I wasn't foregoing my principles by cooperating with the PIC... I was learning.

I was eventually allowed to go back to my normal housing unit about 2 months after "inciting a riot."

I continued to fight for the inmates that could not speak for themselves, i.e., elderly, Spanish-speaking, or from any ethnic group whose numbers were nominal, (Whites were often minorities in jail). This was not a standard practice for a representative of one specific group or another, particularly the Hispanics who hold themselves to a very high standard when it comes to prison politics. Nonetheless, this is what I did, and my policies and procedures were accepted by my car, albeit grudgingly by some of its members.

I realized the Kosher meals for inmates who proclaimed Jewish and Muslim faiths received milk and graham crackers with each meal instead of just water or Koolaid. Before I left Sandoval County, the entire jail was on Kosher meals due to my paperwork submittals.

When the Marshalls finally made ready to ship me to

prison, I was transported to Estancia, NM; an old state prison that was federally contracted to house inmates awaiting sentencing.

Again, I was sequestered away from the other inmates (for inciting riots at Sandoval County) before the Marshalls came for me, placed me on Con-Air at the Albuquerque airport, flew us to the Las Vegas Strip, and then to Pueblo Colorado, where we all loaded up on buses and were driven to Florence.

These were just some of my experiences all *prior* to prison...

HOME, OR THE CLOSEST THING TO IT

"One of the many lessons one learns in prison is, that things are what they are and will be what they will be."

— OSCAR WILDE

The conditions described, both in jail as well as Florence – and the inhabitants one is forced to exist with – are by far the most deplorable aspect(s) of life behind bars. The filth, disease, the Hepatitis C, staph infections, HIV, contaminated drinking water, food that comes in boxes that say "not fit for human consumption," they are all small yet significant parts of a very nasty sum total.

Remember that to "be Japanese" is to be respectful of others, at all times, so when you do lash out or react to an insult, all will know that your reaction was that of an honorable person; thus, equivalent, or on par with the insult itself. But to be Japanese and practice an altered form of *Bushido* also means we are people who cannot live with the shame of being insulted by another. It is for this reason that many of us are placed in the "Hole," and forfeit our chances at an early release.

Allowing a rude or disrespectful person to insult you, intentionally or otherwise, is to lose face with the rather observant and opportunistic prison population. In short, your prospects for surviving prison, honorably, and with easy time as a bonus, have just diminished drastically. It is better to lose good time, than to have a hard time surviving prison.

Men (or women) emulating the Samurai mindset in feudal Japan may not be the best MO for the modern world. But it most certainly provides a great deal of benefit to those who practice it behind bars. The degree to which we demand respect and politeness from others is often measured by the extent to which we give respect and show obligatory politeness in kind.

KILLING TIME

There are many things a prisoner can do to stay occupied while incarcerated, but choosing the right thing to do, as opposed to the wrong, can also provide a more positive resonance on our experience in prison, as well as on our character and subsequent methods we'll employ upon reentering society.

Know, also, that some activities can remove "lump sums" or significant chunks of time from your initial prison sentence, i.e., 90 days for academic participation, or 6 months for good behavior, or 9 months off your sentence in the federal system if you qualify for the drug program.

We must also bear in mind that the wrong kinds of participation are apt to lead to a longer commitment inside than what we were initially prescribed.

One of the few benefits that prison provides is that it actually gives us time to discover ourselves; to discover new interests and hidden strengths that we likely never would have realized had we been hard at work in the world or blindly chasing the Almighty Dollar.

Despite the noise, the filth, and a heightened level of awareness, prison allows for plenty of time to study, to write (or to work on one's handwriting), to discover a talent for painting, music, and other arts. Or to further one's education and strengthen the mind through as many academic pursuits as possible.

If playing chess is preferable to earning a degree, then by all means play chess. It projects the mind forward several moves, and cultivates the ability to multitask, to flank the opposition, and to separate one's thoughts from a single-track trajectory.

We can lift weights or perform calisthenics (if there are no weights). Condition one's self through cardio training, acquire your personal trainer's license either inside or when we return home.

We can also sit in the housing unit all day watching basic cable, politicking, or whatever diversion keeps us occupied until our sentence is up.

Politicking is a practice that some choose to immerse themselves in, participating in and enforcing the policies and procedures in a "car" group, or gang they associate with. And also mitigating the situations that arise as a result of differences between your group and another.

Politicking is a pastime or profession that should be limited to those who are recognized as authority figures in prison, or who are in the employ of authority figures in prison, such as enforcers. And whose lengthy sentence or status among the populace demands an active role in managing the affairs of other people.

It is when someone chooses to pass their time through the practice of politics – without having first earned their bones or having been vetted by their group – that they often find themselves on the losing side of decisions made by shot callers whose words count for more than the two cents thrown in by a non-entity. It is at this point that an aspiring politician might find themselves in trouble.

Wannabe politicians can easily transition to "crash dummies," or people that are hurled at others, with those doing the hurling knowing full well the extent of the use of this type of inmate. Their sole purpose is to commit one, perhaps two acts of violence before they are placed in segregation, and shipped off to another prison. They were not the *politicos* or tacticians they thought they were. They were merely crash dummies, thrown at a problem individual or "wrecks" whose own incompetence cancels out the uselessness of the other.

Tread carefully around those whose readiness to be an "influencer" may cause them to be drafted for some dirty work. Being conscripted for "doing dirt" might garner a lengthier sentence. Or they could find themselves on the receiving end of work performed by those who are already well-accustomed to getting their hands dirty... as well as their shanks.

I prefer a combination of the options listed above. Be active in mind, body, and soul. If invited to a sit-down or "junta" consisting of members of your group, unit reps and shot callers, keep your ears and eyes open, mouth shut, and learn from the ebb and flow of the conversation. Be grateful someone thought it necessary for you to be included, and be prepared to answer questions rather than offer suggestions, at least initially.

Some guys jokingly referred to me as a "health freak" or "bookworm," or any description alluding to the extreme of any pursuit. But in truth, I couldn't imagine doing my time any other way. The only time I'm sitting at the tables in the housing unit – where all the card games are played – is to play a game of chess. But even that feels like some form of training or mental exercise, despite whether the game is lost or won.

Strenuously exercising at least 5 days a week, and casually

walking the yard for the remaining two days is something that relieves all the angst I'm apt to experience if I don't at least provide the illusion of forward momentum. Even if that momentum takes me in circles around the same yard in the same prison year-after-year. My job in the law library also demands more of me than, say, a game of cards would. But no matter how occupied I was with these diversions; they are not a sufficient substitute for interaction with other humans... and therein lies the problem.

UNA PARTE DE ALGO

> "We must become bigger than we have been: more courageous, greater in spirit, larger in outlook. We must become members of a new race, overcoming petty prejudice, owing our ultimate allegiance not to nations but to our fellow men within the human community."
>
> — HAILE SELASSIE

Prior to my incarceration I was quite the social butterfly (sounds gay but whatever) in that my propensity for communication with others provided a distraction from the tediousness of my daily operations. In prison I was quick enough to realize that social butterflies, politicians, crash dummies, wannabes, etc., tend to involve themselves with issues not their own, simply because boredom dominates most of the prison experience.

Being friendly to the point where you are now recognized by the prison population as outgoing and sociable isn't necessarily the worst thing to be known for, but it may cause some to question your allegiance; thus, putting your allegiance to the test.

Even if you're not the sort to be sociable with folks on the other side of the fence, you still have to interact with someone, don't you? Of course you do, because healthy interaction with other humans is preferable to allowing antisocial traits to fester within you. That interaction is most often practiced among those in our particular group.

These groups can either be small and extremely tight-knit or they can be a rather large collection of individuals depending on an array of factors. Again, I employ the word *group* to include cars, gangs, cliques, subsets, races, and some of the other more common analogies used to describe consortiums that are inevitably formed in prison.

NOTE: New Mexico, or "Nuevo" is a rather small car in the federal prison system. We're few in comparison to other states with larger populations but we adhere to the criminal and prison codes of conduct without question, and we are respected for it. We have an alliance with a Mexican-American fraternal order who shall not be named, as well as their foot soldiers.

New Mexico Hispanics see themselves as Spaniards, or people whose descendants can be traced all the way back to the "Old County," or Spain. Many of us contend that we are not mixed with the Pueblo Indians or other Indigenous Peoples that were here before the Spanish came to this region in the 1500s.

While there is a mixture of Hispanics from New Mexico that have red hair, blonde hair, and green and blue eyes, it's also apparent that when the Spanish settled here – much the same as their processes for colonizing other areas – they inter-mingled, married, and procreated with the original settlers; thus, many of us are in fact mixed. But hell, who isn't these days?

Just to further the history lesson a bit more, Hispanic last names ending in "ez" or "es" such as Martinez, Gonzales, Rodriguez, Hernandez, Guttierez, etc., imply that whomever has one of those names is the "son of" Martin, Gonzalo, Rodrigo, Hernan, Guttiero, etc.

For instance, when the Spanish came to the new world, some came from noble houses and some were commoners. If a Spaniard came to the new world without nobility, and established himself, normally they would marry either a Spanish woman or one of the locals. Let's say for instance that the Spaniard in question was named Chavo. If Chavo had a son but he didn't have a surname, they would name his son "Carlos Chavez," meaning, "Charles, son of Chavo." Make sense?

Other nationalities possess this same way of identifying sons and daughters as being the children of Brian or whomever. The Irish and Scottish use "O'" and "Mc." McDonald is son of Donald. O'Brian is son of Brian, and so forth. Swedes actually use the word "son." Peterson is son of Peter. Johnson is son of John. Get it? Now you can go wow your friends over a drink when you explain to them what their last name means.

So, as it stands, Nuevo is primarily a Hispanic Car from a primarily Hispanic State. But New Mexico's population also consists of several Northern European ethnicities, or generally speaking, Whites; hence The Brand is present in New Mexico. There are also Indigenous people hailing from our Pueblos and other Nations. Blacks, Asians, and other ethnic groups who band together based upon race and street gang affiliations are also prevalent, albeit more so in Albuquerque than any other town or city.

The Original Americans have got to be one of the most widespread groups in the federal system, mainly because most reservations are considered Sovereign but subject to Bureau of Indian Affairs and the FBI; hence, many crimes committed on Pueblos and Reservations "go federal." I would love to see a book written from the perspective of a modern Original

American that has done time in the federal prison system. Many of their beefs and grudges with other Tribes and Nations go back centuries, as well as their practices. For instance, we had an Original American prison guard who was despised by all the Sioux Nations due to the fact that his tribe was one that helped scout for the Union Army during the American Indian Wars.

There was a black guy in Florence nicknamed "Black" because of his skin tone. Black, (A.K.A. Derrick Williams) was perhaps one of the last of a type of street boss and prison general who fashioned his family much the same as the Sicilians organized their families. Black's family was from Jamaica but migrated to Brooklyn and several other cities around the United States. When I met Black, he had just been transferred to Florence from some other United States Penitentiary back East.

He had shown me several offers for interviews from Dan Rather to Geraldo Rivera, asking Black if he would tell his story and the story of his family's rise in the United States, and around the world. He refused.

Black's mindset is that of a soldier, a general, a true student who follows the Code without question. He spoke fluent Spanish, some Italian, and spent years behind bars back East and elsewhere with the likes of Carmine Persico, and other mafia chieftains that were thrown in prison and forgotten as the decades rolled on.

Black was not "Una parte de algo" or a part of a prison gang. Rather, various leaders from various prison gangs gravitated towards Black due to his ability to serve several decades behind bars, honorably, and to advise – not necessarily the gangs themselves – but certain leaders if they were of a mind to listen.

I had the good fortune of being in the same housing unit (Mesa Bravo) as Black. I learned from him. I developed a mindset necessary for surviving in a world where being hyper aware and keeping one's head on the swivel were attributes worth cultivating. And yet, Black was Black, and from another race.

Some of my interactions with members of other races were initially frowned upon by my car. I think once they realized that I could move and intermingle easier than they could with other groups, my ability to act as an emissary, as an enforcer (on occasion), and a liaison, became my contribution to the Whole.

I could gain access into another housing unit when I grouped up with the Whites coming back from the gym. When "spice," and suboxone began hitting the yard, I could get a wholesale price on products that we would otherwise have to pay exorbitant amounts for that would make it difficult to profit from.

I was fortunate enough to be invited to sweat lodges with the Navajo shot caller named "Draper" in our unit, and develop a relationship with those hailing from New Mexico, the Dakotas, and beyond.

My mother's half Italian and half Hispanic heritage, and my ability to speak both, earned me an introduction with Vito Rizzuto, the last Sicilian Don to reach the pinnacle of success in the early 2000s.

What few soldiers were there from the Bonanos, Gambinos, or other Families would send for me to come to the yard after the lunch move, and we'd have pasta cooked by the guys who had kitchen detail. Vito would casually pick our brains via providing several scenarios that he would then ask our opinion on.

Vito was Sicilian, and came from the town of Cattolica Eraclea, Sicily. But he spoke several languages fluently, i.e., English, Italian, French, Spanish and Portuguese. His Family had farms in Venezuela that they would use to transport goods – some legal and some illegal – up to Montreal. From there, they would trickle down to the tip of both Coasts through their trucking companies.

This was a guy who consolidated all the street gangs and mafia clans in Canada under one banner. A man who contracted with the Hells Angels, the many different "Reserve Indiennes" in Canada, and other entities to work cohesively and peacefully across the entire continent.

I remember when Vito was set to be released from Florence in the Fall of 2012. They locked the whole place down. Those with views to the street from Pueblo Unit could see the American and international news crews lining the road that led to Florence to cover Vito's extradition back to Canada. Vito died a little over a year later in December of 2013. The news reported that it was pneumonia, but everyone at Florence suspected Vito of dying from what most of us die from if you drink federal prison water and eat federal prison food for too many years... cancer.

I saw a highly stylized show on Netflix about Vito titled "Bad Blood" starring Anthony LaPaglia, Kim Coates, and Paul Sorvino. I think it did a good job of capturing the personification of a man that was in the Life. Vito's son, his father, and several of his associates were murdered while he was serving time in America. He exacted revenge upon returning home, but Montreal's criminal world has never seen the level of peace and prosperity it did under Vito's direction.

What I saw when I looked at Vito was a man, imprisoned worlds away from his home, whose family suffered horribly while he was away. He didn't smoke, he ran and walked several miles a day. And I believe he was determined to set matters right and execute his vendetta before he died.

There are visionaries in prison who come from different ethnicities and nationalities. Most if not all of these notable inmates were deemed largely successful in their ability to influence and build upon their dreams while free. What I find most disparaging is the number of good men I met while I was there. Men such as Derrick "Black" Williams, and Vito Rizzuto. Men who came from nothing and had a vision that didn't necessarily parallel the law, but saw to it that they, their colleagues, families, and even adversaries profited from their ability to move their visions from theory to practice.

Religion, too, is one of the more prevalent factors in deciding what individuals a person is apt to gravitate towards, as spiritual beliefs are based on something much more fundamental than one's racial, geographical, or criminal identifiers.

I found it calming and gratifying to observe the level of respect practiced by people in prison coming from different religious paths. I had an Egyptian-Muslim math teacher who started each class with writing in Arabic "there is one God, and Mohammed is his prophet," or لا إله إلا الله محمد رسول الله.

He would invite someone to end the class with a Christian or other type of prayer, to which someone would readily respond. I mean, this was a math course, not an indoctrination. It was just the way in which he was taught to commence teaching in schools over there.

I have found as a rule, that larger groups are more prone to constant fat-trimming, infighting, power struggles, or as we refer to it in prison, "cleaning the books." This is a term used to describe weeding out snitches, crash dummies, rabble rousers, and generally weak soldiers who would only compromise the strength and reputation of the Whole. Conversely, if a group is smaller, then alliances will tend to be built upon something more than just power plays, and bonds are constructed out of necessity to survive as opposed to mere safety in numbers.

Being a part of a large group, a small one, or even choosing to run independent all have their pros and cons. Large groups generally are in a constant state of housekeeping, that is to say, dealing with internal issues. If they dominate that particular prison, it isn't likely that they will have external issues with other smaller groups that recognize the hierarchy, as well as their place within it.

As mentioned previously, smaller groups tend to be a bit

more genuine and familial than the larger ones. The level of devotion coming from each member can be measured as opposed to the sense of false brotherhood many will hide behind in a bigger pack. Also remember, for any newbies constantly receiving directives from unit reps or shot callers… if they can quote the rules, they better live by them.

NOTE: I had an incident occur in my housing unit, not long into my prison sentence, where our unit rep was laying on his bunk with his boots off and under the covers. Although this is a violation of Nuevo's internal policy, the general mood of our prison was rather calm for the past couple months. Several stabbings had occurred from the Hispanics onto other races that had resulted in those cars cleaning the books, and ridding the prison yard of those that warranted getting stabbed. Although it was just a few minutes before lockdown, I said nothing to my unit rep, but pinched his big toe when the guard was calling lockdown and told him "que tengas un buen noche," or have a good night.

A month or so later I was sick with whatever flu was rolling through that disease infested place during the harsh Colorado winter. I had informed the homies that I wasn't feeling well and to keep watch until I was back on my feet again. Although I stayed suited and booted for most of the day, I rested on my bunk with my beanie pulled over my eyes just before lockdown. I don't think there's a worse, more uncomfortable place to be sick than in prison.

Our unit rep came in and pointed at my feet and verbally proclaimed the violation. I immediately flew off my top bunk, and jumped in his face, and assured him I was ready for whoever, whenever, and that I could beat or stab most people just as effectively with my boots off than on. I also reminded him of when I pinched his big toe during the time his boots were off for no other reason other than he was "slipping."

He backed off and told me he would be talking to our shot caller about it in the morning. I told him to do what he had to do, but that I wasn't in prison for snitching, or for being a hypocrite. He got the message and never took the issue to a higher court within our car.

NOTE: Myself and this same unit rep had the unpleasant duty of smashing out a snitch among our group that was discovered shortly after the no-boots incident. It was winter, we wore gloves, and the investigation failed to yield any arrests. This act of criminal justice bonded us together the way only crime can. Although we weren't friends, we knew we could rely on each other if the shit got deep.

A man or woman who chooses to run independent is a person that elects for a more difficult road to travel, for reasons I'm about to explain. But keep in mind that it also negates the necessity of being obligated to others, being gainsaid by opposing members in your group, or having instant enemies as a result of your affiliation. But it also means the only person who backs your play is You.

Coming to terms with running solo upon entering the prison system is one of the more difficult choices that one may voluntarily make, if they are not already affiliated, or, if any group they would most likely associate with deems them an unacceptable candidate.

Running solo is often times viewed with a skeptical eye, as inmates will want to understand the logic behind a decision that runs in opposition to 99% of those who come to prison. Prior to acceptance to most respectable and feared prison groups, we are screened, a background check is performed, and someone from your city, town, or region will vouch as to what they've heard about you in the streets so that others may consider you to be a criminal in good standing with the Code.

Being an independent means that you have no one to answer to (or no one to run a background check on you). This places the independent under immediate scrutiny, and it is often up to that independent's fellows coming from the same race or area to perform due diligence and ensure that a child molester, rapist, or some other bad criminal is not walking "freely" among us.

NOTE: There was a White in Florence who came from Wyoming and represented for all of the Wyoming Whites, if not the entire white prison population, excluding specific white prison gangs of course. One day, he comes into the chow hall, and I'm sitting at the New Mexico table with all the other Hispanics. He's in line, I shake his hand over the waist-high metal banister, and rather than take his place among the sea of Whites (there were a lot of Whites in Florence), he takes his tray and sits at one of the two independent tables. There's a couple of flamboyant gay men there, an older guy from New Mexico that ran independent named "Armijo," and a couple of other randoms.

I think the entire chow hall lowered a few decibels, from the inmates to the guards, at this act of independence. He was never questioned by the Whites, or the prison staff. I asked him why he made that decision when we were shooting the breeze in the law library one day. He explained that he had always been alone, and that it was the color of his skin, his reputation on the streets, and where he came from that caused the other Whites to gravitate towards him.

Now that I think about it, Black, Vito Rizzuto, Wall, Chills, (both from New Mexico) and the other "real deal" shot callers weren't necessarily associating with their respective groups. It was the groups themselves that associated with them. Of course, Black and Vito had seats at certain tables. But it was the Midwest and East Coast Blacks that associated with Black, and the Tri-State area guys, (mostly Italians and Irish) that associated with Vito.

For all intents and purposes, these guys walked alone.

Chills came from Roswell, New Mexico. Roswell is as about as "Wild West" as it gets and there is a large following of guys coming from that city and its surrounding towns and villages, all loyal to Chills. When he was the shot caller for

New Mexico, he easily had 100 soldiers or more that would do his bidding, (and that was just in one prison). But the core Roswell members knew they had a captain in their crew that was repping for the entire state; thus, they stayed close to him and were more active in doing dirt than guys from other cities.

If a guy like Wall was in power, and who was a shot caller from Albuquerque, the core members from that city will be the ones making decisions and administering direction for the rest of us.

The same occurs with different crews in organized crime families. The Ozone Park crew was just one amongst many in New York where one prominent member became the boss of the entire family. So too is this hierarchy mirrored with most cars in the federal prison system.

Vito's crew was, for years, considered by the Five Families to be a branch-off of the Bonannos; despite the fact that it became clear Vito and the hundreds of other Sicilian members in Canada were most definitely *not* a part of what the Italian-American families had going on in the States. In fact, Vito was considered by INTERPOL and other international law enforcement agencies to be a mega boss, beholden to no one with the exception of self and his Sicilian clan.

If you were an Italian-American in the federal prison system, and were housed in Florence in the early 2000s until 2015, chances are I knew you.

Whether in prison or any other social setting, belonging for some people is more important than not belonging to anything at all. To belong is to be accepted. And to be accepted is to feel something that many in the prison system have never really experienced heretofore... inclusion by one's family.

COROLLARY

Side effects that stem from incarceration are just that: side effects, or nuances that should be peripheral irritations. They are not, by any means, "front effects," or "in-your-face effects" or ripple effects that determine and shape the course of our lives subsequently.

Yet for many of us, that is what these side effects have become. And regrettably, we have permitted ourselves to be governed by symptoms which have arisen as a direct result of our time behind bars.

Envision if you will what your life would have been like had you never fell and gone to prison, or even better, if you had never been *criminally activated*. Every day I think about what *could* have been, what *is*, and what may come, and how much harder life is going to be due to my inclination to go against the grain.

To consider our lives from a past-perspective, however, is to perform a review of things that have already occurred. And while there's nothing wrong with examining the past to approach similar future instances differently, bear in mind that when we live in the rearview, we are not projecting our thoughts towards a future that is boundless in regards to its opportunity and prospects.

I have to be careful when I rearview glance at moments in time, as the feelings of self-contempt, regret or frustration over what cannot be undone can often obscure the reason(s) behind the remembrance.

This negative and cyclic self-reflection is one of the leading side-effects of time spent incarcerated. And these feelings, reinforced with negative activity, i.e., self-medicating, harboring grudges, directly or indirectly starting shit with others, and/or bringing ourselves into the "mix" with those in our sphere of influence are all practices that inevitably make us unpleasant to be around, much less recognizable as the people we once were at the outset of our time behind bars.

Add to this soup the external stresses and anxieties that often accompany being in prison, and it becomes easy to see the events which shape a second fall to our own machinations.

Feelings of vengeance, hyper-aggressiveness, tough-guy posturing, speaking loudly when there is no background noise which to talk over, reacting on impulse as some prison environments have trained us to do… these are all traits, or symptoms rather, indicative of one who has spent time behind bars.

They are also components of a defense mechanism that no longer possesses value or utility beyond the framework of the prison in which it was created.

These symptoms can be identified simply by understanding the purpose they once served, and in the setting they were necessary for being crafted – much like the snitch is to the police – and then discarded, or unlearned, as soon as we realize the template of their design is not patterned after survival in the World. It simply does not fit.

We as people have such an admirable ability to adapt to almost any habitat on earth, that is to say this ball of rock, water, and gasses making its revolution through the tiniest region of space. We possess the ability to adapt to environments that are man-made or synthetic in comparison to what is natural. And yet, it is often that ability to adapt that we must practice anew when we enter an environment that is less of a construct than that of prison.

Have we all seen the mounting number of commercials advertising prescription medications for any and all ailments? I'll also assume that you've heard the narrator in a friendly yet rapid tone informing the listener of side effects including but not limited to, 'thoughts of suicide, difficulty operating machinery, or driving an automobile, difficulty breathing, anxiety attacks, heart attack, stroke, or in rare cases, even death.'

The thought of enduring side effects that might seem worse than the affliction itself would also cause me to reconsider the severity of my ailment, as well as taking a medication in hopes of remedying whatever discomfort I might experience.

When I consider, in correlation, the treatment for criminal inclinations that prison has afforded the majority of its patients, I also question whether the "cure" is worse than the illness.

REMEDIES

Judging from the amount of data collected from inmates, (their friends and families) and correctional and P&P officers, law enforcement and behavioral health practitioners, there appears to be Three Major ailments analogous with the time one has spent incarcerated.

It is also acknowledged that these disorders were not always thus; but attributes or qualities derived out of necessity and reliance, that have since "mutated" or altered in scope and purpose, more so when they shift from dormant to active in the free world.

The First can be perceived as an aloofness or icy character, and at times irritable or stand-offish demeanor that can prevent FFC from getting too close. This behavior, when practiced in prison, is generally used for two purposes: one, it keeps what little privacy you still have relatively intact by closing the door to an overabundance of conversation. This is because other inmates, conscious of it or no, will kill as much time as possible by filling it with trivial chit chat. And secondly, being somewhat aloof or reserved will prevent others from phishing you for information. This will also ensure that their problems do not become your own.

The Second symptom is the need to organize and direct the random complexity of FFC into a routine – or units that can be controlled – much like we attempt and succeed to make sense of our time behind bars via organizing and regimenting everything within our sphere of influence for the duration of our sentences.

The Third is substance use disorders and habitual addictions to things that stimulate or numb the senses such as drugs, alcohol, antidepressants, sex without attachment, physical or emotional combat, the Life, or anything that is not being practiced in moderation which grossly upsets the balance in an otherwise normal reentry into an old and familiar habitat.

Unlike the first two, addiction and self-medication were never forged from every fiber of one's being needing to adjust and survive; rather, they metastasized from a flawed means of coping with the pressures that were often too much to bear.

Side Effect No. 1. Detachment/En Guarde

To fight, to never give ground, to never concede to demands, threats, or the implication of force; and to be as ruthless and unyielding as possible was the way I thought I had to be in order to survive immersion in the criminal world prior to my incarceration. Needless to say, this was not the best practice for surviving in prison, despite what stereotypes would have us believe. It did, however, change me from the youth I was into something, I myself, did not recognize.

The detachment method of survival precluded me from having a normal relationship with the few remaining people that still cared for me. Those FFC whom I successfully indoctrinated to this philosophy would then possess the same beliefs as I; hence, we grew apart from one another, and subscribed instead to the power and monetary gain we collectively or independently sought to acquire.

The detachment and defensive posture(s) are practiced

among the majority of prison populations. It was practiced by myself prior to coming to prison in hopes of reducing the amount of loss I was apt to experience when I eventually fell. And it is practiced still by many of us with our FFC upon returning home.

Reflect for a moment on the manner in which we maintain a constant display of strength, independence, and emotional detachment in prison, and the way in which we keep friend and foe alike at arm's distance. Now, imagine how that same MO and interaction, or lack thereof, would be received by those who consider us their friend or family member in the free world.

Those we feel friendship, affection, or deference towards should mostly be *within* arm's distance for a hug, a handshake, an embrace, or an earnest conversation between two people moving in the same direction, if not on the same path.

None of my colleagues in prison would think it necessary for me to be closer than arm's reach unless I'm telling them something I don't want others to hear. As soon as an initial greeting or handshake is performed, we automatically step back a pace out of consideration for our respective personal space.

It is almost comical for me to consider practicing this same form of "space provision" around family and friends on the outside. And I suspect they would view my behavior as being a barrier to our efforts, and attempts at reforming bonds and communication, which it is.

Although this particular side effect is perhaps one of the least damaging of the three, its subtlety and ability to continue unchecked can have long term impacts on otherwise healthy relationships. It can also derail career pathways if allowed to suppurate.

<u>The Remedy: Relax</u>

The cure for this subtle yet hard-to-identify symptom of incarceration is to train ourselves to let our guard down when at home, or when among FFC. Conditioning ourselves to be more at ease can feel counterintuitive to one's survival, at least initially. But if our survival in the World depends on our ability to relax a little, then finding security in one's self-assurance is key.

I often see this hyper-awareness and guarded posture more in friends returning from combat in the military than I do from folks returning home from prison. But it is definitely prevalent in both sub-populations.

I want to emphasize that I would never suggest letting our guard down completely; nor in public, and particularly not with everything that seems to be escalating on political, criminal and other socioeconomic levels. To fall victim to crime in the world, because of our obliviousness to our surroundings, *after* honing our vigilance while incarcerated, is to fall victim to a state of complacency that even our civilian counterparts are not careless enough to entertain.

Yet to have others shy away from us because of asocial behavior – which derived out of a need to endure in an asocial environment – is to fail to properly adapt to the latest environment we suddenly find ourselves in; one I might add we knew previous.

Make the effort to understand and truly *know* whom our FFC are. Know the difference between a stranger's proximity to us out of a desire to be friendly versus one's proximity with intent to do harm. Understand how easy it is these days to do harm from a distance, virtually, or without you even being privy to the name of the person perpetrating the act.

Training ourselves to be at ease around others is a virtue. Maintain an inner vigilance that is not outwardly displayed via "mean-mugging," standoffish posturing, or direct eye contact with the implied threat in your sights. Learn to use peripheral vision and other senses apart from direct contact to ascertain threats, be they real or a byproduct of our heightened awareness.

In addition to these, practicing and then mastering the ability to flex and adjust one's personality to better relate to others, or "code-switching," will help curtail the excessive wariness and mistrust many experience upon reentry.

<u>Side Effect No. 2. Control</u>

The need to control our surroundings and those within our sphere of influence stems from existing in a controlled environment where pecking orders and hierarchy are more readily apparent. Controlling friends, family and relationships has very little to do with dominance on our part, as it does obedience or subservience on theirs.

Speaking for my own group- domination, authority, or even influence is not so much an obvious and violent power struggle; but rather, a subtle yet never ending cold war between those of us who have yet to establish our place and rank in the respective prison group's hierarchy.

NOTE: It's interesting to witness a person's popularity or influence impact another person's validity within the group, more so if the two are at odds and the latter's sway is offset by the former's impressions... like middle school all over again. Think the film "Mean Girls" but with convicts.

This strife among members breeds competition, and strengthens those who are at odds as strife often does. It instills in us the need to be seen as something other than a non-entity – whose actions may not demonstrate domination – but that are meant to convey an immovable force in their own right, thus gaining acknowledgment and recognition as one who will *not* be dominated.

Should we choose to practice dominion over friends and

family, it will only be met with the same resistance as one in prison who would not be moved by another. And I imagine FFC would view us through a similar lens – as one who is now attempting to manage and control the lives of those we abandoned – much as we were managed and controlled by the prison system.

It is a curious human quality to observe an individual successfully thwart any attempt to be subjugated, only to witness that same individual in their newfound independence attempt to dominate another.

Many who practice domination and control in prison do so for no other purpose than to have one more voice or vote in alignment with their point of view. Upon arrival to prison, it is almost a prerequisite that we establish ourselves; not so much as The One who runs the show, but as someone who will not be unduly ran or managed by another.

Control and management are not needed for something as bilateral as relationships. Rather, fostering those relationships, and practicing patience and understanding should be the order of the day.

<u>The Remedy: Acceptance that some things are beyond our control</u>

Be mindful of the reality you enter upon returning home. And concede that you may no longer be the man or woman of the house. Your wife, husband, or even one of your children may have stepped up and filled that role for the duration of your imprisonment. In truth, many of us have relied upon their efforts to experience a more comfortable time away; hence, it would be better if we assumed the role of a grateful and reciprocating house guest until we have proven we can toe the same line our families have been toeing for a good while without us.

To believe that our families are the types that would

welcome, with open arms, an uncouth and demanding individual, such as the one exemplified in the person you might become, is to believe that our antediluvian form of survival could possibly work in the modern world, and with people whom we should be regarding as equals and ones that we are most assuredly indebted to.

The Serenity Prayer, which I stumbled across while skimming through an Alcoholics Anonymous book seems to fit so many troubles in life, albeit it is a bit longer and more eloquent than simply "throwing it to crazy." The Serenity Prayer is as follows: Grant me the serenity to accept the things I cannot change, the courage to change the things I can, and the wisdom to know the difference.

I don't imagine a better creed exists when confronting new environments with old practices, or vice versa.

Prior, during and after our reunions with family, we should reflect upon our own times of identity crisis and rebellion – particularly as we cultivate relationships with children or young people – as it makes us consider the reasons behind our own resistance when authority figures, such as parents, tried to dominate or manage us. And how well did that go...?

If those reading this were anything like me, or like most young people of a certain age, then you know that whomever we attempt to control will rebel to the point where it ruins our relationship with them- not to mention the fact that their rebellion, initiated by you, might lead them down a path similar to our own.

Symptom No. 3 Addiction

Whether it had its beginnings on the streets or it developed as a coping mechanism in prison, know that this disease – for it surely it is one – has a tendency of turning one's life upside down. Addiction slowly, or quickly, replaces everything else in life that was once worth enjoying with a need for something that will forever be beyond our reach.

The addiction to opium was once referred to as "chasing the dragon." I think this description is befitting of every addiction that one indulges in, because it is indeed, a chase, or a pursuit rather, of something that the pursuer will never attain- at least not the way it was caught and experienced the first time they were seduced by its effects.

What's tragic about those of us afflicted with this sickness is that we are more than aware of our infirmity. Painfully conscious of the transient nature of the remedy, as well as its symbiotic relationship to that which makes us sick... What a paradox.

Addiction is not something that hides in the shadows of our peripheral. It is an insistent thing, one that constantly reminds us of its presence, so much so, that we eventually become unaware of everything else.

<u>The Remedy: Resolve to Heal, Alone if necessary</u>

There isn't and probably never will be one defining cure for one specific addiction. I have experienced addictions of my own with varying degrees of intensity. To fanatically pursue something that can never permanently satisfy, only to have it elude you once it has been obtained, is to be addicted to an object, substance, or feeling that will inevitably bring about our ruin.

My worst addiction by far was greed, second only to emotionless sex with equally emotionless women. Greed thoroughly ruined me as effectively as fentanyl, alcohol, or heroin have ruined those who are dependent upon them. I ruefully admit I was wrong when I told friends and colleagues to pursue money and success rather than getting high. The way in which I chased these pursuits was nothing short of harmful obsession, or addiction rather, that brought about my own demise just as effectively as injecting one's favorite narcotic into their veins.

It something brings pleasure, then by all means, pursue it. For pleasure or contentment in life is something that is not often obtained by everyone. But examine it, and examine your thoughts immediately following the recovery from experiencing that pleasure. If we find that that one singular pursuit affects other aspects of living that were once satisfying – but have since become void of gratification – then beware. As this is the first indication of pursuit of pleasure transitioning into something other than what it was initially intended to be.

To put it in even plainer terms, this is the first sign that *we* have begun to change into something that no longer enjoys that which used to bring pleasure, in lieu of something that we now are simply pursuing but falling short of obtaining.

The ability to practice moderation in everything is key to keeping things that we find enjoyment in doing, well... enjoyable.

When we are no longer tempered by moderation, the balance between indulgence and control become offset, and excessiveness is the emotion which now has free reign over impulse. Thus, consideration for indulgence in small doses dissipates into nothing.

To resolve to be moderate in all matters of fulfillment is to be a person in control of their feelings and compulsiveness. To use or indulge in a practice, act, or substance to the extent where it no longer satisfies – even though the urge to pursue it still exists – is to replace reality with something as fanciful as chasing a dragon.

IRON AND WATER

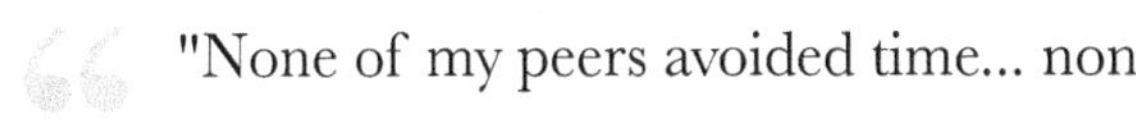

"None of my peers avoided time... none of 'em."

— NIPSY HUSTLE

"All I did was pray to God, every day. In prison camp, the main prayer was, 'Get me home alive, God, and I'll seek you and serve you.' I came home, got wrapped up in the celebration, and forgot about the hundreds of promises I'd made to God (and to others)."

— LOUIS ZAMPERINI

My intent in writing this chapter, and bringing it to a conclusion, is not to paint a horrible picture of prison as a whole, but the people that many of us temporarily or permanently become as a result of the prison experience.

By conceding that we are in constant state of flux, analysis, and improvement, we acknowledge faults within us that then become easier to repair.

I want to also impress upon the reader, the inmate in particular, that prison will not be the end of you. Should it be your fate to end up here, imprisonment will either be the event that frees you and causes you to rediscover yourself anew, or, it will shape you into something unrecognizable to the person you once were.

As a consequence of your imprisonment, that which you are unable to recognize will inevitably be your undoing.

As I write this from my cell in the Mesa Bravo Unit of FCI Florence, I have yet to be reunited with friends and family. Subsequently, much of the advice that I have included thus far has not been attempted by me, and has left me feeling a bit apprehensive as to the outcomes I'm hoping it will produce.

But to have knowledge of a thing, prior to experiencing it is to have a better inkling as to what your future may hold (this includes imprisonment and subsequent freedom thereafter). And to grasp the basics of such a life-altering event is to ensure our survival when we come out the other end.

NOTE: Yesterday was August 7th, 2024. I have been home since 2015. (9 years, 5 months, and 30 days). I was searching for rare car parts for a 1967 Buick Special (a one-year car), and found what I was looking for in Canyon City, Colorado. I awoke at 4:30AM, jumped in my truck and left Santa Fe bound for Canyon City. When I got there, me and the old man I spoke with on the phone exchanged pleasantries and came to a deal on a "shell" or body of the car I was looking for. I asked him how far we were from the Federal Prison to which he responded, "Just follow 9th street until it ends. Take a left and head straight to Florence. And signs'll direct you towards the prison." I decided to stop by and see my old "housing projects" that I had lived in for over 6 years. The guard was a Velcro-wearing, chewing tobacco-spitting hillbilly with a plate carrier and way too many accessories to count. Not to mention "sleeved" color-tattooed forearms paid for with his federal salary. He told me he didn't give a shit if I took pictures from the highway but I could not do it from the guard house. He impolitely asked me to leave after which I took photos from the road. In those 9 years, 5 months and 30 days, I have implemented the plans, ideas, and advice laid out in this manuscript- without a hitch, stutter step, false advice, or bad recommendation.

As humans, we are affected by external stimulus, even when we tell ourselves that no effect has taken place. And yet, the law of causality is a principle that implies we are subjects of, and reactive to, every stimuli beginning with cause.

If we find ourselves existing in the environment of prison, the day-to-day occurrences may seem to have no effect on us. But in truth, if these happenings are nothing like what takes place during the course of a normal day in the normal world, then we must allow that what we are experiencing is quite abnormal; hence, the way we process these abnormalities, too, will run in tandem with the aberrations that preceded them.

Acknowledging that there is nothing normal about prison is to appreciate that the resulting behavior we display is also an anomaly.

I'd like to suggest that – apart from us subconsciously practicing psychology on a daily basis from the day we begin to think and interact – that we also become conscious students of the same, and of the human condition, and our position within that collective. For to not study the environment and the people that we are in the midst of is to not adapt to an atmosphere that is surely more complex, dynamic, and *real* in comparison to the one we will be leaving behind.

To not swiftly and succinctly acclimate to the world will also increase the likelihood of our recidivism back to a place where we are apt to better function and exist... if you could even call it *existing*.

I'll suggest also (and not for the last time) that we use our time behind bars to morph, to change, and experience, quite literally, a physical, spiritual and mental evolution that most are never given the good fortune to attempt.

An older, square-jawed, overly-muscular Brand member in federal holding once told me, "You owe it to your family and to yourself to come out a better person than the one who went in. Do not fail them, or youself."

We owe it to them and to ourselves to be more than a flawed individual whose invalidity, bad habits, and addictions will keep us separated from them long after the forced separation that prison provided.

Know that with practice, patience, and active listening comes a mutual respect and understanding for people, for partners, and even for adversarial relationships. Understand that your physical reunion with your people is just that; physical, which is nothing compared to the reunion based upon understanding and comprehension of the soul.

When reading this I suppose some ex-offenders might inquire as to why I have not broached the subject of adverse behavior on the part of our relatives and acquaintances, as if by becoming inmates we are the only ones held accountable for disagreements amongst those whom we once had healthy or unhealthy relationships with. But I feel that our departure may have been the thing that brought about emotional and financial hardship, and may have led to bad habits, addictions and character flaws of their own.

Imprisonment has a much more lasting effect on the imprisoned rather than on those deprived of us. And as such, I feel that directing my attention towards a situation that I am intimately familiar with would better benefit me and mine, and you and yours. To overcome this challenge from the perspective of the prisoner, as opposed to the family's point-of-view, is also an opportunity for us to take responsibility for the welfare of something other than ourselves. Hence, reintegrating with the family unit by way of an approach that includes us as part of them, and places duty – not control – for a successful reunion within our means.

To identify *our* faults rather than theirs is to identify troubles whose priority should take precedence prior to focusing our attention on the shortcomings of our families and the new environment we're getting ready to enter.

Only when we are healthy ourselves are we able to heal others, and the process of healing and reuniting with families is no exception.

To be as firm and unyielding as penitentiary steel is to be one whose uncompromising behavior demands little explanation for their own mistakes while leaving much to argue concerning the mistakes of others.

To be fluid, and as lithe as water, is to be a person who flexes, molds, and fills the space provided by those (family members) whose indentions were made for the sole purpose of allowing room for one such as yourself: one who could fill the voids left in our wake and absence should we choose to allow them within arm's reach.

This chapter isn't solely about *doing* time, but *spending* what time we have left adequately...

FCI Florence shortly before my release in 2015. I had lost a lot of weight from doing time in the Hole. Left of "Charolas" displaying Nuevo Mexico tattoos on his forearms. Winter of 2014.

Federal Correctional Complex in Florence, CO. Bottom Left, the
Satellite Camp, Top Left, The United States Penitentiary. Top
Right, the Supermax, and Bottom Right, F.C.I. Florence where I
did the majority of my time.

Burqueno homies to the right, and Roswell homies to the left.
My celly and Unit Rep for most of my time at Florence directly
behind me, "Bouncer."

Nuevo homies from every corner of the state. September 11th, 2011. I'm in the Center, Middle Row. Our Original American (Navajo) homie to my left, Eric.

April of 2014. I'm probably counting down my last year's worth of time in prison. The homie Chewy from Los Padillas to my right, and Fimby, one of Albuquerque's shot callers in the Federal Prison System, second row to my right with glasses on. Good men, All.

Another photo opp. From 9/11.

Marcelio "Big Chills" Jimenez, Roswell shot caller for Nuevo.

My return Florence in search of classic cars in Southern
Colorado, 2024. Mesa Bravo Unit is the 4th building on the Far
Right

My return to Florence, 2024. Pueblo and Otero Units behind me.

10
FOUND

"Whatever you are by nature, keep to it; never desert your line of talent. Be what nature intended you for and you will succeed."

— SYDNEY SMITH

"Getting ahead requires avid faith in yourself. That is why some people with mediocre talent, but with great inner drive, go much farther than people with vastly superior talent."

— SOPHIA LOREN

"If you have talent, use it in every which way possible. Don't dole it out like a miser. Spend it lavishly like a millionaire intent on going broke."

— BRENDAN FRANCIS

"The saddest thing in life is wasted talent."

— CALOGERO LORENZO "CHAZZ" PALMINTERI

MOST OF WHAT is fractured psychologically is fixable. And repairing that within us that is fundamentally broken is far easier, than say, repairing external elements for which there is limited control over.

One of my worst idiosyncrasies is my ability to take constructive criticism from others and twist it into an insult or offense than for the benefit with which it was originally prescribed. Unfortunately, my behavior was essential in keeping me in the dark as to my own defects, and it often bred more stupidity than it ever fostered intellect.

When a person provides earnest constructive criticism, the purpose is twofold: one is to make the recipient aware that they are acting in a way that is damaging to themselves and contrary to their own advancement, be it social, occupational or otherwise. And two, constructive criticism often times provides an example of how we should proceed in lieu of the behavior or reaction we normally display.

My defensive response would only further convince people that I was beyond help, which, at the time, they were right in assuming.

Another difficulty I encountered was my inability to make the distinction between helpful advice of any kind, versus the same responses I exhibited when reacting to deconstructive criticism. Any kind of counsel or guidance was never taken under advisement. Instead, I continued to rely upon my own defective outlook.

The displays of defensive and offensive posturing, coupled with my inability to see the symbolic assistance that others offered in the way of advice, examples and so forth, are some of the chief character flaws found in prideful people. It is definitely the most disparaging trait exemplified by the prideful criminal.

As successful criminals – before our fall – the indifference shown towards innate talents we all possess often breeds a curious form of casual confidence that loosens our grip on reality, awareness, and the precarious realm in which criminals function.

As we either breeze through this chapter, or compare its similarities to our own behavior and conditions, bear in mind that emotion called *pride*, and the resulting consequences of allowing such a feeling to pervade waking thought. Compare this sentiment and its uses, or lack thereof, to your talents that are often stymied or disregarded as a result of pride. Examine the two pathways of refined talent versus self-flattery, and project where each will take you.

APTITUDE

There are an estimated 8 billion people on the earth whom are living, working, consuming, not-working, consuming alcohol and other substances, procreating, having sex without procreating, and merely existing without any real course or pathway in mind. And of course, those of us that are in the throes of death whether we know it or not.

Of those 8 billion, 4,058,360,359 are women representing 49.72% of the total population. The other half are males. There is a growing minority of people that are non-binary or genders that don't fall into the category of male and female.

It is also estimated that a total of 109 billion people have lived and died on earth- add to that number those of us that are still alive for a total of 117 billion humans.

Consider for a moment what percentage of 8 billion are inventers, entrepreneurs, innovators, visionaries, and contributors on a scale that would impact the remainder of the planet's population. How many of us are simply born, mature, consume, and then perish after our time here expires? How many of us join the ranks of employers, corporations, manufacturers, armies, etc., only to follow in the footsteps of the billions of people that came before us?

Perform a bit of basic math and consider your own age,

how many people you have possibly interacted with thus far, (they say we remember each meaningful encounter since the age of 5) how many more you will meet and interact with before your death, and what sort of influence your existence has had on those who have had the good or bad fortune to encounter you.

Let us now consider – out of the 8 billion souls still living – what our contribution is to the world. What talents were we imbued with that could possibly impact that many people, not to mention the small handful that are within our current sphere of influence?

For me, and for most, I would say that my impact was minimal from the ages of 1-12. I was no child genius so any lasting impressions were within my immediate four-member family. I would say I affected my older brother's young life dramatically when he was almost 3 years of age, when our parent's attention suddenly shifted to the new addition.

As I reached my preteens, my influence began to grow among classmates and others as my intellect and ability to communicate likewise grew. But again, this influence is almost non-existent when measured against the entire population and the small percentage I was unaware that I even existed within.

My greatest and most obvious ascendancy, albeit mostly negative, was the influence I exuded over those whom I peddled narcotics to. The realization that cocaine opened more doors than my affability or willingness to work for others ever did came as quite the epiphany for me.

As stated previously, buying something for a dollar and selling it for two is not necessarily the greatest talent, but it's a talent nonetheless. Coupled with this ability the strength to resist an occasional line, crack rock, or injection of the product one peddles, and the opportunities for one who was relatively poor for much of their young life suddenly appear boundless.

It was this initial success as a salesman – who sold a

product that basically sold itself – from which a feeling of self-worth was generated, and later a pride and confidence that would inevitably suffocate and replace any innate talents I may have been fortunate enough to be ingrained with.

Talent can also asphyxiate and wither under habits and addiction, or simply because it possesses little or no foreseeable use in the life one is currently living.

NOTE: It took coming out of the other side of prison before I was able to rediscover the ability to network in a positive fashion, to reach people outside of my sphere of influence using online meeting platforms for discussions and presentations; to understand that that feeling of panic and anxiety when speaking in front of strangers was a catalyst to achievement, rather than the paralyzing agent I once took it for.

How many of us are aware of inherent talents that are taken for granted on a daily basis; never given them time to grow into something greater than a second-nature inclination? How many of these skills are used as pastimes rather than passionate pursuits to an end that is gratifying both for yourselves and for others?

I know guys in prison that can create masterpieces of art with a few pencils and pieces of charcoal. And yet, these talents are reduced to tattoos or sketches on paper when today's technology and communication could distribute these works of art beyond prison and across the globe.

Even on the outside I've seen glimpses of inestimable genius as regards people's ability to create art, compose music, or make others laugh to the point of crying with the sheer genius of their humor. There's a guy I met in Santa Fe who could freestyle rap and hold his own against the best lyricists in the world. This person has also created some of the best graffiti masterpieces known around the Southwest, and California.

But he squandered his talent. He began selling heroine and was "courted," or jumped into a street gang in his late-twenties in an attempt to build bullshit street credit for the sake of his music career. What the fuck is that?

I came home from prison around the same time as an infamous local gang leader. The leader called me and we later met in person, asking me if I would vouch for this rather talented individual, as the gang was cleaning the books and checking backgrounds on new members. I laughed in the leader's face and told him if they were recruiting the likes of guys in their late 20s that weren't legacy members or grew up in that neighborhood, then this particular gang had really fallen from the "middle" echelons of gangbanging. Wasted talent...

I have always been fascinated, and a bit envious, of those who are inherently gifted with the ability to draw, paint or sketch; or who can sing, or play musical instruments effortlessly, or figure out a math problem in their head without counting on their fingers. It blew my mind when I witnessed kids in their pre-teens excel in sports when the rest of us would attempt the same and fail horribly.

When I would ask why they were not using their talents to benefit themselves, or others, they would simply throw my question back at me, which, I suppose was the most accurate and obvious answer I could hope for. Why the hell did I never use my gifts and skillsets when I had the time?

I suppose the short answer and truest in nature is that my talents died under the success and confidence I found in my criminal activities.

In candor, I became too comfortable, too confident, and too complacent within my own fabricated idea of what reality for me entailed. I began to believe that the world and everything in it consisted of chemicals and chemical reactions. Chemicals in the brain that generated thought, chemicals in the atmosphere that we consumed to live, and chemical combinations of gasses such as water that we drank to stay hydrated and survive. Chemicals that we derived from plants and other substances, that we sold to grow rich, or that we ingested to alter our state of mind. Any skills or talents I possessed and enjoyed doing were now viewed as worthless in comparison to the rather "black and white" construct I had surrendered to.

The belief that a comfortable existence is founded upon nothing more than being moderately competent at a profession is often the point where we turn our backs on, and disregard, skills and talents that now take a back seat to that which provides a higher standard of living.

I drafted this hoping that the reader discovers skills and talents in direct relation to the amount of happiness and success they are capable of accruing. Mainly for those of us who have either engaged in criminal activity, or something as mundane as surrendering to a "normal" education, followed by a "normal" job, and ending with a "normal" life fashioned out of what pathways and opportunities were available.

This chapter is also meant to be used by Us, to recognize and nourish the talents and skillsets we see in others. And how best to shed light on their prowess; to master it, and perhaps bring it to the surface of consciousness. It otherwise might become buried underneath the economic structuralism and demand that defines existence for the majority of the world's 8 billion souls.

If at this point, if we have taken the necessary steps to transition our own lives, then our ability to help others should be just as strong, if not stronger than it was when we made the decision to help ourselves.

Electing to help others realize their full potential can be a rewarding accomplishment. It could be that this person or persons prove stalwart allies and colleagues that uplift us in our own endeavors, amplifying a positive ripple effect that gains momentum rather than lessens as it moves beyond us.

Such an attempt should only be performed for selfless reasons, and only if we are in a position to adequately guide. Although teachers often learn more about themselves from the mentoring of others, choosing to help someone should not be done for the purpose of self-emulation, or even for furthering our own learning processes. Rather, we should assay to elevate and guide after having successfully completed an irreversible transition- one that guarantees our role as contributors. Only then will our experience, strength, and knowledge be of use to someone else.

PREREQUISITES

Before I begin waxing philosophical, let's do a quick review to make certain that steps are indeed being taken in the right direction.

Even if we're only *thinking* about these steps rather than actually taking the plunge, at least we're considering alternatives to the current MO.

Prior to taking these steps, our need for legitimacy must first be substantiated through our own resolve. We must see our criminality for the self-deprecation it represents. If at any point we're still considering the possibility of crime as an option, we need to weigh the pros and cons; our current living situations, levels of fear and uncertainty – or pride before the fall – and revaluate how we might benefit from a transition that parallels acceptable and lawful forms of "making it."

Substituting our criminal activity (or thought processes) and replacing them with positive thinking and action is a good preliminary step, be it in theory or practice. A good measurement for this step's effectiveness is seeing a steady regression from all things illegal, including *thinking* about that next "lick" or score. To this day, I'll see a large drug bust on the news and place myself, in my mind's time machine, at the scene where tens of thousands of dollars were confiscated. I'll imagine knowing those who were just arrested and justify my thought process as to taking their profits for myself and leaving the drugs, or finding the drugs and being satisfied with selling those at a discount to other dealers in order to reap the profits.

All I'm really doing is going down a rabbit hole of "what-if" scenarios that would never happen because the targets in question have already been arrested! It's like waking up from a dream where I found hundreds of thousands of dollars in my closet, only to discover it was only a dream. Why entertain that sense of loss over something we never had?? To that same thought, why consider future criminal scores if there's another way?

Next, making certain that our cost and standards of living meet, but do not exceed or drain our nest eggs. Or a means of legitimate income is sustaining us during our transition. If expenditures are proving likely to exhaust savings, or if legitimate occupations cannot fulfill financial obligations, then we have not successfully budgeted and downsized our lives to the extent where they are now manageable through legal methods of survival.

Conquering our fears, or at least using them as the vehicle to advance into the unknown, rather than as gatekeepers holding us back, is essential to familiarizing one's self with a wide world which extends beyond the microcosm of crime we operate within.

To remain inconspicuous throughout life in its entirety – particularly between the regression stage and avoiding a final arrest – is tantamount to existing and indeed, advancing in an unremarkable and completely ordinary fashion. This is to assure that our criminal past does not negatively impact the present and future that we should, at this stage, be striving for.

Upon reentry into society, effectively managing everything that is expected of us can be an overwhelming feat to accomplish; specifically legal obligations. But dealing with these issues by giving them the attention they deserve is to make a difficult milestone to reach far easier than we tend to make it. And by mastering something as demanding as Probation and

Parole is to make most other complications in life appear trivial in comparison. By keeping a record of our day-to-day activities, we also bear witness to the fact that we are doing exactly as we are tasked in the event our actions need to be verified in a court of law.

Learning to flex and adjust our personality to better fit others is also detailed in Chapter 5. And mastering this ability is, in essence, perfecting the art of communication, thereby expanding our networks, increasing our influence, and assuring that those whom we interact with will support, uplift, and vouch for our character when the time comes.

To know what assistance is available to us through the same local, state and federal governments that persecuted us, is also knowledge that is in complete accord with providing assistance to others. FCC may be following our path from prison to the streets; and guidance upon their reentry provided by us, rather than P&P and/or criminal elements, is to ensure that they don't stumble or falter in the areas where we might have.

Distinguishing ourselves from the bad criminals of the world – many of whom are perhaps, beyond a cure – is to recognize ourselves as worthy of the citizenship and freedoms that we were once in possession of. This also makes us experienced candidates for helping others realize their own worth and possible transition.

Choosing to adhere to a higher set of principles than those we relinquished for financial gain, or those that law enforcement suggest we renounce – as outlined in Chapter 8 – empowers us to make genuine and principle-based arguments for those we hope will follow a higher path, rather than speaking from a financially-driven or deceitful lectern.

And finally, recognizing the road we travelled from the outset > to imprisonment > and beyond is to see in ourselves just one of the many pathways people embark upon without thought as to where it will take them. Only having travelled that road – in some instances, for decades – before perceiving the damaging effects it embodies. To reroute, and seek alternate, optimal pathways at any juncture is a feat that is better manifested late than never at all.

Once this stage, this understanding, has been reached; and every other step followed in sequence, it is feasible for us to consider that a transition has commenced, and may even be concluded; hence, if we've come this far, perhaps we can go a bit further towards helping another.

REFLECTION

I have a friend on the streets I've known since '94 whom we'll call "Dario." When I met him I was 14 years of age, and Dario was a couple years behind me. We became very close and much of what people didn't know about me, or much of what police suspected but couldn't prove, Dario was privy to. He was one of my truest friends.

Like many relationships young people are a part of, ours was based solely on enjoyment of each other's company. There was no benefit to our friendship aside from the mutual geniality we both shared.

We also shared the same clothes, fought each other's fights, and got into varying degrees of the same shit that most teenagers get into.

But somewhere along the line, Dario's priorities became vastly different from my own. Whereas I was constantly trying to make something out of nothing, Dario was content to be a part of the nothing that we came from. His proclivity for heavy drinking – and later, heavy drug use – wasn't concerning at first, as we all drank and smoked weed rather heavily in my opinion.

When I look back on the mid-90s, we were all overindulging *something*. But Dario's enthrallment with drugs gained momentum faster than the rest of us and quickly devolved into a repetitive and disastrous cycle. It would prove to be his greatest downfall.

As the years went on, it seemed as if he was stuck in a time warp. His inability to hold down a job or fulfill the minimum number of responsibilities imposed upon him by his father was concerning to say the least. We later learned that his drug abuse was really the only thing that ever motivated him.

His crimes became ones of such insignificance that they barely yielded more than a few bucks for the next bag of dope. It started with cheap beer and booze, cocaine, then crack > heroine > suboxone, and now fentanyl or a meth bubble depending on whether he's getting high or getting low.

Before we knew what was happening, bench warrants were being issued and the cops were looking to arrest Dario for all sorts of petty crimes. If he was with me and I got pulled over, it was usually because they were looking for him. My car would also get searched but I wasn't carrying anything while in transit.

NOTE: I owned a fleet of Dodge Neons in the late 90s. You could pull the heater vent covers off and stick dope or anything small enough to fit down the vent back behind the stereo. I would have to use a dope fiend's arm or a hanger with tape around the end to "fish" large bags of dope out of the ducting. I had those cars torn apart during searches but they always had to let me go.

I began viewing Dario as a liability rather than a friend and crime partner. We even stopped using him to assault, strong-arm and rob other addicts whose debts were overdue. It got to the point where we would give Dario a bag of coke to watch him and one of his new friends (always another junkie) fight in his front yard for amusement. Dario would always win and win big. He never was one to lose a fight, but we could all tell the partying was beginning to take its toll.

I had a policy of bailing out our troops for first-time offenses. If their bail was too high, we'd have our attorney file motions until it was low enough for a cash or surety bond. This was taught to me by my "plug." The rule was, if someone working for you got pinched, you bailed them out, lawyered them up, and they plead guilty to their first offense which usually resulted in a year of unsupervised probation and some piss tests. If they got pinched again, they were a liability and you washed your hands of them.

At first, either myself or Dario's pops would bail him out, without a second thought. But it became apparent that he was indifferent towards our attempts to help him. If we bailed him out, we would lose our up-front money due to his missing appointed court appearances.

I talked with Dario until I was blue in the face. And, as was our standard method of keeping all of us in line (myself included) I beat him up a few times before realizing that this too had no effect. I tried bringing him around successful people, both legit and criminal, in hopes of igniting some enthusiasm within him concerning a different pathway besides the one he was on. This resulted, more than once, in Dario robbing their home when they weren't there or when he "went to the bathroom."

I remember giving him one of the fleet Neons. I had it painted a MOPAR gun metal grey, with paint-matched wheels, a decent system, pretty ghetto fab, and something he could be proud of. About a week after I gave it to him, he got into a chase with the police, rolled it, and that was the end of that little Neon.

I hit my stride at about 22 years of age and I was busy enough with my own problems that Dario's became somewhat peripheral. I still hung out at his house, as we used it for a drop off, test site, and drug house from which we all reaped profits.

I now reached a level of success where I could afford to practice some benevolence with friends, family, and sometimes complete strangers and non-profits if I felt they needed it. If

I'm being truthful, I think I donated to ease my conscience and help balance the old Karma Scale.

I also found that my capacity to practice philanthropy was something I found great contentment in doing. It made me feel good supporting causes or providing things for people and animals (I love animals) that made their lives easier to endure.

Dario was still going in and out of jail, still unemployed, and still a willing test subject when the new shipment arrived. We would cook it, ensure that it rocked-up nicely, and Dario would smoke some before giving us the thumbs up to distribute. Sometimes a "dart boy" would be present and this person would inject the cocaine before giving us his approval as well.

NOTE: The usual sign(s) of good coke being injected was the test subject's vomiting and feeling the urge to defecate immediately after injecting it, followed by an increased body temperature and an extreme rush of euphoria. To each his own, I guess.

I pretty much absolved myself of any obligations to Dario with the exception that I still considered him a friend. I gave him money for his kid's diapers (or dope) depending on what story I chose to believe. If I went to eat anywhere and no one was joining, I would bring Dario. If I had an extra bag of dope I didn't want to drive home with, I gave it to Dario.

Unfortunately, this trend of friends becoming addicts and customers repeated itself over the years. It just began with Dario.

There were other instances, apart from getting a decent car – or a year's worth of county jail time – that I thought would turn things around for him; such as the birth of his daughter. None of this had any real impact on him, and he continues, to this day, to destroy himself.

NOTE: I drafted this chapter around 2012. It's now 2024 and Dario was just released from a rehab facility in Española, NM. He moves back into his mom's public housing building in

Las Vegas, NM whenever he is released from rehab or jail to resume the same cycle he's practiced since 1995.

Whether it was tough love from the homies, or from his father; or coaxing, patience and positive encouragement, or by imprisonment, nothing and no one seemed to have the slightest effect on Dario's disposition.

I suppose the reason I continued to try and help and advise him throughout the years – even if that help was haphazard and slipshod in its approach – was because I saw within him the kid I once knew. The kid who took state in wrestling championships at his middle school, the kid who had trophies and framed pictures galore of various competitions, church gatherings, and other events.

Apart from what his addictions drove him to, he was and still is one of the most selfless persons I have ever met.

Dario was a guy who would give you his last ramen soup if that's all that was in his pantry. A person who would receive you graciously whether it was 3PM or 3AM; a person who, without fail, would give you a plate of food whether you were hungry or not (this is a practice common among Hispanics in Northern NM. If they're cooking... you're eating).

Dario hung out at the local Boys Club and mentored youngsters, taught them to wrestle, and looked after most of the children in his neighborhood. Of his many girlfriends – when he was still handsome and charming enough to snag em – they all were wooed by the attention he showed children, babies, etc. If there was a child around, Dario would make sure that they were acknowledged, rough-housed, and made to laugh uncontrollably. I can recall on several occasions him breaking out his colored pencils and sketch paper so kids could draw and scribble.

Granted, you couldn't leave your wallet around him but there was still that genuineness and willingness to help others that was unparalleled. Before Dario became a street-level gangbanger and drug addict, he was a pretty good kid. Those qualities shone through every once in a while.

The level of easy cordiality he showed to any and everybody could have landed him a job in any customer service or service industry position had he taken up one of a thousand offers. His uncanny insight and ability to connect with children; with training, could have led to a career in child therapy, child-care, social services, or even teaching.

His endearing personality was by far the chief reason I made so many attempts to bring him back from the brink.

I think the truth is he is either beyond help, or the trigger or moment that changes his life for the better has yet to be realized. Some would argue that he hasn't hit rock bottom, but those who know him know that he's been at the bottom for several years now. And how he can remain alive and enduring without coming up for air is beyond any of us.

For some people, external help is something that is not helpful, but hurtful; and which only enables the continuity of instability. As is the case with Dario, I believe the only thing that can help him is that which has hurt him all these years... self.

YOUR CANDIDACY

Following our own transition, the selection process in choosing one who would benefit from our efforts must first begin with an evaluation of self, and our intent behind electing to help someone else. If our reasons are selfless and our motivation founded on providing another with a stronger likelihood of success and achievement, then the first step has already been taken.

Always be cognizant of the fact that our own needs must never take precedence over the needs of the person we've selected. Our own needs should never be something our candidate is made aware of, as our role in this relationship is that of a mentor who provides direction for another, and to require something of your target recipient – other than to help them realize their full potential – would be counterintuitive to the task at hand.

We must also determine what level of devotion we are prepared to offer; what amount of time and resources we are prepared to give. If this is just a once-a-week meeting where you and your candidate meet for coffee and discuss prospects then so be it. If those meetings evolve into something that requires more effort, then be prepared to take the initiative and follow through with what your candidate's realistic expectations are.

The person whom we select should not be chosen solely for reasons of affability or compatibility, but rather because we see within them that which they may not see, or that needs nurturing or brought into the light in order for them to know its value. Taking a shine to an apprentice or someone we're fond of isn't a deal breaker, but it should not be the sole premise upon which our selection is based.

NOTE: Chef Fernando Ruiz (featured in the bio section) created a culinary training program that begins while candidates are still incarcerated. He then performs job placement for graduates upon reentry, either at his restaurant or one of the growing number of restaurants participating in the program. Chef Ruiz continues to work with participants to set up bank accounts, debit cards, gym memberships, and more. This is perhaps the best possible example of a returning citizen making a successful transition, and being at a vantage point to mentor others.

Finally, the candidate whom you select should be made aware of your interest, intent, and involvement with them. It should be made known that we perceive in them talent, or talents, that when honed and cultivated, might prove beneficial to them and others. And in an environment other than one that crime would either bond those talents to, or suffocate entirely.

This selection and subsequent bilateral arrangement do not have to be set in stone. But it should be made clear to them your reasons behind their selection. And it should also be made clear that you are making this effort with the intent of facilitating their transition from either criminal, or to improve their less than favorable holding pattern.

If requirements and conditions on behalf of both parties are agreed to, these contractual components will become an indispensable foundation upon which much of the relationship is cultivated.

I might also point out that if you are in prison at the time of your own conversion, there are plenty of inmates who would benefit from an unofficial mentor who provides sound advice in preparation for one's reentry.

No matter the environment, it is best to feel your candidate out, as much as possible, prior to taking that leap of faith.

As is the case with everything, preparation, past experience and a positive outlook is yet again key. Be absolutely certain that our own transition is fixed and permanent, and that our willingness to help another make fundamental and meaningful adjustments in their mode of operation is based off of our legitimate evolution, and not predicated upon failure.

Candidacy is often determined by the relationship or association between ourselves and those we select. Often times we encounter these individuals through shared criminality. If our reputation as a criminal is something that is envied, feared, or respected by others, the amount of weight our word carries concerning this particular caper is apt to be substantial as well.

On the other hand, if our criminality resembles that of Dario's or something similar, the reputation that preceded us is probably not a good one. But, if our transition was successful, one that demonstrates just how drastically we veered from our previous course, then our success story will be that much more impactful to our target audience.

Granted, providing assistance of the caliber I'm suggesting requires knowing that person's strengths, weaknesses, proclivities and disposition on a very in-depth level. But how could we ever hope to accomplish this if we are not intimately familiar with our own?

THE MOMMAS AND THE POPPAS

Anyone who has ever been to prison is aware that there are "prison poppas" and "prison mamas." The mommas and poppas are the older, more experienced convicts that take under their wing younger, less-experienced convicts, and show them how to "program," i.e., how to get off their tits and be suited and booted before the cell doors pop. How to have their bunk made and mattress rolled up so as not to feel tempted to sit or laydown when they should be ready for any and every eventuality that comes with doing time.

Often times the prison dad is the prison son's "celly" or cellmate. They may even be an older relative, uncle, our cousin, or one of the son's "big homies" on the street. More often times than not, the prison dad or mom has a greater reputation and influence than the son or daughter- more money on their books, and holds more sway within the prison itself.

It is not uncommon to see prison sons and daughters with two plastic mugs filled with instant coffee, waiting at the hot water machine or microwave to heat the mugs' contents. And return to the cell to give the prison mother or father the cup they provided with coffee from their canteen.

This relationship is not, by any means, a "you're my bitch" type relationship that is often idealized and stereotyped as commonplace in prisons around the world. Rather, it is a symbiotic relationship that is often founded organically rather than contractually between two people coming from different generations. I have never witnessed one that entailed sexuality either, as this would indicate a form of symbolic incest between a parent and child.

I've often seen it as a chance for fathers and mothers to attempt to be better parents than those that went to prison and left their children behind. I've also viewed it as an opportunity for adult children to demonstrate a level of respect and gratitude towards paternal figures that are kind enough to show them the ropes and offer them a cup of coffee if they don't have money on their books.

Even in prison gang culture this symbiotic relationship exists, perhaps more so than in regular prison culture. You see the big homie, or the OG, the *llavero* ,shotcaller, or mafia chieftain educating, honing, and strengthening the younger soldiers in a fashion that will ensure their prison career is a successful one, as opposed to them being successful criminals.

If you have ever been a prison father or son, mother or daughter, or witnessed this rather singular occurrence first-hand, then you have also been party to one of the most effective forms of mentoring in one of the most difficult environs one can mentor another.

Never have I witnessed in one of these relationships a negative context, i.e., the encouragement of drug use, debt accrual, enforcement, or the like. It is always performed by a qualified mentor and a willing mentee who demonstrates some level of promise, talent or intelligence worth sharpening.

This may sound hypocritical to the average reader, and contradictory in nature, i.e., a gang leader mentoring a novice soldier on how to be a better gang member. But that is not the role I am describing between prison mentor and mentee, nor is this manuscript meant for the average reader's conclusions. The teacher/student correlation that exists within prison walls serves a more positive purpose than one's personal agenda.

THEIR CANDIDACY

Feeling your candidate out with a little chit chat or situational Q&A is a great way to determine what misgivings they may have about their current state and how best to improve them. As was the case with my assignation to unit rep in federal holding, the representative before me would provide scenarios to which he would gauge my reaction and analyze the solutions I provided- much the same as Vito would create scenarios to hear the responses from the guys that looked up to him.

NOTE: My status on the streets was known... My credit in prison was, at first, non-existent.

It will need to be determined that said candidate is eager to make some kind of positive shift prior to moving forward. If they are content with things being as they are there is no need to convince them otherwise, and to do so might sour their feelings towards us in the future when they are actually ready to consider life adjustments.

If they have the foresight to desire change prior to experiencing a life-altering event (such as imprisonment), then it is also safe to assume that they might be more receptive to your approach than not.

Apart from varying minute indicators, a candidate's eligibility really consists of only a few requisite conditions. For one, they must acknowledge their current existence as something that could be improved if not completely disregarded altogether. Secondly, they must be willing to take the same or similar steps as you. And thirdly, they must be encouraged to see their own worth and how best to use it to their advantage; thus, jumpstarting a new course through encouragement and self-motivation.

Remember, one's candidacy does not rest so much on our ability to mentor as it does our aptitude to help others realize their potential. Even if those we select can see within themselves certain inherent qualities, they may also perceive that the proper channel or outlet for their gifts is more difficult to chart than the talent itself.

This is where our experience and expertise is likely to prove useful. By providing information, advice and ways to avoid pitfalls that we at one time stumbled into, we chart a course with the most optimal routes to take. And it helps to ensure that their chances of success are just as good, if not better, than our own.

Keep at the forefront of your consideration just what exactly your candidate's eligibility entails, and how best it would mesh with your own approach to mentoring. Respecting their decision to accept or reject our assistance is part of their qualifications as well.

HEADWAY

Let us assume that those reading this are doing so, because, despite our imprisonment, we are more or less free from the criminality that at one point kept us in thraldom as thoroughly as prison keeps us isolated. Let us also assume that – even if we are still in cages – that life has reached some modicum of a regimented lifestyle, or close to normalcy as a thing as tumultuous as existing could possibly be.

Then, let us assume that we are at a crossroads where we have taken it upon ourselves to consider instructing and guiding another. At some predetermined time, the two of you will have to take stock of the situation, or assess if you will, to determine what headway is being made.

There are a number of ways to measure one's progress, but the most prevalent are Emotional, Social, Academic and Financial Progression, or stabilization.

EMOTIONAL PROGRESSION

It is practically guaranteed that if an individual is taking up new or past interests and pursuing these as a means to either improve their mindset or divert attention to activity other than crime, most will experience a subtle but near instant improvement in their emotional disposition. This normally occurs for two reasons: one, the more time a person invests in positive thought and action, the less crime they're apt to commit or even entertain; hence, the less they have to worry about the repercussions of those crimes. And secondly, the more activities a person is involved in that are based on positive self-starting, the more focused they become on pursuits of a constructive quality, as opposed to those that are deconstructive.

If such progression becomes noticeable with your candidate, then it's important to bring to their attention their newfound enjoyment in what they're doing, because it can often be imperceptible to the person experiencing it. Such is the subtle nature of these effects. It is often in hindsight, or after we revert back to a previous mode of thought that we see our emotional progression for the tangible and favorable outcomes it produces. Unfortunately, if we do experience recidivation, it is often in jail or some similar setting where the knowledge hits us that we were, for a time, on the right track.

Be sure to point out and encourage progress where progress is made. If the steps are minuscule or fewer and farther between, then we may need to reevaluate the chosen course, interests pursued, or the mindset of both- the one who has already made the transition and those who are in the process of transitioning.

SOCIAL PROGRESSION

Social progression can be an extremely important indicator. Especially when we consider just how many of us are apt to be social outcasts. Or ones who have only gained social status because of the amount of drugs we sold, crimes successfully committed, or by material accumulation via illegal activity.

Successful criminality is often hard to relinquish, because without it, many of us experience feelings of social irrelevance. And our first attempts at legitimacy can leave us dispirited on many levels.

The first step in measuring ours (or another's) social progression is to first disregard previous concepts of what is socially acceptable, particularly if they are concepts that somehow correlate to stature or recognition through financial, or worse, criminal achievement. As it hits home that our criminality is no longer an acceptable measurement for determining our social or economic status, we begin to gauge our social significance through more practical means.

These means, incidentally, are the same methods that the majority of people use to determine their relevance in relation to others, as opposed to the flawed manner in which most criminals calculate theirs.

Proper social progression equals criminal regression; which is to say that criminality in itself runs contrary to our true representation of worth. And to perceive people's desire for our company, or to seek out our advice or fulfill another need other than that which our criminality provides is to have acknowledgment of social progression- not just by people in general, but by the right people for the right reasons.

Social status (not progression) in prison is often measured by the amount of credit or weight we carry as criminals. It was difficult at first, but I was able to make the distinction between social status versus progression as my ability to provide counsel increased both in, and outside of the prison system.

Everything I advise people on has nothing to do with my success as a criminal, and everything to do with concepts that run in opposition to criminality. And yet, this has not lowered my esteem in the eyes of my peers, but increased it, as heretofore I was only valued by what I could provide, the damage I could inflict, and the amount of deception I could practice while staying under the radar.

My social development evolved in spite of my former status, not because of it.

Explain to your candidate that some people may view their transition, at first, as something that might diminish the amount of esteem or influence they possess. But also explain that we are in pursuit of social progress, not status.

Even the hardest of hardened criminals saw my transition for the value it promised, both to me and others. Those that saw me as going straight, or legit, or not having what it takes to persevere in the shit and the darkness were usually far beneath the level of crime I ascended to, or descended to depending on your point of view.

Making legitimate headway is a great thing to experience. It can be immensely gratifying to go through several phases of advancement in all things. But to be at a vantage point to observe another experience it, your candidate no less, is comparable to few achievements in life.

To measure the progress one is making, or lack thereof, is to also measure the continuity and effectiveness of our own social progression.

ACADEMIC PROGRESSION

Academic Progression is perhaps the most simplified progression to measure via grading of one's academic pursuits.

I started learning Spanish in prison with one simple phrase, "como se dice?" or "how do you say?" and I would point at the item or action I was referring to. Now I can read Spanish flawlessly, hear and listen to it fairly well, and speak it perhaps not as well as the first two. Conjugations kill me.

When you speak English, it is the subject that changes rather than the verb, i.e., we, you, I, they, he, she, *ran* to the store. In Spanish it's the verb "to run" or *correr* that changes. I'll get the gist of it one day...

In the federal prison system, there are people from all over the world. It brings the world to you in a nightmare vacation sort of way. Spanish seemed like the most prevalent second language I could learn, but I also picked up Navajo or *Dine' Bizaad*, Sioux, Russian, Hebrew and some Arabic. I have an aunt from Morocco I use my favorite Arabic phrase with at every opportunity, *inshallah* or "God willing."

If we're learning another language, it also broadens and expands our social and academic circles like never before.

FINANCIAL PROGRESSION

Measurement of financial progress is a tricky one. When we're in the world and we commit to our transition, we're not often hired initially as a high-earning executive, and the financial downturn we experience as a result of going legit is perhaps the most discouraging aspect of one's transitional phase.

Then again, if your candidate is socking away money and cutting back on expenditures, and reducing overhead; their transition might not be as discouraging as it is for others.

There are many of us that use their ill-gotten income as a

means to start legitimate businesses; and while, granted, none of mine are in existence any longer, I at least had the presence of mind to plan for a future that consisted of something greater than my previous MO

Financial progression is not just about making instantaneous, boat-loads of money. Rather, it entails planning and making financially viable choices, both during our criminality as well as after. If money is being saved for future investments – even if that investment is merely surviving – then said money is building interest, and financial and intellectual equity.

If we are foregoing present comfort for future security, then we are experiencing financial progression. If financial gain can be measured by the amount of money saved, as opposed to the amount being squandered, then we are seeing financial progression.

Efficient record keeping is a vital component in measuring the level of advancement one is making concerning their financial security. If a candidate is living well within their means, while striving for an amount of income that would place them beyond their current standard of living, then this is indeed a formula–albeit a very basic one–for determining one's economic advancement and/or stability.

DARIO

I often think about Dario and just how little progress he's made over the years. I have a friend that I met post-prison, who is on the autistic spectrum, but who is a savant when it comes to common sense, philosophy, different types of tequila, and basically any and everything imaginable.

He explained to me that growing up affluent he experienced the same "level plane" of living that I described when talking about Dario. He further explained to me that super wealthy kids grow up and spend much of their life in school, in training; law school, medical school, art classes, traveling the world, studying art, different periods of history, dabbling in real estate, development, following in mother or father's footsteps, philanthropy and so forth. But that many of them never truly embrace these experiences and opportunities for what they were meant to be.

They do this because there are no proverbial hills and valleys in the life they were born into. There is no struggle, strife, suffering, hunger, or other experiences that contrast feelings of joy, achievement, fulfillment or contentment. As a result of this, their life is an even, never-changing, flat and featureless landscape that often leads to self-medication, alcohol consumption, the prescribing of antidepressants by their psychiatrists as they grow older, or Adderall when they were younger.

What good is joy if we've never experienced pain? Do the affluent suffer the same as the impoverished once each reaches the conclusion that their respective constructs hold the same level of empty promise, lack of opportunity, and nothing hard nor made of stone with which they might sharpen themselves against? Is our struggle for financial security just as vain as the one with privilege who struggles with their own relevance? How do you measure success if you've never had to strive to achieve it?

When I reflect on my relationship with Dario and the decades it spanned, I also think about the opportunities we provided him with, the cars, the sacks of dope he could've sold rather than used... and the always dispirited "thanks" he gave in return.

I reflect also on how my criminality probably left a greater impression on Dario than the material things and so-called "opportunities" I thought I was providing.

How can you tell someone to *only* sell drugs and not do drugs when you yourself drink every night and have indulged in recreational drug use with the same person you think you are trying to help?

What a hypocrite... I mean, here I was telling this guy to get his act together, while at the same time committing acts that ran contrary to what I was preaching. Essentially, "do as I say, not as I do."

At least Dario's nature and criminality was such that he brought more harm to himself than he did to others, not so much the case with my own. At least his generosity and personality were something that made him desirable to be around. I, on the other hand had a personality that exuded greed and mistrust of those I hoped to profit from; my true inner person having little or no use in the world my alter ego flourished in.

When I thought of Dario, (pre-prison), I thought of weakness, and of a person possessing no drive or motivation to move passed the conditions we found ourselves in. The fact that he could have been so much more than what he resigned himself to be disgusted me. It caused me to resent and look down upon a person who had been my friend; who gave me a place to sleep, food to eat, and who supported and made me feel better about myself- more so than I ever gave him cause to feel better about his own situation.

Despite his addiction causing him to thieve and rob – even from those friends among us who were unfortunate enough to leave a purse or wallet laying around – I know that the sincerity he represented was in direct opposition to the illusion of success I marketed to those I interacted with. Because the things I was telling him were surely perceived as lies, if not words spoken by a hypocrite, who by no means practiced what he preached.

When I picture Dario in my mind's eye looking at me during those half-ass attempts to "reach" him, I know now that it wasn't indifference or apathy that he regarded me with, but pity rather, and perhaps even a resigned form of contempt for someone who had the audacity to think that he was actually helping another, when it was plain to see I was only furthering my own interests.

It was easier for us that knew Dario to concede that he was simply one of those people whose addictive personality was the thing that caused a decades-long downfall, rather than to admit that there were other aspects of his life we didn't know about that may have contributed to his self-medicating.

Granted, the "assistance" I provided was the only effective method I knew of that proved beneficial to me; hence, I concluded that it would prove beneficial to others. I'm not sure if the vehicle I used to convey it, nor the package I presented it in was the most appealing, but I knew of no other way. Furthermore, how much of that help was relayed in a responsible and conscientious manner?

Was it given because I cared, or was it simply offered because I was in a position to give it? If I'm being honest, I think it was flung at people carelessly, and in such a way that I didn't care if it was intact or damaged at the time desperate people struggled to catch it.

I was perhaps the worst possible example of what a mentor is supposed to be. I peddled poison to him, to his family, and to our friends, while preaching the benefits of selling it rather than ingesting it, knowing full well the addiction that was overwhelming most everyone I knew.

It amazes me to consider that what I believed I was offering was genuine concern for the welfare of others when their very addiction was the thing that assured my success...

If any attempts are made by us to help people while we are still living life contrary to what is lawful and morally acceptable, then I'm sure those around us will see the hypocrisy in our actions, even if only on a subconscious level. And any half-ass attempts to mentor another will more than likely keep candidates on unfavorable pathways, as advice preached but not practiced is hardly advice to be followed.

I see now, more than ever, that my help was nothing but a barely-concealed marketing strategy, whose real intent was to make myself appear benign and supportive at the expense of those who could have used a helping hand. Instead, those around me sustained grievous injuries from a companion whose vigorous and concentrated form of criminality was perhaps the biggest detriment to their welfare and survival.

A chilling epiphany occurred when I realized that my thinly-veiled help was nothing more than criminality practiced while owing to the morality and principles I lacked.

Would it not smack of lies to us if someone of high criminal and social status told us that crime doesn't pay? All the while that person is wearing clothes, driving cars, and living a lifestyle that is completely immersed in materialism of the highest standard?

The illness of hypocrisy and the folly of trying to cure another, when we ourselves have yet to be cured, is a circumstance that will ensure those we think we are helping will never convalesce. Our help will continue to suppress their talents, long after the effects of being underprivileged and socially marginalized.

To practice this form of assistance is to essentially ruin a person, or further hinder them, much the same as I contributed to the ruination and hindrance of my friend Dario... and countless others.

AUGMENTATION

I think it vital to learn what our character truly consists of, and where we hope to be tomorrow, or the next day, or next year. To understand what our value, intent, and worth means to those around us. But it should be with the most passionate of spirits that we come to recognize the worth, talents, and skills of others, more so when they have trouble identifying these qualities on their own.

We are often blinded by daily duties and responsibilities, jobs we work that define us, or the overindulgences we fall victim to as a means of coping with the demands of our corporeality.

Performing our occupations at high proficiency, or merely surviving through drudgery don't necessarily define us so much as they sustain us. A police officer may only see themselves as a police officer unless he or she has other functions besides their profession, such as a parent or a coach. Does not this same eventuality also apply to those that society has labeled as criminals, drug addicts, and transients? Are not those people also children, parents, and definable as something other than the label they are assigned?

When speaking in terms of one's candidacy, the objective is to make it possible to show your candidate in a radiance that better displays a multi-dimensional person, rather than the two-dimensional shadow a normal light would cast. The aim is to identify and showcase the talents they possess that reveal themselves either subtlety or in a flash of brilliance that is often eclipsed by something as commonplace as their day-to-day lives.

Once those talents are distinguished, our job is to amplify and encourage them, and to unveil them to the candidate and/or to the world at the most opportune time.

Our description as mentor is also one of a Facilitator that paves the way, connects people, networks, and augments, and increases the impression cast by those we genuinely and wholeheartedly believe in.

Our experiences, our past, our present, our future aspirations, and anything relating to our transition should be shared should your candidate wish to know, think full disclosure. Depending on your own progression, they may find it hard to believe that we were even in the same position they are in now. But the proofs will be apparent in the person standing before them, which can often times be the incentive needed for them to more fervently seek out their own dreams and aspirations.

Remember your role as facilitator. Remember your duty to assist, to listen, and to offer advice. Remember that you yourself were once in a position similar to that of their own, and remember that the feelings of doubt, frustration and uncertainty they are experiencing, we also experienced. Use this as a means to better identify what needs fixing in their lives, and make it known to them.

Also keep in mind that we are not to become a crutch or permanent support from which they can lean on; but rather, we are the conveyance of the message of self-motivation. We are not the means to a better life. We are simply the message bearer, or reminder, of that which we already know and have already experienced. Even if *knowing* is a speck or shadow in the peripheral of our awareness compared to the insistency of the present- the understanding that life can always be better than its current state, for us, and for others.

The more one succeeds the less likely it is they are going to feel discouraged when faced with setbacks or defeats. And the amount of progression made is measured not only by social, financial, academic, and emotional advancement, but by a regression in criminal activity, thought, and behavior. We are here to win the war, not battles.

Know that confidentiality when working with your candidate might very well be a prerequisite between the two of you, and to compromise this arrangement is to break the trust and consideration upon which much of this agreement was built.

Our guidance may demand of us the teaching of steps taken in our own transition, and how best to thwart relapses or feelings that arise as a result of stress and certain triggers, that would cause someone to revert back to their previous lifestyle, or to give up their transition entirely.

I want to impress upon you that this isn't an exact science, nor is anything in relation to treating or improving the human condition, much less someone else's rather than our own. A success story – if one is to result from this – might not even include you or I in its retelling. <u>What is of consequence is that your candidate is in a position to recount their past from a now favorable present.</u>

We are fallible, incomplete, unshaped, and should be in a continuous state of flux and improvement until we exhaust our energy and perish- only to transition again from this state into something else.

And be prepared for an eventuality that might smack of defeat. Perhaps a failure or two is just the thing we need to adjust fire, approach from a different position, and experience victory.

DARIO II

The talents of the world are out there – hell, sometimes they're in here – like seeds in the desert, waiting for the monsoons or some other rare advent as the instrument that spurs their growth.

Then there are others, like Dario, who, despite their potential, their ability to bloom may have come and gone. Or it is a once in a lifetime event that, without the perfect combination of elements, we may not have the good fortune to experience in our generation.

There also exists impressive specimens of the human condition, that, despite the odds, have been able to grow and survive even if in a dark and desolate place. And there are those that, in spite of all the talents in their possession, they lack the means needed to showcase their potential to the rest of us. And so, they lie dormant and undiscovered.

I have elected to take on this task myself in an environment that many would see as unfit for any kind of growth other than the stunted and distorted variety. And yet, the amount of progression I see in those I try to build up, and by the way, who help themselves, is astounding. I can only imagine the progression they'll experience once transplanted to a place that fosters growth rather than hampers it.

It is only a fact of life, however, that some of us will never take root in more favorable conditions; but will anchor ourselves to a construct and an environment that we feel we are best adapted to, such as crime and prison, where many have a sense of worth that would be impossible to duplicate elsewhere.

As a result of being removed from this controlled environment, many of us will wither and shy from exposure that otherwise would have encouraged the proper development. First, beware that this doesn't happen to you. Secondly, hope that it doesn't happen to those you hope to influence.

As was the case with Dario, it wasn't only his environment that stunted his growth but also the number of weeds that surrounded and suffocated him, myself being one of those weeds. We absolutely need to make sure that our own successes – criminal or otherwise – do not lead to feelings of overbearing, confusion, or negative influence that would have the opposite effect on a target recipient.

We are not movie-style criminal overlords, seducing volatile and promising young criminals to the Darkside. We are nothing, and no one. And what we offer others is our unadulterated perspective; trials already won-or-lost. Errors and incorrect pathways already identified, nothing more.

Any progressions on my part are not due to helpful prison staff, or the overabundance of positive advice and support from fellow inmates. Nor due to the concept of "corrections" being successfully implemented in regards to the amount of rehabilitation it provides. But because I realized that each of us have the ability to be motivated by a yearning for something greater than that which previously motivated us. And to recognize this is to discover a drive from within rather than being *driven* by wants, needs, and desires for things of an external and temporal nature.

Upon my reentry I'll have many responsibilities that will keep me preoccupied for the first four years subsequent my release, if not for the rest of my life. But to seek out, talk with, and tentatively offer my assistance to Dario will be somewhat of a high priority once my own requirements have been met.

If that help consists of devoting what little free time I have left to listen, and be attentive, then so be it. If it involves seeking out professional assistance or counseling that he would otherwise not feel inclined to seek out on his own, then that's what I'll do. Knowing Dario, I get the feeling that a simple session of catching up might be a good start, ending with a genuine and heart-felt apology. Yes, a simple apology might work.

Lil Moe A.K.A. 'Dario' with Michelle Lujan-Grisham, Governor of New Mexico.

11

ENDGAME

 "Only the wisest and stupidest of men never change."

— CONFUCIOUS

I've TRIED to fill this work with every possible bit of information I could that would be relevant to a successful transition, and while it could probably use a bit more, I don't feel that more would necessarily be better.

Apart from the information provided concerning job/career acquisition, assistance programs, and successful reentry tactics, much of what I've written we already know. It just helps when that knowledge is placed in perspective – and outlined in detail – remaining cemented in our minds, as opposed to fleeting and soon dissipating as more pressing concerns dominate our thinking.

I wanted a handbook that we could use that I could refer back to, as a means of measuring my own progression, and where I am at year-one post prison. Year-five. Year-ten, until I'm in the grave and another generation is faced with how best to tackle these problems.

When I first resumed this project, I wasn't exactly sure

why I was doing it or towards what end it would take me. I look back on last October, 2023, (a year ago) when I knocked the dust off the draft I had mailed out piece-by-piece, sitting on a top shelf of my closet. I placed it on the dining room table I'm working on now.

I think I groaned or sort of sighed out loud when I thumbed through the pages and resolved to type, rather than scan, the entire draft into a WORD doc.

And so I began what I thought I had finished almost 13 years ago, 3 years prior to my release from Florence. In hindsight, the decade-long intermission was probably a necessary waiting period, as it proved every step of my reentry plan to be accurate and effective.

I want to impress upon you just how difficult it was to even get this manuscript – page-by-page, chapter-by-chapter – through the federal screening process for all mail that comes into and out of the Florence Prison Complex. When I think about the hundreds of dollars in stamps I couldn't afford to purchase – and the likelihood that a guard or US Marshall would sight my work as inflammatory and prevent it from being sent home – it was a miracle each time dad would confirm that he got a couple more pages over the phone by saying, "I got your latest letter, all 14 pages."

When I went to the hole for disciplining a homie who was riding the coat tails of an up-and-coming shot caller within our ranks, I thought for sure that my original draft would be taken and thrown away. Or that if I was shipped out to another prison, my property would not contain the one working draft I had in my possession.

And here we are...

I dream of a paperback version of this making its way from inmate-to-inmate, becoming more frayed, dog-eared, and highlighted as the copies spread. I see Nuevo convicts tagging it with Zia symbols, and members of other prison cars further tagging and scribbling on its pages, highlighting areas that make sense to them while calling "bullshit" for other arguments of mine. Drawing sketches of women, (female inmates adding their own art and ideas to the notes sections), and people in general using it for its intended purpose; or merely as a paperweight, or filling space on a bookshelf... much the way we fill space in prison.

Perhaps attempting to lessen a never-ending cycle of failure and recidivism isn't the worse task I've undertaken. Even if the initial impact is minimal, my hope is that the ripple effect will gain momentum rather than ebb with each successive wave.

My expectation is that the uptick, or pendulum, of more-and-more people going to prison will, at some point, experience a downtrend and swing the other way. My further hope for us is that we establish ourselves as citizens of worth, contribution and principle. Citizens that far exceed the levels of contribution our legitimate counterparts were capable of providing under normal circumstances, and within the construct we are all subject to... and subjects of.

OF WAR

"It is fatal to enter a state of conflict without the will to win it."

— DOUGLAS MCARTHUR

On occasion, I have used the terms "war" and "hostile environments" when describing the, at times, bleak condition of the criminal's state of affairs, because I feel that this comparison and indeed, the consequences, are so alike that to paint it in any other contrast would dilute the seriousness of the situation.

As long we think, live, and breathe criminality, rest assured that we exist in a perpetual state of conflict. And as a soldier in any war of attrition, our fall is imminent if it hasn't already occurred.

I speak with all candor when I say that we are at war. We are at war with conventionality. With society. With legality, and with other criminals and other criminal organizations. We are at war with law enforcement, and most perplexing- we are at war with *ourselves.*

Such a continuous state of hostility is bound to provide the ones fighting this conflict with defeat heaped upon defeat. Even if we're winning battles, I assure you the war was lost a long time ago.

I suppose the one disparity in armed conflicts between different groups and the practice of crime on a never-ending continuum is that you don't often see every soldier in it for themselves. There is always a clearly defined mission objective, or an assignation of "us" versus "them."

When we see conflict within The Conflict; people fighting side-missions, forming separate factions, and self-serving interests despite allegiances or affiliations suggesting otherwise, your conflict has digressed into pure and individual criminality... every person for themselves.

The point I want to drive home is that this form of warfare will, for the most part, be fought alone. From the time we make the decision to go against the grain, our solitude and our criminality will often be the only things that remain constant, or that keep us company.

I've witnessed and participated in plenty of organized criminality. And I've seen that when individual interests veer from one another, or when mutual benefit is no longer pursued in tandem with criminal activity, those partnerships or organizations often come to an end. It was not uncommon that the termination of such partnerships resulted in misunderstanding, resentment, jealousy, and sentiment which held no semblance of camaraderie or brotherhood.

At some juncture, we come to the conclusion that we can

have anything if we're willing to take it. We can have what has eluded us if we're willing to sacrifice our civilian existence and replace it with one that uses force and unlawful means to obtain our objective.

With the death of our civility comes the birth of practices that benefit a person whom we are unfamiliar with, but whom we are fast becoming acquainted. And conflicts that are often resolved through violence.

Conventional comforts are soon replaced with a hyper-awareness and mistrust of those around us. Materialism gained at the expense of others is now a daily pursuit, and one that our new visage welcomes. It is our privilege, our entitlement rather, to be imprisoned, preceded by the stripping away of a citizenship that meant nothing and provided minimal conciliation at the outset. Raw ambition becomes a flame through the darkness in an obscure microcosm that is harder to define than the real world. This "becoming" will be experienced alone as we drift further away from those we knew, and ourselves.

Alone is how we entered this state, and by our own volition is how we will leave it.

OF TRUTH

In order to reemerge from this intact, a stronger individual than the one who elected to pursue this pathway must be born from choice. We must openly face, and arm ourselves with certain truths that are the basis of our transition, and what may well be the rest of our lives.

These truths do not elude the majority of criminals. They are not hidden from us, nor foreign in concept. They are but basic and rudimentary tools that are often overlooked, misplaced, or unused; nothing a little dust-off and sharpening won't cure.

The First weapon in our arsenal of truth is the truth itself.

If we're armed with the truth, and are aware of it in any circumstance, how could we ever be defeated or misled by something as transparent as deception and/or self-deception? The ability to self-deceive is most often the untruth that brings about downfall long before we fall victim to the deceits of another.

To see our rather precarious position within the microcosm of crime is to perceive the insecure footing that we are perpetually imbalanced upon. No number of conflicts won will provide a more secure footing if the campaign is lost. To overlook this truth, rather than to face it, is perhaps the greatest acquiescence to the criminal pathway, and to defeat.

The Second truth one must arm themselves with is the acknowledgment of our own abilities to advance and succeed within the parameters of the law. We sell ourselves short via the practice of crime and the asphyxiation of talents that could otherwise be used legitimately.

Because an illegal activity is profitable, it does not mean that it is more profitable than a legitimate trajectory, less so when we take into account the consequences of arrest counterbalancing the profits gained. Remember that crime caps your income, and devalues it, because it becomes more difficult to invest it in legitimate enterprise.

I gave up on so many childhood and young-adult aspirations of mine to become a salesman whose product sells itself. Where is the achievement in that? Where is the challenge, the struggle, and the reward? To know that my current state of living in sunny Colorado derived from nothing more than the buying and selling of illegal goods is something that has effectively removed any of the status I may have attributed to my criminal career.

That I voluntarily elected to pursue this course causes me to feel shame for the impudent and self-assured fool that I was, and may possibly still be.

The world is filled to capacity with talented people that

never amount to anything for lack of self-motivation. If we experience trouble discovering those talents and skills that lay dormant beneath our daily routine, perhaps it is the determination itself that is the true talent. Pointing it in the right direction might be just the thing to jumpstart innovation.

The Third truth is not the truth itself, but the truth of *Self*. If you are anywhere near a mirror (even the scratched and stainless-steel variety will work), I'd like to suggest that you walk over to it, look deep into the eyes staring back at you (for several minutes if necessary), and see what the Truth is...

Do we recognize the reflection staring back at us? Do we see the child we once were? Do we see the ambition that thrived inside of us before countless arrests exhausted the steam that kept us going? Do we acknowledge that there is still some fight left in us? If so, allow yourself a smile, allow for some crow's feet to show at the corner of your eyes, and be comforted by the knowledge that we *Know Thyself*. For the truth is so many of us are born, live, and die without ever truly knowing who we were, why we're here, or what struggles we overcame with the time provided us.

Sometimes independence and peace begin with a blowup mattress on a bare floor and your first smart TV in your first apartment since coming home; trying to figure out your first smart phone. By yourself, with no celly. Enjoying the silence. A pizza pie and a bottle of wine. Or some food truck tacos and a Modelo on a cheap table with candles glowing rather than the noxious gas-emitting light from overhead fluorescents... there is nothing wrong with this starting point. On the contrary, it is nothing-but-nothing but right.

Every morning when I awake, I look at my reflection in the mirror and I spend a few moments gazing back at that ridiculous face of mine. Sometimes I laugh at my rounded features and the eyes that are set just a little too close together. I try to understand this individual. I try to see what makes him tick, what drives him, scares him, and what makes him feel of worth or significance.

I tell myself that the *awareness* of self might be as close as I'll ever get to truly *knowing* someone. To be ignorant of self is to be alone as perhaps as much as anyone can possibly be in the world.

My ignorance of self, who I was, what talents I possessed, and how best to navigate the environs I found myself in kept me ill-informed and inept at that navigation. I stumbled rather than glided. I lurked with malice rather than walking with assurance in the light of the sun. I dead-panned a room rather than smiling when I entered.

Free yourself of fear and walk tall; chin up, shoulders back... and glide. Know that the opposite of this posture is fear, and its governance of the path you take if you allow it to steer you.

Take a few moments out of the day and reflect upon the person you are, and if the choices we make are in conjunction with the person you believe yourself to be. If your choices provide intrinsic reward and are direct results of the talents you practice, chances are you know more of yourself than most. And, perhaps you find more contentment than most.

If our choices provide us with the opposite, and our efforts frustrate rather than reward, we may need to spend a bit more time discovering the stranger who stares back at us in the mirror.

An often-sad truth is that as long we exist within a state of criminality, we exist in a state of constant conflict. And we fumble around in a perpetual fog, where our ignorance of self and of the world precludes us from seeing things with the clarity that Truth provides.

OF THE ENEMY

In any situation where strife sharpens our edge, there is going to be struggle in which one individual, or a group of individuals will seek to gain an advantage over another. When we find ourselves at opposition with those attempting to best us, or to gain advantage at the expense of our safety, finances, or welfare, such forces should rightly be identified as adversarial.

In regards to crime and those who practice it, our enemies become manifold, and can consist of people, public opinion, rules, laws, policy, and procedure. The most obvious – though, by far, not the greatest threat to our criminal continuity – is law enforcement. At this point in our reading, (as well as in our progression or digression as the case may have it), we should all know just what to expect from this particular adversary.

If we are caught in the act of breaking the law, or an investigation results in arrest and prosecution, we are going to face punishment in accordance with our judicial system.

Law enforcement embodies adversarial properties that are not only apparent but justifiable. Apart from some of the methods used to investigate crimes, their approach is pretty straight forward. Most importantly, they are (or should be) your adversary only so far as we continue to commit criminal acts.

NOTE: There are instances where local and federal law enforcement entities will pursue targets long after the accused has proven themselves innocent of any wrongdoing. An attorney once told me that the FBI in its investigation of certain Italian American sub-cultures believes that those associated are guilty as a way of life, and that rehabilitation does not exist unless members cooperate, are imprisoned, or are murdered. This is one reason why many mob affiliated convicts are placed on probation, literally, for Life.

As was the case with John Gotti Jr., Federal Prosecutors

spent millions, employed over a dozen US Attorneys, and over one hundred cooperating witnesses, many of whom were violent convicted felons, who in total, had committed almost 100 murders, assaults, and robberies. JGJ was eventually acquitted of all charges.

Even if you elude law enforcement and make a successful transition, they don't have to convict you so much as they can investigate, charge, and force you to seek representation in defense of your actions. This attack on an American Citizen by the government ultimately breaks them financially. It can also break you mentally, physically, and spiritually if allowed to continue unchecked.

It wasn't so much JGJ's continued criminal status that made him a target several times over, but other factors, i.e., his name being synonymous with his father's. His associations in the Life, and law enforcement's inability to grasp that someone could successfully put an end to their criminal career – not by cooperating, nor by being sent to prison for life, nor by getting killed – but by *choosing* to do so.

Being federally investigated doesn't have to result in a conviction in order for it to cause the target to become poor and destitute as a result of having to legally and lawfully defend one's self from government attacks.

There are exceptions, but in most cases, targeting will only continue so long as our criminal career does.

There are other enemies, however, whose intentions and methods at thwarting your advancement are far more effective than law enforcement working alone. Their reasons can vastly differ from those the police may have for wanting to put an abrupt end to our criminal careers.

These enemies represent the criminal competition that—whether we know it or not—are dedicated to the same mission objective as law enforcement, but for different reasons.

Competition in crime can be synonymous with espionage and other cold war tactics, more so when demand is high, supplies are limited, and profit margins are tight due to geographic constraints on those operating within blurred lines of their respective market shares.

Apart from the competition's more obvious incursions into our piece of the pie, simply being in proximity to us, to me, would be enough of an encroachment into my personal space to preempt a rather violent and conclusive pushback. Again, always out of fear and a sense of hyper-awareness.

Even if we're not experiencing open turf wars, we are likely to face other, more subtle oppositions, and on several fronts. This makes it difficult to know who can be relied upon versus those that are fast becoming liabilities, as subterfuge and deceit are weapons that can and will be used just as fast, if not faster than say, a knife or firearm.

Now that the basis for external threats has been identified, let us cast these aside for the minor inconveniences they symbolize.

If possible – and maybe even during a gaze-in-the-mirror session – I would like each of us to take a look at the greatest opponent we will ever face... Yourself.

Just as I am convinced that the greatest and most effective tool of our transition is choice, and self, so too are the most ruthless and deceptive enemies I have ever known. How I've allowed myself, my wants, my thought process, and my negative knee-jerk reactions to outside stimuli shape my avarice and direct my path, are perhaps the purest form of betrayal I have ever known.

The internal voice we hear telling us whatever it must to move us to action is the greatest threat to our ability to advance and to prosper in a meaningful and legitimate fashion. And the more we indulge our inclination to survive, to provide, and to prosper, the more powerful it becomes. And the more likely it is to overwhelm conscious thought and reason without you knowing it was there.

That voice is not our own. It is a conjuring made up of

emotions such as greed, pride, fear, hate, and external gratification knowing that the street is watching. And Her estimations of you are either raised or lowered with each decision
you make.

OF MICE AND MEN

"All of humanity's problems stem from man's
inability to sit quietly in a room alone."

— BLAISE PASCAL, PENSÉES

Long before I came to prison I was an avid reader of basically
anything that caught my interest. I never sought out those self-
help books on "how to influence and control others," or any
of that elementary school psychology and gaslighting
nonsense. I've seen guys read these, then try and head-trip
another inmate, and find themselves in a fist fight or worse
over an obvious attempt at manipulating another.

Whether I was reading Sun Tzu's "The Art of War,"
Marcus Aurelius' "Meditations" or classic historical fictions by
John Steinbeck, or Gary Jennings; what I enjoyed most was
stepping into the past and getting a glimpse of how we
thought and operated in times before the present. It was interesting to interpret how Sun Tzu incorporated psychology and
practical thought into the art of war.

What interested me most about many of these reads was
not so much the information they provided, but the insight I
gained into the minds of those who wrote them.

It amazes me to experience the things people create,
simply from thought; and how that thought, once projected
into the world, shapes and influences those who consider its
import and application. I wonder what an author such as Sun
Tzu would think if his work laid dormant for generations,
suddenly to explode to consciousness in the minds of corpo-

rate employees and businesspeople who then applied his observations on war to an environment that most of us would have difficulty identifying as hostile. And yet, this is what war has become for legions of people that wield pens instead of swords, and designer business suits rather than armor.

During my immergence into the competitive and sometimes violent world of crime, I never once referred to these studies as guides that I could perhaps utilize in order to gain the upper hand over my adversaries. Instead, I read them for the sake of entertainment and diversion. Some might argue that if I had actually used them for their intended purpose that I might be in a far better situation than the one I am currently in, but I beg to differ.

Remember that war itself, or the state of war, rather, is often a matter of how one interprets their environment; or worse, how we define ourselves through conflict. Bear in mind, also, that a continuous state of war is not an environment, or mindset, that one should perpetually exist within, lest that person become shell-shocked and unable to recognize advancement without conflict, much less socialize and interact as a normal person would.

For many people today, their perception of day-to-day struggles in an aggressive or overly-competitive workplace is often times the stimuli that causes them to believe they exist in a hostile environment; when in fact, it is their interpretation of reality which allows feelings of threat, intimidation and aggression to persevere. Add to this mixture a little self-help in the form of military tactics that are then applied to your daily routine, and what we have is a bunch of normal citizens, or convicts even, being far too militarized than is necessary to achieve small victories on a daily basis.

Waging war over who closes the next business transaction, or who gets to sell dope on which street corner, are often unnecessary acts of aggression.

I found that my own enmity, and belief that I existed

within a state of war, was often projected as a result of my inability to simply *not* react to stimuli and situations that didn't deserve or require a response.

There are prisons, environs, and habitats that contain hostile elements for which people existing in these habitats must be aware of. As a result, most make preparations to deal with those hostilities via training. Such training usually consists of exercise to prepare the body and defend it against physical attacks.

Maintaining a defensive posture and quickly going on the offense is a preemptive method used to neutralize threats, both imagined and real. Unfortunately, our projection of feeling threatened – and our subsequent battle readiness – unknowingly marks us as a competitive threat to others, and in instances where there was never any real threat to begin with.

I have witnessed several inmates being thrown in the hole, or shipped out to another prison, or receive additional time on their sentences as biproducts of gearing up for a war that never came; or would never had come to fruition had they not initiated a state of conflict through obvious outward preparation.

This is a perfect example of a self-fulfilling prophecy, or people being dictated by their fears and perceived threats, rather than basing their course and desired pathway on past experience, confidence, and the ability to not react when no reaction is necessary.

I would never be so presumptuous to assume that this manuscript would be of the caliber and quality of the great reads previously mentioned. But should you ever find yourself reading this or others that are likened to the "self-help" genre, I would suggest reading them first for enjoyment, second to glean what useful information you can from their pages, and lastly, that we take every suggestion – including my own – with a grain of salt.

For to use another's thoughts, in such a way that they

replace your own would be to completely disregard the purpose and meaning of *self-help.*

I would suggest rather, that we take under *advisement* each and every bit of advice and information that is assimilated. And that we see the benefits it provided those who have first practiced, and then preached it, only after having proved its worth in the real world, and in real time.

To deal in absolutism when considering suggestions is to transform advice into doctrine and/or a dogmatic point of view. Once this occurs, we deprive ourselves of the flexibility needed in order to survive, circumvent, and disregard the conflict that will surely manifest throughout the course of our lifetime.

Weigh what others suggest against that which you yourself deem to be fair, right, or in accordance with your own beliefs and MO. And know that free will exists for the purpose of making our own way in this world, rather than following or allowing others to pave the way for you.

OF PEACE

At present, there is nothing more valuable to me than what little peace and quiet I experience when they lock the prison down for the night. Sometimes a fellow inmate is screaming. Other times another inmate is yelling in response to the screamer to "just kill yourself!" And on those rare occasions, my insomnia notwithstanding, I might actually get a few hours of sleep in between the guards taking pleasure in shining their newest brightest flashlight into the cells, or kicking the doors at night to ensure none of us took the quick way out.

It's a curious feeling to reflect on what items and experiences I hold of value in here as opposed to the importance I placed on certain amenities while I was free. I know when I was free that I took my downtime for granted, and that I usually saw any lulls in activity as space that needed to be filled, rather than time that was supposed to be enjoyed doing absolutely nothing.

The supreme pinnacle of financial success was reached when I purchased my first home in 2007, just before the real estate market crash of '08, and my own fall shortly thereafter.

All of my efforts were bent towards that one purpose: to have a place of my own.

A strange occurrence happened, and on a grander scale that paying cash for that first new car (as is often the marker for financial progression for most impoverished folks). I was not as comfortable in my new home as I thought I would be. And the void that I was sure home ownership would satisfy was still empty and unfulfilled.

I found that I often grew anxious and agitated when I was there for longer than a day or so. And my desire to be around others or involved in some activity, preferably of an illegal nature, would precede my venturing out in search of *something* rather than to stay home and enjoy the peace and security I had finally achieved.

I remember coming back to that house on the Westside of Albuquerque (or Rio Rancho to be exact), and it would feel as if I were walking into a stranger's home. That feeling of apprehension usually necessitated a security sweep where I would walk through the entire house and investigate every nook and cranny where someone might be able to hide and waylay me.

I can recall the exact moment when it occurred to me that the chief purpose of my life – financial security and a place to call my own – did not provide me with the comfort and peace that I thought it would. And the nausea it left in my stomach concerning what I had sacrificed, only made the void that much more vast and unrelenting.

How could a house and money possibly provide me with peace and a sense of security when the very means they were obtained by relied on a heightened sense of awareness and conflict in order to ensure their continuity? How could I be so naive as to believe that home ownership and ill-gotten gains could somehow release me from the obligations which provided those things in the first place?

My brand-new bullshit house didn't feel like home, and my illusion of financial security didn't feel secure, because I was still immersed in a lifestyle and a *modus operandi* that ran contrary to anything resembling serenity, stability, or peace.

Rest assured that the permanence of peace or stability will never last so long as having it requires of us an inordinate amount of risk-taking. Nor will any amount of material conciliation ever rid us of the feeling of insecurity that is the constant companion of our criminality.

Notions of peace, be they home ownership, a family, spiritual contentment, or simply a few extra bucks tucked away for incidentals are directly connected to the fashion in which they were obtained or realized. Their temporary or lasting nature can be discerned by their correlation to their criminal or legitimate means of acquisition. That is to say, if we *earned* it, it is likely that we will keep it, maintain it, and value it. If we did not, then we will not.

Our willingness to adhere to legitimate ways of "making it" in the world will allow us to possess peace and security permanently, acts of God or happenstance notwithstanding. Purchasing, renting, and leasing the *idea of* peace and security through the haze of criminal activity is something that we have all been sold on, hook, line, and sinker.

Peace comes from within. Never will it come to us through externalizing that particular sentiment, or state rather. Peace comes almost as an afterthought, and as a result produced by correct and earnest choice, rather than by consequence of corporeal possession and desire.

Peace is not the end result of a battle won, but of a war that need never have been fought had we elected to make the right decisions. Casting aside intellect, talent, and reason, and flinging ourselves recklessly into a state of conflict because we believe we are stronger than those who oppose us is something that the capitalistic criminal cannot help but to be a part of.

War is, at best, an artform, to be dabbled in and observed; to create scenarios with from a military state of mind, and practiced when all attempts at diplomacy fail.

Peace, on the other hand, is not an art form, nor even a way of life; but a state of being, that each of us has the right to pursue and the capacity to experience.

OF HEARTH AND HOME

I examine these two states (or conditions) of war and peace at the end of my writing because it is important that we remember the former in order to fully experience the latter, and to devise ways to remain in a state of peace; to defend it, and to encourage its omnipresence as much as possible.

Pain, unless it accompanies a terminal illness is quickly forgotten once it's genesis is identified and remedied. So too are the damaging aspects of our criminality forgotten without constant reminders of just how thoroughly it infiltrated our person.

I used the example of my long fought for and long sought after home, because the idea of homeownership encompassed so many other concepts of favorable conditions. If I had a home, I might also have started a family. I would have a place to rest and recuperate, and I would finally be in a position where I could enjoy some peace and quiet, or so I reasoned.

Did I mention that the home I purchased was gone 6 months later when the Feds arrested me at the strip club? Forty-six thousand dollars as a down payment, and 6 months after I bought it, and it was gone. The foundation upon which I acquired it was crime, and upon such a foundation no home, dream, or concept of peace could possibly stand for long.

I never imagined that the comfort and sense of ease and wellbeing my parents provided could ever again be duplicated, least of all in a place such as prison. But places are just that, places; or settings rather, that should never dictate the feelings of those who occupy them. They are merely backdrops for the stage of life.

I won't deceive, or embellish, and tell you that prison is a wonderful place, filled with wonderful people. But nor is it the nightmare parodied in film or illustrated by the police. What I will tell you is that neither places, nor people, nor "commitments" to our imprisonment should be the basis upon which our conflict or tranquility stems from. Rather, our disposition, our composure, and our non-reaction to impetus is what affirms our stability and permanence, no matter the environment in which we realize such a pursuit is worthwhile to attempt.

I imagine that I will have to apply these beliefs, yet again, upon my exit from prison and entrance into the halfway house. And upon my release from the halfway house into the world. From the ankle monitor to probation, and from probation to freedom, these convictions must carry me. And they must carry you.

SUSTAINED

Now that we are on the home stretch, and this particular bit of work is coming to an end, I feel that the real work for us is finally beginning. The labors that positive change will demand of us will not be easy, and sometimes the rewards will be difficult to discern from the labor itself. But know that if you are reading this, that your transition began over a hundred pages ago.

And although you may be reading this from prison, or from the state of conflict which your criminality has demanded of you, know also that you are – regardless of conditions – moving on a correct trajectory of your choosing.

For who among us considers change when the profits reaped from our illicit efforts are as good as they are? Who even considers going legit when the proofs of our success surround us like so many material trophies? We are allowed at least one arrest, one slap on the wrist, from which we can rebound and improve our methods, our approach to crime, are we not?

Why then would we even consider an MO other than crime until that first wrist slap occurs? Because the one who perceives their criminality for the illness it is, *before* the illness becomes terminal, is a thousand paces ahead of the rest of us. We who were naive in believing that one slap on the wrist would not veer us from the penchant for crime, nor damage our eligibility for other more legitimate pursuits.

The prudent among us are those who dismiss their criminality the moment they realize that it caps our income, marginalizes our prospects, and pigeonholes our opportunities. The smart criminal is the one who considers other options before resorting to something that is really no option at all.

In order to sustain this train of thought, or to refrain from thought that would lead one back to the Life, we must reinforce the belief that our transition is already imminent, underway, and possible. Some of us need simply to move forward in the right direction. Others, such as myself, need constant reminders, certificates of achievement, or other indicators that milestones have been reached and surpassed.

I can't say for certain what I will require concerning my own transition upon reentry to society, but in prison, I measure Social, Academic, Financial, and Emotional progress by the influence I wield, the degrees under my belt, the books I read, the pushups I do, the miles I run, the pennies I save, and the relationships I foster and maintain. Because without these, it would seem as if my life has been at a standstill for literally years' worth of time; which, if I choose to look at it from a pragmatic point of view, it has.

I also keep track of progression by the number of pitfalls I have thus far avoided. The times I mediated beefs between us or those outside our car. Or when I abstained from selling or ingesting "spice" or suboxone; *pruno*, or a snort of heroin.

If those reading this are in prison, or in another environment where measuring advancement can prove slow or difficult, remembering all the harm that we've thus far avoided will give us some measure of progress. Albeit imperceptible in some cases, I promise progression is underway.

Granted, the accomplishments I've detailed may seem trivial, but when they are weighed against all the opportunities to do dirt and hone our criminality, the comparisons between each path become apparent. Hence, one pathway widens, and its tributaries multiply, while one diminishes and becomes nothing resembling a path whatsoever.

All I'm really doing is preparing for the day of release when I can hit the ground running without looking back. I'm eager to see what advancements I can make and what contributions I can provide.

For those of you reading this, I can only hope that I have been comprehensive and thorough in my approach to this problem, and the subsequent solutions I've offered. I can pray, focus on you as a collective, and hope that you see your preparation for the future progress it represents.

I pray that your transition will sustain you indefinitely, if not far longer than crime ever will.

When I consider what I want out of life, and when I take into account all else that others have told me they hope to gain, I've found that what we all desire, on some level, is peace. Peace, and peace of mind, and perhaps even a little more peace. Thankfully, I am not as demanding or as insatiable as I once was, and much of what my idea of peace consists of has already been realized. The rest, *Inshallah* or God willing, will come in time.

And if it doesn't come, I can find no fault in venturing out in search of it.

Do you know what your version of peace consists of? And are you ready to obtain it? If so, let me suggest you stop reading another's thoughts and ideas, and go out and find it. Once it's yours, I pray you never let it go. I pray you fight for a worthy cause, and die for it if necessary.

Were we not soldiers at one point or another? If not soldiers, then mercenaries? Citizen mercenaries who fought and were imprisoned, who lost our freedom and sense of self for something as fleeting as status and financial gain? Were they worth fighting for? Worth being imprisoned or dying for? I think not. But I know that peace and the right to pursue one's dreams most assuredly are.

I hope this is read with the same open heart and mind with which it was written. I can only hope that you gain a fraction of the benefit from reading this that I have gained from writing it. I wish nothing but the best for All of you. And, if chance should have it, I'll see you on the Outside.

November 11, 2012 2:30 PM MST, Florence, Co.

Initial Edit Completed 9.16.24

POST SCRIPT

In closing this final chapter of my criminal life, one step remains. I applied for a Presidential Pardon several years ago. I check the website every now and again but have yet to be affirmed, or pardoned rather. I've gotten clarifying questions from staff via email at the US Pardon Attorney's Office, but nothing follows. As of today, January 20th, 2025, on the exit of the Biden Administration and beginning of the Second Trump administration, I received the following email. I will reapply immediately:

Re: Case No: P300974

            Notice of Clemency Denial

Dear Jason Everett Grinage:

Your pardon application was carefully considered, and the determination was made that favorable action is not warranted at this time. Your application was therefore denied by President Joseph R. Biden, Jr., on January 20, 2025, in accordance with the procedures set forth in 28 C.F.R. § 1.8(b) (providing for notices of denial). If you wish to reapply for pardon, a new application form is now available through the Department of Justice. Your application should include any new or updated information since you previously applied."

PERSONAL
ACKNOWLEDGMENTS

First and foremost, I want to thank my fellow inmates from New Mexico that, at times, had to "break out the handbook on this vato" during my year in federal holding at Sandoval County and the old Estancia penitentiary. From Crazy Town Roswell, Artesia, Carlsbad, Las Cruces, Silver City, T or C, and all the homies from the Southern and Central parts of the State. From Grants to Hobbs and Portales. Albuquerque "Burque" to Santa Fe. Las Vegas, Española, and every town, village, and Pueblo in between. We-are-Nuevo.

"Bouncer No. 1," played an integral role in schooling me between the different nuances of street versus prison survival. His guidance in preparing me – and countless others – entering prison for the first time was quite literally, a lifesaver. Charles "Charolas" Lucero, for being my steady companion from sentencing, to prison, the halfway house, and present day. Gabe "Bouncer" Ortiz. You are a true *Llavero* and friend. Because of you my "prison career" was ever intact, and I can walk the line in any prison the world throws at me... or throws me into.

Marcelo "Chills" Jimenez. Thank you for the direction, guidance, support and advice you gave. Not only to me, but to the hundreds of other New Mexicans under the umbrella of leadership and respect you provided for All. Roman "Wall" Muraga, the same gratitude extended to you Señor. John

"Knucklehead" Lovato. Every Hispanic Car needs that one quiet *Chino*. I'm glad you were ours. Your progress since coming home, your daughter... some accomplishments just can't be measured.

To Don Vito Rizzutto. *Mi dispiace, signore, di non aver potuto imparare di piu da te quando sono tornato a casa... Riposa en pace.*

To Derrick "Black" Williams. Never has there been another more dedicated to the principles of war, the mindset to survive, and the conviction that you will one day be free. Please give "Swazi" my best hopes for an early release as well.

To the Original Americans, the Indigenous Peoples. From the members of each Pueblo, Tribe, and Nation. Draper, Swallow, Runs Against the Enemy, and Dwayne Bear. You are the original Warriors, still fighting the same battle that your Ancestors elected to fight against the same federal government hundreds of years ago. I pray that that fighting spirit never dissipates.

To J.L. Burkholder. Thank you for showing me a darker pathway to a different version of myself.

And to Ralph Martinez. Crazy how fast 30 years went by. What we went through- to think that we're here again, decades later. Only both of us doing so much more for ourselves and New Mexico. Proud of you, Señor.

Javier Quihuis. Another 30-year saga, beginning as kids. From fist fights, turf wars, and God-only-knows-what else. I'm glad we bridged the gap. Salud compañero.

To Lil Moe, A.K.A "Dario." I'm glad we had that talk, my friend. Just you, me, and Eden left out of the original group.

Jesse Sandoval. Thank you for your service and your friendship. From this desert to the Middle East.

To Lucious Lavern Pettway, 1977-2007. I wish I never would've said "Let's" to you. May you Rest in Power.

My Father, David Grinage... from East Baltimore to West. Mt. Holly St. to Vietnam. Back home and thence to Denver by way of hitchhiking across the country. And Denver to Tacoma where you and mom made me. If the world knew your story it would demand that, at the very least, a screenplay be written about you. You served enough time and put in enough work for all of us... for generations to come. I am convinced you are the best man I will ever know.

To my Mother, Michele Grinage, who taught me the value of dancing and laughter, playing a recorder and learning to embroider (a talent many employ in prison). Singing hippie tracks, Motown, and 70s rock with you on the way to school, and later music from the 80s. You are definitely the Spanish/Italian Momma that gives sons "mother issues," and full-satisfied tummies. I love you Ma!

To my Brother, Oley J. Grinage. You did it right. You did it legal, and yet... You were the real gangster.

HGF...FHG

To Anais Mendez, the one girlfriend and only friend out of dozens whom I thought were my friends... thank you for making the trip to see me in Florence. I am so grateful we're still in each other's lives... Boricua! To Allison Morgado, my sincere thanks for showing me the inner workings of the Justice System, and what it truly means for survivors of criminal acts. I may not be the feminist you had hoped for, but I have a much deeper appreciation for the human condition, thanks to you.

To Roger & Denise Newman, my second set of parents. I'm looking forward to our next nightcap together after a good dinner and during a good movie. Your mirth, candor, and genuine friendship always leave me craving our next visit. Many, many thanks for seeing me in Florence, and stuffing me with cheeseburgers and other extortionately overpriced "delicacies" from the visiting room vending machines! I love you both very much.

To Emma. Thank you for reminding me of Light, Love, and Laughter. I had forgotten what these were. Mind-blowing to consider how much of the Three you injected into six short months. My sincere apologies for the 18-months of hell that followed. Thanks to you I believe these sentiments should be continuously sought after and experienced by all.

PROFESSIONAL ACKNOWLEDGMENTS

Dan Marlowe, my criminal defense attorney... we beat them all anyways! I hope you're enjoying retirement.

Jeff Spelech-Martinez, United States Probation, District of New Mexico. Hands down the most professional and supportive Probation Officer I ever had the good fortune of reporting to (and I have reported to several during my tenure as a criminal).

Sheriff Billy Merrifield, Rio Arriba County Sheriff's Office. It takes a guy from the streets to properly and professionally serve and protect those that are still subjects of the streets. Police and Sheriff departments the world over might better serve their fellow citizens if they took a page from your book.

Lt. Colonel David "Dave" Sedillo, United States Army (Retired). I thank you for your tutelage and instruction while employed in state government.

Former police officers Cecil Sena and Ben Chavarria of the Santa Fe Police Department. Thanks for cutting me a break when warranted, and cutting me no slack when I needed to learn a lesson. May you both Rest in Power.

Judge Francis Gallegos. I greatly appreciate the leniency when I admitted guilt. Your programs worked, and are sorely missed in the City of Santa Fe.

Officer Martinez from Raton who acted as Mesa Bravo unit guard on several occasions at Florence, definitely a good man.

And that one-cool-guard at Florence who was a Pittsburgh Steelers fan. You would open the housing unit doors in the Winter if constructive torture was occurring where staff cranked the heaters up to 90+ degrees. Or when they turned the air conditioner off during 100-degree Summers. You shot the breeze with us and remained respectful during shake-downs. And you maintained your professionalism and training no matter what went down. I hope you guys get a Superbowl win soon.

Para Ti